FUTURE IMPERFECT

HOWARD P. SEGAL

FUTURE

. . . .

The University of Massachusetts Press   Amherst

IMPERFECT

THE MIXED

BLESSINGS OF

TECHNOLOGY

IN AMERICA

Copyright © 1994 by
The University of Massachusetts Press
All rights reserved
Printed in the United States of America
LC 93–2265
ISBN 0–87023–882–5 (pbk.)

Designed by Rebecca S. Neimark
Set in Caledonia and Futura by Keystone Typesetting, Inc.
Printed and bound by Thomson-Shore, Inc.

Library of Congress Cataloging-in-Publication Data

Segal, Howard P.
    Future imperfect : the mixed blessings of technology in America / Howard P. Segal.
        p.   cm.
    Includes bibliographical references and index.
    ISBN 0–87023–882–5 (pbk. : alk. paper)
    1. Technology—United States—History—Case studies. 2. Technology—Social aspects—
United States—Case studies. I. Title.
T21.S43   1994
303.48'3—dc20   93–2265
                                                                                        CIP

British Library Cataloguing in Publication data are available.

This book is published with the support and cooperation of the University of Massachusetts at Boston.

For Deborah D. Rogers and for
Richard William Rogers Segal

CONTENTS

. . . .

ILLUSTRATIONS

. . . .

PREFACE

. . . .

"Make use of whatever advanced technology is available." As I was
completing this book I received that unsolicited advice in, of all forms, a
fortune cookie from a local Chinese restaurant. I ordinarily ignore the
wisdom of fortune cookies, yet the timing of this suggestion—or perhaps warning—made it hard to forget. As clearly as I had ever seen it
stated, here was the doctrine of the technological imperative, which
this book repeatedly rejects. That the conventional wisdom regarding
technology of at least the past two centuries had filtered down to fortune
cookies in Maine made me momentarily question the value of the book I
had been working on for nearly two years. Nevertheless, I quickly
reassured myself, finding this traditional justification for unceasing
technological advance in a fortune cookie might actually represent its
removal from the mainstream of American society and culture and its
relegation to the periphery. That kind of progress I could readily endorse. In either case, the fate of the technological imperative lies at the
heart of the growing contemporary debates over technology and progress to which this book is, I hope, a modest contribution.

Despite my aversion to the fortune cookie's advice, I am not a
latter-day Luddite. I may not be enamored of technological advances for
their own sake, but I do appreciate the beneficial uses of many of them
and do not advocate a return to a simpler life. Nor am I impressed with
more radical critics of technology who see no contradiction between
advocating a return to a simpler life and utilizing the latest transporta-

tion and communication technologies to spread their message of modern technology's inherent evils. As several chapters of this book make explicit, we are long past the point of debating whether to live in some kind of pervasively technological society; the real question is what kind of technological society do we wish or can we afford?

What nevertheless concerns me throughout this book is the painfully naive assumption that the technological optimism that has historically characterized American society and culture will or must continue unabated. If I have learned any basic lessons from my professional studies over the last two decades, it is that the past is profoundly discontinuous from the present and that the attempted recovery of the past by the present in the name of imagined historical continuities is utterly futile. In this book I have applied that overall historical perspective to the history of technology, a relatively new field that initially suffered from but quickly outgrew such naiveté regarding the past and the present. It is a tribute to the maturity of the history of technology— and, not least, to the field's founder, Melvin Kranzberg, a longtime mentor and friend—that historians of technology are among those now suggesting that technological optimism may be the hallmark of an era that has ended. In many of these chapters I consider the dilemma this poses to those who still believe in unadulterated technological progress, but I discuss it most fully in the final one on high-tech culture.

This book uses case studies to analyze and illuminate my principal points. However pervasive technology both is and has been in American life, it remains ill-defined, poorly conceived, and misunderstood by many. In place of additional vague generalizations I therefore offer concrete examples. Each of the chapters treats some specific aspect(s) of the historical relationship between technology and progress and the contemporary implications of that relationship. The focus of the chapters moves from American history to technological museums to visionary writings to high-tech culture.

This book represents a reconsideration not only of technology and progress but also of much of what I have written over the past fifteen years about this subject. Far from merely reprinting what I have previously published, I have systematically revised, expanded, updated, and cross-referenced every one of the articles and essays that form the chapters of this book. That process has naturally forced me to rethink— and in several instances to alter—my original ideas and positions.

I am greatly indebted to Paul M. Wright, acquisitions editor of the

University of Massachusetts Press, for encouraging me to pursue this enterprise when it was just a proposal and for supporting me throughout what became a far lengthier effort than either of us had initially imagined. He and his associates at the Press have been professionals in the best sense.

I am also much indebted to Melvin Kranzberg and Warren Wagar, who each read my manuscript. Their detailed suggestions have been taken to heart. The book is much better because of their helpful evaluations. In addition to Kranzberg and Wagar, fellow historians Alan Marcus, Everett Mendelsohn, Arnold Pavlovsky, Rosalind Williams, and Solomon Wank have helped me clarify my ideas in various discussions and conferences over the years. My history department colleagues William Baker, Jerome Nadelhaft, and David Smith have also assisted and encouraged me in my intellectual pursuits since my first days at the University of Maine.

As a self-confessed "low-tech" writer, I am often dependent on the kindness of others to assist me in word processing. Although I am proud to have written much of the book on my own computer, I required considerable technical assistance along the way and, in the case of articles and essays published before I had a computer, it was necessary to create new disks and files. Suzanne M. Moulton and Deborah L. Grant of the University of Maine's Department of History were enormously helpful at every stage.

Several University of Maine students were invaluable to me as research assistants as I sought recent materials on all the major topics discussed in this book. Undergraduate and graduate students Frank Campbell, Glenn Davis, Bart Hollingsworth, Thomas Kinney, Jeffrey Melanson, Deborah Stiles, and Michele Wehrwein repeatedly sought out and obtained pertinent books, articles, essays, reviews, and other items. They were invariably helped, as was I, by the reference and interlibrary loan staff members of the University of Maine's Fogler Library. In addition, Deborah Stiles also proofread every one of the chapters in draft and final forms and provided excellent stylistic and substantive comments on the manuscript.

A 1992 summer research grant from the University of Maine's Faculty Research Funds Committee enabled me to devote several months to this project and expedited its completion. I am most grateful for this support.

Paradoxically, I am indebted to two current university presidents who, a decade ago, eliminated the Department of Humanities of the University of Michigan's College of Engineering, in which I formerly taught. Presidents James J. Duderstadt of the University of Michigan and Charles M. Vest of the Massachusetts Institute of Technology, in their earlier positions as dean and associate dean of Michigan's College of Engineering, deemed all nontechnical courses in their college "inappropriate" for engineering students, who were expected to find equivalent courses in other colleges—when, in fact, most of these courses, including mine in the history of technology, were not offered elsewhere on campus.

Obliged to move on to pursue my career, in 1986 I had the good fortune to be offered a position in history at the University of Maine. There I met a very different kind of engineering dean, Norman Smith, who not only recognized the importance of the history of technology to prospective engineers but also enthusiastically supported the establishment of the technology studies program I now direct. Since 1988 we have team taught courses on technology past and present to growing numbers of engineering and nonengineering students. As I knew from my experience at Michigan, students who are exposed to rather than shielded from basic questions about technology will become more responsible citizens—and, in the case of engineers, better professionals. Dean Smith accepts the reality of different points of view and does not feel threatened by criticisms that imply that technology leads to a less than utopian world. More than he knows, he has restored my faith in the intellectual integrity of engineering educators.

Two grants from the National Science Foundation for the improvement of undergraduate education for engineering and nonengineering students have enabled Dean Smith and me to plan and implement several courses that speak to the issues raised in this book. These grants (USE-8953617, 1989, and USE-9156081, 1992) are gratefully acknowledged.

Shortly after I arrived in Orono I met the woman who, two years later, became my wife. More than anyone else, Deborah Rogers has helped me with this book. A professor of English at the University of Maine, she has read and reread every line of every chapter and has made invaluable stylistic and substantive suggestions. The book is infinitely better because of the untold hours she took from her own research and writing to do this. No less important, her faith in my ability to transform diverse essays and articles into a unified volume has sustained me throughout the enterprise. She is richly deserving of the book's dedication.

As someone who became a father relatively late, I had not fully appreciated the difference a child could make. Having my precious son, Rick, in my life has been an unqualified joy, and that is why this book is also dedicated to him.

Orono, Maine
January 1993

ACKNOWLEDGMENTS

. . . .

This book represents the extensive revision, expansion, updating, and cross-referencing of the following prior publications. Permission to reprint (some version of) the original has been obtained in every case and is gratefully acknowledged here.

"The American Jeremiad of Technological Progress: Historical Perspectives," *Alternative Futures: The Journal of Utopian Studies* 3 (Spring 1980): 139–52.

"Leo Marx's 'Middle Landscape': A Critique, A Revision, and an Appreciation," *Reviews in American History* 5 (March 1977): 137–50, by The Johns Hopkins University Press.

"The Automobile and the Prospect of an American Technological Plateau," *Soundings: A Journal of Interdisciplinary Studies* 65 (Spring 1982): 78–87.

"Tocqueville and the Problem of Social Change: A Reconsideration," *South Atlantic Quarterly* 77 (Fall 1978): 482–503, copyright 1978 by Duke University Press, Durham, North Carolina.

"The Machine Shop in American Society and Culture," *Henry Ford Museum and Greenfield Village Herald* 14 (Summer 1985): 44–49, by Henry Ford Museum and Greenfield Village.

"'Made in Maine': A Professor's Perspective," *Technology and Culture* 31 (July 1990): 463–68, copyright 1990 by the Society for the History of Technology.

"Exhibition Review: Computers and Museums: Problems and Opportunities of Display and Interpretation," *American Quarterly* 42 (December 1990): 637–56.

"Bellamy and Technology: Reconciling Centralization and Decentralization," in *Looking Backward, 1988–1888: Essays on Edward Bellamy,* ed. Daphne Patai (Amherst: University of Massachusetts Press, 1988), 91–105.

"The Feminist Technological Utopia: Mary E. Bradley Lane's *Mizora* (1890)," *Alternative Futures: The Journal of Utopian Studies* 4 (Spring/Summer 1981): 67–72.

"Vonnegut's *Player Piano*: An Ambiguous Technological Dystopia," in *No Place Else: Explorations in Utopian and Dystopian Fiction,* ed. Eric S. Rabkin et al. (Carbondale and Edwardsville: Southern Illinois University Press, 1983), 162–81.

"Mumford's Alternatives to the Megamachine: Critical Utopianism, Regionalism, and Decentralization," in *Lewis Mumford: Public Intellectual,* ed. Thomas P. Hughes and Agatha C. Hughes (New York: Oxford University Press, 1990), 100–109, copyright 1990 by Oxford University Press, Inc.

"High Tech's False Nostalgia," *Science and Public Policy* 15 (June 1988): 189–90, by Beech Tree Publishing, Guildford, Surrey, England.

"Are Fairs Obsolete?" *The New York Times* Op-Ed Page, June 3, 1981, 25, copyright 1981 by The New York Times Company.

"Utopian Fairs," *Chicago History: The Magazine of the Chicago Historical Society* 12 (Fall 1983): 7–9.

"The Several Ironies of Technological Literacy," *Michigan Quarterly Review* 27 (Summer 1988): 448–53.

1

INTRODUCTION: THE AMERICAN IDEOLOGY OF TECHNOLOGICAL PROGRESS: HISTORICAL PERSPECTIVES

. . . .

When I published *Technological Utopianism in American Culture* in 1985, I thought that the historical phenomenon I examined in that book—an uncritical faith in technology's ability to solve all problems— would soon be a relic of a more hopeful if more naive era. I believed that increasing numbers of Americans were beginning to seek healthy, mature limits on unadulterated technological advance and were starting to express greater concern for nontraditional realms crying out for equivalent attention, enthusiasm, and funding. As I elaborate in chapter 3, I then sensed movement toward a "technological plateau." I still believe that, but my optimism, never overwhelming, has since been tempered further.

As I detailed in my book, the commonly held conception of America as a potential utopia to be brought about by technological progress is old and familiar, with many European roots. It long predates the actual technological wonders that to so many here and abroad promised to transform this fantasy into reality. And it is a conception apparently still shared by many Americans (and non-Americans) despite growing doubts about both America's and technology's future. Indeed, for all the now familiar criticism of technology generated by such developments as the proliferation of atomic weapons, the pollution of the environment, and the malfunction of nuclear power plants, there remains considerable faith in American technology's ability to solve problems and to improve society.[1] This faith was evidenced in 1991 by the national outpouring of zeal for the computerized weapons systems that initially appeared to have been decisive elements in the Persian Gulf War. Overnight, it seemed, any doubts about at least military technology's prowess evaporated amid numerous examples of its "high-tech" achievements. Suddenly the dormant spirit of technological utopianism had been revitalized, thereby legitimizing the otherwise questionable advertising claim of a high-tech company that technology is still "the romance of our age." As chapter 12 argues, high tech has an ongoing need to assert historical legitimacy in its advertising.

All of this is not, however, sufficient to dismiss technology's contemporary critics, among whom I count myself. Nor, for that matter, does it warrant endorsement of what I and others, paraphrasing historian Herbert Butterfield, like to call the overly optimistic "Whig Theory" of the history of technology.[2] Rather, it is to suggest the extraordinary complexity of the fundamental problem all the chapters in this book treat: the indeterminate relationship between technological progress and social progress. It is also to suggest the continuing utility of placing current concerns for that relationship in a historical context.

Technology, it must be emphasized even to engineers and engineering students, to say nothing of most other persons, consists of more than structures and machines alone,[3] more than just "hardware." It includes the uses of those structures and machines in the organization, evolution, and sometimes destruction of society. Technology also encompasses the technical skills and knowledge needed to invent, produce, improve, and repair those structures and machines. These constitute technology's "software." Thus all structures and machines, primitive or sophisticated, exist in a social context and, unless designed for the sake of design itself, serve a social function.

Throughout history, the initial social function of structures and machines has been to enable people to survive and adapt to the natural environment, later controlling it to enhance their quality of life. Another social function has been to enable people to construct an environment to replace, at least in part, the natural environment—but for the same beneficial purpose as controlling the natural environment.

It nevertheless comes to many as a revelation that technology, understood as such, has been present to some degree in every society. To contemplate a return to a primitive paradise without technology—an attraction to some simplistic contemporary critics of technology—is thus to indulge in a historical fantasy no better than that of the technological utopians. A nontechnological society *might* be possible in a genuine Garden of Eden. Elsewhere, technology's presence is a "given" that cannot be removed.

The existence of technology to some degree in virtually every society does not, of course, mean that its relationship with every society has been uniform. Quite the opposite: its relationships have been almost infinitely varied. In fact, the term "technological society" popularized by Jacques Ellul's book of the same (English) title[4] applies, I suggest, only to those societies in which technology has become not just the material basis for society but in a real sense its social and ideological model as well. Such societies include twentieth-century America and its comparatively few imitators. As chapter 4 argues, the efforts of the United States after World War II to "modernize" less technologically advanced societies in its own image were ill fated.

Moreover, whatever technology's impact on American and other societies, all societies and their cultures have had an impact—often profound—on technology. This likewise is a revelation even to many engineers. Just as specific structures and machines do not come about in a social vacuum, neither does technology more generally come about without needs and desires to be filled and values to be promoted on the part of at least some persons or groups in a particular society. To be sure, the structures and machines developed to meet those needs and desires and to promote those values may fail to do so. No less important, the advance of technology may have social consequences, which need not necessarily be negative, unanticipated by those responsible for it. Yet the fact that there are unexpected consequences undermines the Whig Theory's fundamental assumption of smooth unceasing technological and so social progress toward some kind of technological utopia. This in turn illustrates further the complexity of the relationships between technology and society in the past and present alike.

In terms of the relationships between technology and society in American history, it is reassuring to observe nowadays an unprecedented appreciation among historians of that complexity. The maturation since the 1960s of the history of American technology as an area of scholarship has naturally contributed the most to this reevaluation of American technology.[5] But the pervasive loss of faith among historians in the Whig Theory of American history as a whole has contributed as well. So, too, has the overdue concern for the lives of workers, women, minorities, and others previously neglected by most historians. If, then,

American history in general is no longer conceived and described as an unadulterated success story,[6] American technology in particular—hitherto deemed not just the principal means of progress but the very embodiment of progress—is inevitably being reconsidered too. In this respect the appearance in 1978 of Daniel Boorstin's *The Republic of Technology*, a sometimes pedestrian collection of essays and addresses not all of which even discuss technology, is a significant event. Boorstin, perhaps the ablest post–World War II historian celebrating the American past, here questions, if only briefly, both that Whiggish interpretation of American history and the contribution of technological change to it. His fundamental optimism remains intact, but growing concerns over American technology have forced him to reexamine what he and other historians traditionally took for granted.[7]

Concurrently, the maturation of American Studies, an area of scholarship that began at roughly the same time as the history of technology, has also contributed to this reevaluation of American technology.[8] The appearance since the 1960s of learned, penetrating, and frequently critical studies of the "American Dream" from the seventeenth through the twentieth centuries has deepened and altered the conception of America as a potential utopia.[9] Of special importance here, as will become evident, are Sacvan Bercovitch's *The American Jeremiad* (1979) and Cecelia Tichi's *New World, New Earth* (1979). Although Bercovitch's book is only peripherally concerned with technological advance, both works are extremely useful in illuminating American culture from its Puritan origins in the 1630s to approximately 1900, the historical backdrop against which serious twentieth-century critiques of American technology must be scrutinized.

Since its discovery and first settlement by Europeans, America had clearly been the object of utopian hopes abroad, and it was those hopes that fed America's own. What made America a potential utopia was its alleged status as a tabula rasa on which a new society could be impressed and its possession of enough natural resources to provide material plenty for all.

Nevertheless, the *potentiality* rather than reality of America as a utopia must be emphasized. Too many historians have assumed both that the sheer possession of abundant natural resources guaranteed that America would become an advanced society, perhaps a utopia, and that virtually all Americans from the seventeenth century on agreed with that proposition. In an earlier work Boorstin, for example, suggested that newly arrived Europeans and, in due time, their American-born descendants simply took stock of their natural resources and proclaimed the entire land utopia. Going further, Frederick Jackson Turner and his disciples made the same connection but defined those natural resources as free land alone.[10]

Unfortunately for Boorstin and Turner, there is a considerable gap between the appreciation of abundant resources on the one hand and the proclamation of them as utopian on the other. It is a gap that cannot be bridged by the naive Baconian views of American values held by these historians and others: that is, that values are culled from the natural environment rather than read into it. In the American case, in fact, the sources of that gap are fourfold: (1) the inheritance of a European tradition of utopianism, which gradually altered the prospect for the realization of utopia from the "impossible" to the "possible" to the "probable";[11] (2) the need to convert natural resources into finished products; (3) the existence of another civilization—the Native American—that viewed European civilization as an invader and as a rival for territory; and (4) the consequent existence of a partly inhabited territory rather than a "virgin land."[12]

Even had the sheer physical impact of European settlement been more benign than it was with respect to the Native American civilization, the threat to the new arrivals and their offspring of permanent scarcity frequently loomed far larger than the promise of eventual abundance. This fact has generally been ignored by those historians who read nineteenth- and twentieth-century paeans to abundance back into earlier periods of American history. Indeed, contemporary concerns about possible future scarcity in a society not long ago proclaimed "affluent" primarily account for whatever reconsideration of past affluence has occurred.

It is nevertheless apparent that, until at least the mid-nineteenth century, considerable numbers of European immigrants and their American-born descendants did not take abundance for granted. Instead, many of them conceived of even America's natural resources as finite, not infinite. The finished products derived from those resources and the wealth that might accrue from their manufacture, purchase, and distribution they conceived of as finite too—not merely because the raw materials were limited but also because other sources for the development of wealth could apparently not be created. Hence these Americans conceived of America as at best a *potential* utopia, but hardly a probable or an existing one.[13]

What, beginning in the mid-nineteenth century, changed these early American assumptions about scarcity was not the discovery of ever greater natural resources beyond the initial areas of European settlement. Rather, it was the invention of technological devices that not only converted raw materials into finished products at an unprecedented pace but also provided opportunities at last to create new wealth. New wealth could be created in three ways: (1) by the use of structures and machines to locate, extract, and transport otherwise unknown or unmovable natural resources; (2) by the invention and manufacture of synthetic "raw" materials like steel and in turn finished products; and (3) by the use of structures and machines to build canals, steamboats, and railroads and in due course farms, towns, and cities, all of which transformed much of America's vast lands into fluid—and infinitely expandable—capital.[14]

The result of these technological advances was the reconceptualization of America as an open rather than a closed system. It is hardly accidental that the first American technological utopian writings appeared just as those advances appeared in antebellum America.[15] Those and later technological advances were precisely what transformed the prospect for realizing utopia from the "impossible" to the "possible" to the "probable." As America as a man-made rather than a natural utopia became a distinct prospect, the originally Puritan notion of America as the site of God's millennial kingdom, the notion examined with great subtlety by Bercovitch and Tichi, became partly secularized. Human beings, not God, would be primarily responsible for transforming America from a potential to an actual utopia. Still, what Tichi rightly calls an "ideology" of environmental reform by no means became wholly secularized, and Bercovitch properly emphasizes the persistent fusion of the sacred and the profane throughout nineteenth-century America. Unlike their European counterparts, he observes, the "American Jeremiahs obviated the separation of the world and the kingdom, and then invested the symbol of America with the attributes of the sacred."[16] Yet dependence on people (and on their technology) rather than on God, which distinguishes utopianism from millenarianism, is a more than technical distinction and one that cannot be ignored even in the face of persistent and still influential millenarian rhetoric.

As Bercovitch and, more explicitly, Tichi demonstrate, a number of influential Americans from the Puritans through Whitman saw no necessary conflict between nature and technology. On the contrary, these Americans—whose ranks included clergymen, politicians, scientists, landscape architects, and men and women of letters—wished to alter the natural environment precisely to improve it; and not just the natural environment but the man-made environment as well. More to the point, realizing the apparently pervasive utopian vision of a genuine new world in America required utilizing nature and technology alike— not for the purpose of exploitation or economic gain but for the purpose of uplifting America and, ideally, the entire Western world. Damming streams, clearing forests, draining swamps, erecting towns and cities, and inventing and manufacturing the structures and machines necessary to accomplish those tasks were consequently acts of national—and, in America's millenarian tradition, spiritual—fulfillment. Those acts at once reflected and generated an overall though not unqualified optimism about America's destiny.

Not surprisingly, the specific relationships between nature and technology that Tichi and, to a lesser extent, Bercovitch treat were as varied as the relationships between technology and society noted earlier. Tichi's insightful analysis of those changing relationships from the Puritans through Whitman correctly includes a consideration in each case of the connection between the literary imagination and "real world" conditions. Although that connection varied over time as well, most of Tichi's examples confirm my own findings for the nineteenth and twentieth centuries of numerous actual attempts—not merely technological utopian visions—to preserve, enlarge, and refine what Leo Marx aptly calls the "middle landscape." By this Marx means a reconciliation between technology and the pastoral, a reconciliation which, as detailed in the next chapter, he unfortunately restricts to a handful of efforts between colonial times and the Civil War.[17] Though by no means always successful, these additional attempts to reconcile nature and technology further undermine simplistic interpretations of American technology. If the millenarian ideals that Bercovitch and Tichi describe did not avowedly motivate most of the utopian and "real world" reformers I examined, in their own, more secularized fashion all of them sought a radically improved America. The terms Tichi uses to describe the subjects of her study, such as "literary engineers" desiring an "engineered millennium" and an "engineered New Earth,"[18] could, if altered slightly, readily apply to the subjects of my (and other) more purely historical studies as well. And where, as Tichi shrewdly observes, we today equate environmental reform with restraint, earlier visionaries equated it with activity.

The industrial designers whom Jeffrey Meikle discusses in *Twentieth-Century Limited: Industrial Design in America, 1925–1939* (1979) represent a logical extension of this faith in evolutionary technological progress leading to a new world. Walter Dorwin Teague, Henry Dreyfuss, Raymond Loewy, and above all Norman Bel Geddes deemed a technological utopia of some kind not merely possible or probable, as it was conceived by the late nineteenth- and early twentieth-century visionaries I wrote about in my earlier book, but a world practically here. Its achievement, quite literally, simply awaited their design. Beginning with individual components of a new world such as streamlined appliances, vehicles, and buildings, they moved on to comprehensive design of an altogether new and avowedly man-made environment, one which would replace much of the natural environment. The 1939 New York World's Fair, as Meikle convincingly shows, epitomized these collective efforts and was definitely intended, as its slogan stated, as a preview of the "world of tomorrow." After visiting the dazzling exhibits designed by Teague, Dreyfuss, Loewy, and Geddes, especially Geddes's General Motors Futurama, thousands of Fair visitors readily agreed that the world of tomorrow was at hand.

The gap between this fantasy world and the real world proved far wider than the Fair's designers, its government and corporate sponsors, and probably most of its visitors ever anticipated. In general, the America of 1960 that Geddes envisioned has not yet been realized in the 1990s. This is one of several reasons for the obsolescence of world's fairs, as chapter 12 argues. More precisely, and most ironically, although the physical dimensions of the world of tomorrow have largely come about or, where not yet in place, readily could come about, given sufficient funds and desire, the social dimensions of that utopia, which Geddes, like the earlier technological utopians I studied, naively assumed would be the inevitable by-products of technological progress, have not yet materialized and could not readily do so. Consequently, the fate of Geddes's vision and the somewhat less explicit visions of his fellow industrial designers parallels the fate of the prophecies of those late nineteenth- and early twentieth-century technological utopians. This is not surprising, for the visions of the two groups are strikingly similar, especially in the physical layout of the world of tomorrow.

If Bercovitch convincingly interprets the American Jeremiad as both more optimistic and more influential than hitherto believed, this was confirmed twelve years later, with the resurgence of technological utopianism during the 1991 Persian Gulf War. In my view, however, the Jeremiad's traditional sense as a warning of doom ought now instead to apply, ironically, to the very modern technology once deemed a principal means of creating a heavenly kingdom of sorts on American earth. Technological progress surely *has* brought social progress, but it has not brought as much social progress—or as much happiness—as its fervent nineteenth- and twentieth-century advocates repeatedly predicted it would. And technological progress has obviously left a considerable share of social regress—and unhappiness—in its wake. *Twentieth-Century Limited*, the clever title of Meikle's fascinating book, a double-entendre referring to the premature end of both the streamlined style of industrial design and the legendary New York–Chicago luxury train which embodied it, might apply further to the centuries-old dream of technological utopia that has found its partial fulfillment but perhaps its permanent limitations in twentieth-century America. [19]

The critical issue, all told, is how to live sanely and humanely in America's pervasively technological society. That is where serious discussion about America's and technology's future ought to begin. And that is the focus of this book.

I

TECHNOLOGY AND AMERICAN HISTORY RETHOUGHT

2

. . . .

In the study of American history at all levels nature and technology are commonly treated as antagonists. Nature in whatever form is almost always portrayed as technology's enemy and, usually, its victim; as inevitably retreating before technology's unrelenting advance. My research on technological utopianism initially suggested to me that this polarity was inaccurate and that its perpetuation was unfortunate. If, as I discovered, the American technological utopians, the supreme believers in technology's right to progress anywhere and everywhere, themselves reconciled nature and technology in various ways, which Americans did not? And if comparatively few Americans actually viewed nature and technology as wholesale antagonists, how were the two reconciled? In pursuing these questions I eventually found the greatest assistance in the writings of Leo Marx. Yet I ultimately rejected as itself inaccurate his conclusion that nature and technology, once reconciled, were later permanently split. I instead discovered that their reconciliation took different forms over time and that illuminating those forms required revisions and reformulations of one of Marx's central concepts.

Nearly three decades after its publication, Leo Marx's *The Machine in the Garden: Technology and the Pastoral Ideal in America* (1964) has become a classic in the field of American Studies, along with such other works of the post–World War II era as Henry Nash Smith's *Virgin Land* (1950), R. W. B. Lewis's *The American Adam* (1955), and John William Ward's *Andrew Jackson: Symbol for an Age* (1955). Like them, *The*

Machine in the Garden utilizes literary and historical materials to define and explore the "meaning" of the "American experience." Marx asserts at the outset that what he calls "the pastoral ideal" "has been used to define the meaning of America ever since the age of discovery." His aim is to analyze the changing uses of that idea: to trace "its adaptation to the conditions of life in the New World, its emergence as a distinctively American theory of society, and its subsequent transformation under the impact of industrialism."[1] Marx's grandest claim is that the pastoral ideal embodies the meaning of America. Such a claim is scarcely provable, for it is metaphysical. My concern, however, is to evaluate not this claim but his more modest, if still grand, argument that the pastoral ideal has long best characterized the meaning of America for many Americans.

To analyze the "pastoral ideal" Marx employs above all the concept of "cultural symbol": "an image that conveys a special meaning . . . to a large number of those who share the culture."[2] He contends that the principal cultural symbol of the pastoral ideal has been "the machine in the garden." The machine stands for industrialization, and the garden for pastoral America. The machine *in* the garden represents the intrusion of industrialism, especially in the form of the railroad, on rural, preindustrial America.

Marx's particular concern is with the responses of certain Americans to that intrusion. Far from being complacent about it, Americans in general experienced the intrusion as "dissonant" with their existing beliefs and sought to overcome the dissonance. Indeed, Marx is as interested in the "consciousness" of dissonance as in the situation that created it.[3] The dissonance arose during the period from roughly 1800 to 1860,[4] when the pervasive assumption that the nation would continue to be a predominantly rural, agricultural society—a "garden"— seemed increasingly contradicted and threatened by the apparently relentless spread of industrialization—the "machine." Some Americans staunchly retained that assumption in the face of experience to the contrary. Others, after similar experiences, relinquished it. The most interesting response, however, and the one that most interests Marx, was that of those who neither retained nor repudiated that assumption but instead redefined it to meet the changing circumstances. The new cultural symbol embodying their redefinition was what Marx calls the "middle landscape." Though it derived from the pastoral ideal, it was an "imaginative and complex" version of it. In Marx's clearest definition, the middle landscape was "a new, distinctively American, post-romantic, industrial version of the pastoral design."[5]

The middle landscape did not differ from the traditional pastoral in fusing nature with civilization. The traditional pastoral itself had done that. Pastoralism never meant a yearning for outright primitivism. By definition it means a mediation between primitivism, or nature, and civilization. Hence its characteristic setting is not the forest but the farm. Although, as Marx notes, some late seventeenth-century and early eighteenth-century Americans like Robert Beverley periodically *turned* to the wilderness for inspiration, like Rousseau they harbored no wish to *return* there.[6] And by the late eighteenth century sophisticated Americans like the younger Jefferson and sympathetic Europeans like Crèvecoeur were finding greater inspiration in farming and the yeoman farmer than in the wilderness and the Indian. (The pervasiveness of technology in America by this point is largely ignored by Marx, as is colonial Americans' generally positive attitude toward it.)[7]

The middle landscape, then, differed from the traditional pastoral not in fusing nature and civilization but in fusing them in new ways and in response to a new condition: widespread industrialism. The originality of the middle landscape lay in its accommodation of nature to this condition, which was the severest form of civilization yet to appear. That in the process of accommodation the middle landscape transformed nature and civilization alike is a point missed by Marx and others.

In reconstructing the middle landscape, Marx implicitly qualifies the view of his mentor, Henry Nash Smith, that (quoting Marx) "down to the twentieth century the imagination of Americans was dominated by the idea of transforming the wild heartland into . . . a new 'Garden of the World'"—that is, a garden minus the machine. For if Smith satisfactorily demonstrates that (again quoting Marx) "Americans were unsentimental about unmodified nature"[8] and were eager to transform the wilderness into a garden, Marx shows that, contrary to Smith, the kind of garden they sought not only varied over time but gradually made room for the machine. Hence Smith's lament at the conclusion of *Virgin Land* that the exclusively agricultural garden he describes "was powerless to confront issues arising from the advance of technology"[9] is unwarranted.

Thomas Bender has refined Marx's own analysis by emphasizing what Marx barely notes: that the ideal of the machine in the garden did not necessarily mean the city in the garden. For Jefferson and his contemporaries carefully distinguished manufacturing and commerce, which most of them favored, from cities, which most of them did not, given the known ills then plaguing the major English and continental European cities.[10] If, as the Jeffersonians conceded, an initially rural republic must for economic reasons become semi-industrialized, then "workshops in the wilderness," as Marvin Fisher, Marx's student, calls them, would suffice.[11]

From 1830 to 1860 both Americans themselves and, as Fisher shows, their European visitors shared and appreciated this distinction between industries and cities. The initial success of Humphreysville, Lawrence, Waltham, and especially Lowell, plus other early factory communities set amid rural landscapes, seemed to confirm their faith that America could absorb and perhaps advance European industry and technology while avoiding Europe's crowded, diseased, and grimy city life. Consequently, the equation made by Jefferson and Tocqueville of republican virtue with good land and honest labor now included honest commerce and manufacturing as well.[12]

After 1860, however, this dream of the middle landscape became distant, at least according to Marx. Rampant industrialization, immigration, and finally urbanization—to recite the worn litany—overran and spoiled the real landscape. Marx reads all major American writers from Hawthorne to Fitzgerald as successively predicting, observing, and bemoaning this fact. The incompatibility of the machine and the pastoral is for Marx "the great issue of our culture. It is the germ . . . of the most final of all generalizations about America."[13] After 1860, he concludes, the middle landscape was no longer a realistic social and cultural ideal but a cheap rhetorical device masking a painfully different reality. In effect, it became a "popular and sentimental" version of the pastoral. Required instead were new cultural "symbols of possibility."[14]

Where Marx contrasts the literary and intellectual rejection of the middle landscape to the popular retention of it, Bender demonstrates that ordinary citizens as well as extraordinary writers were affected by the "cultural crisis" which its fate precipitated. Many reformers, businessmen, factory workers, and Lowell "mill girls" were sensitive to the delicateness of the balance between garden and machine and often fearful that it had been tipped permanently in favor of the latter.

Bender's most important revision of Marx, however, is his recognition that there existed other responses to industrialization and urbanization beyond the single middle landscape Marx depicts. If the Lowell of 1840, a mere fourteen years old, was, as Bender contends, no longer "a 'middle landscape'"[15] but already an authentic and problem-plagued city, there nevertheless persisted well beyond 1840 imaginative efforts by thoughtful Americans—and, again, not only writers—to create what I will term three new versions of the middle landscape: urban, suburban, and regional. Bender treats only the urban version, and treats it as only a variation on Marx's version, not as a new version in its own right. But as far as he goes, he shows, albeit implicitly, that the middle landscape was not, as for Smith and Marx alike, a static symbol ever less in accord with reality. Rather, as Smith wished *his* "master symbol" to be, the middle landscape was (quoting Smith) an "intellectual apparatus for taking account of the industrial revolution."[16] Marx himself grants twice that the concept of the middle landscape was continually redefined to meet new circumstances,[17] but nevertheless limits it—and so its capacity for redefinition—to antebellum rural America.

The urban version of the middle landscape preceded the suburban and regional versions. It arose after 1830 and as a "movement" lasted until about 1900. Where the original version—Marx's exclusive version—of the middle landscape meant a fusion of nature and civilization, or garden and machine, the urban version meant, instead, their juxtaposition. Where, however, civilization in the original version did not include cities, in the urban version it did; the virtual inseparability of large-scale industrialization from urbanization was now conceded. The aim of the urban middle landscape was not to escape from the cities but to balance them against the country. Manifestations of this new middle landscape included "rural" cemeteries, "rural" walkways, and city parks. Their purpose was to alleviate city problems without leaving the city: the country was either brought inside the city or, more commonly, established just at the city limits, as a temporary, not permanent, relief from the city. More than its predecessor, this new middle landscape "offered the attractions of rural life without any of its liabilities: the beauty and freedom of the country without the arduous labor, the loneliness, or the cultural poverty of farm life."[18]

It did so, however, because the country was not only adjacent to the city but also as "civilized" as the city, thanks to the kind of scrupulous planning that had characterized certain "workshops in the wilderness" like Lowell. This new planning of the country, which Marx and Bender, among others, ignore, was itself a technological achievement and so figuratively if no longer literally another example of the machine in the garden.

The illustrious career of Frederick Law Olmsted (1822–1903), ignored by Marx but discussed by Bender, spans the emergence of both the urban and the suburban middle landscapes. And not surprisingly, for as Albert Fein contends, Olmsted was nothing less than a pioneering planner of the entire American environment.[19] Even in his original career as gentleman farmer Olmsted was, or tried to be, "scientific." When, after 1850, he gave up farming and turned to the city as the fresh focal point of American civilization, he retained this concern for treating the landscape scientifically, including where, as in his designs for parks, parkways, playgrounds, campuses, estates, and suburbs, he retained much of the natural setting. In this respect, as Bender, Fein, and others correctly note, Olmsted's many city parks—capped by his masterpiece, New York City's Central Park, 1857–58—are significant as countrysides adjoining or surrounded by cities. What has, however, been ignored is that these city parks are themselves scientifically planned tracts with *man-made* footpaths, bridle paths, pavilions, streams, and ponds akin to the *man-made* buildings adjoining or surrounding them. To have left Central Park and other parks in their "natural," "primitive" state would have been to polarize nature and civilization. Instead, while keeping actual factories and large machines out of his parks, Olmsted nevertheless "civilized" nature and transformed country and city into an urban version of the middle landscape.

Yet Olmsted's observations of contemporary city life convinced him that, notwithstanding his own contributions to urban amenities, American cities suffered from insufficient spontaneity, congeniality, and "sense of community," and from excessive noise, dirt, and crowding as well. He therefore shifted his energies from the urban landscape to the suburban one and designed several suburban communities, beginning with Berkeley, California, in 1866 and Riverside, Illinois, in 1868.[20] Olmsted never turned antiurban, however. He not only continued to accept the inevitability of cities but envisioned suburbs inside as well as outside city limits, and as integral parts of cities in both cases. At the same time he viewed suburbs as autonomous and distinct neighborhoods, not complete cities writ small or sprawling large. Like his parks, Olmsted's suburbs were, needless to say, well planned. They featured modern homes on carefully landscaped sites; walkways and parkways; playgrounds; public spaces; and drainage and sewerage systems. As such, they represented a further refinement of the American urban environment.

For Olmsted, the suburbs were a means of improving urban life. But for those after him, who witnessed the decline of the cities, the suburbs constituted the opposite: a means of escape from urban life. The balance between country and city, which Olmsted forever sought and temporarily achieved, was soon toppled. Nevertheless, Bender's concluding lament about the "lost heritage" of this second middle landscape, so similar to Marx's lament about the first, fails to recognize that the suburban and later the regional versions of the middle landscape emerged to take its place.

To be sure, Olmsted's suburbs were not America's first. A considerable number had arisen before 1866.[21] Olmsted himself was strongly influenced by the example of Llewellyn Park, New Jersey (1852–53). But with this exception, along with Riverside, Berkeley, and a few others, these early suburbs were *only* retreats from the city and not, as Olmsted wished, means of revitalizing it.

The fullest development of the suburban landscape did not come until 1880, with the comprehensive planning of suburbs. Earlier suburbs were haphazardly planned—houses and buildings were simply erected, without regard to the environment—and Olmsted's suburbs, which *were* meticulously planned, were too much a part of the city to qualify as full-fledged suburbs. Because American suburbs have always been architecturally, economically, and socially disparate, none embodies the third, or suburban, middle landscape the way Lowell embodies the first and Central Park the second.

There are, however, various ways of categorizing comprehensively planned suburbs. The most common is the division into three varieties: the commuter suburb (Shaker Heights, Ohio; the Country Club District of Kansas City, Missouri); the industrial suburb (Pullman, Illinois); and the "garden cities" inspired by the English reformer Ebenezer Howard as garden suburbs. Historians have analyzed each of these examples but have failed to examine them in the context of the middle landscape.

In all three cases the site of the middle landscape is the country, as in the original version, rather than the city, as in the second; and the country is generally beyond walking distance of the city, as in the original version, rather than surrounding or surrounded by it, as in the second. Yet the country remains accessible to the city, and precisely through technology—through railroads and, later, cars. And the countryside itself is in all three cases well planned and modernized—the machine making possible the modernized garden.

The electrified street railways of the 1880s, along with cars in the early 1900s, spurred the rise of commuter suburbs outside of Boston, Milwaukee, Norfolk, and other cities.[22] These vehicles were the logical successors to the omnibuses of the 1820s and the horse-drawn street railways of the 1850s, neither of which could travel as quickly, as comfortably, or as far as growing numbers of disenchanted city dwellers wished. Although the commuter suburbs were better designed than most cities, they were usually drab and uniform, commercialism ordinarily governing their construction. The best planned commuter suburbs were Shaker Heights and the Country Club District.[23] They balanced aesthetic and environmental concerns with financial ones and thereby fulfilled the ideal of the commuter suburb.

Commercialism also governed the construction of the Chicago suburb of Pullman (1880–85), named after the railroad magnate who founded it. Yet so much planning and expense went into its construction that it seemed the salvation of industrial America and the harbinger of *industrialized* utopian communities. George Pullman himself, though, harbored less sublime designs. Like his counterparts in other "company towns"—above all United States Steel's Gary, Indiana—and, for that matter, like his predecessors in Lowell and elsewhere, he viewed his creation as primarily a financial investment, which, despite its enormous cost, would one day prove profitable. Once worker discontent loomed too costly, however, Pullman, like United States Steel, simply abandoned his "model city," consigning it to the sad fate of ordinary industrial communities. Nevertheless, his company town, more than any other in the nineteenth or early twentieth century, set machines and buildings in carefully landscaped parklike sites, with lakes, fountains, greenery, and boulevards carved out of the flat prairie. If only for a brief time, Pullman seemed an exemplar of the second of the three varieties of suburban middle landscape: the industrial suburb.[24]

Only in the case of the third kind of suburban middle landscape, the garden city, did planning regularly take priority over profit. That its founder, Ebenezer Howard, was a genuine visionary rather than a businessman doubtless accounts for the fact. As Howard envisioned in his landmark book *Tomorrow: A Peaceful Path to Real Reform* (1898), each garden city was to be a well-planned community of thirty thousand, with a balanced industrial and agricultural economy circumscribed by fields and a forest, or greenbelt. All of the garden cities were to be interlinked by rapid transit systems and superhighways and linked in turn to a regional center of sixty thousand. The most prominent American garden cities were Forest Hills Gardens, Long Island, New York (1911), Sunnyside Gardens, Queens, New York (1929), Radburn, New Jersey (1929), Greenbelt, Maryland (1937), Greenhills, Ohio (1938), and Greendale, Wisconsin (1938).[25]

For varying reasons, no American garden city completely fulfilled Howard's original dream, which *was* realized in the garden cities he himself established at Letchworth, England (1903), and at Welwyn, England (1920). Forest Hills Gardens, for example, proved so expensive to construct that it became a predominantly residential, noncommercial community and a sanctuary for the prosperous rather than a home for wage earners of all kinds. Similarly, Sunnyside Gardens and Radburn eventually became predominantly residential suburbs. The American communities that adhered longest if not most faithfully to the garden city ideal were Greenbelt, Greenhills, and Greendale—the three established during the New Deal at the urging of "Brain Trust" member Rexford Tugwell, who in truth sought three thousand greenbelt cities instead of just three. Though none of the three made provision for agriculture or industry, all did include a greenbelt and well-landscaped pastoral settings. Moreover, despite their individual deviations from Howard's ideals, all of the six most prominent garden cities together brought country and city, and machine and garden, into a more stable balance than either the commuter or the industrial suburbs did. The garden cities were, then, the most successful variety of the suburban middle landscape.

The fate of the countryside in an increasingly urbanized and suburbanized society was the initial concern of advocates of the fourth version of the middle landscape: the regional. Like Olmsted and his fellow pioneering landscape architects, such early ecologists as George Perkins Marsh, William John McGee, John Wesley Powell, and Nathaniel Shaler were neither "against" cities nor "for" nature.[26] They were simply seeking to preserve a countryside that, they feared, was fast disappearing. Their views bespeak the regional middle landscape because it was with vast areas of land that they were concerned. They were in fact the first conservationists, and, as Samuel Hays has shown, their opponents were as often an indifferent public as greedy developers. They were not merely romantic nature lovers, as traditionally portrayed, but hard-nosed scientists and technicians determined to apply scientific techniques to their ends.[27] They rejected older notions that the optimal relationship between people and nature lay in primitivism, or even classical pastoralism. Instead, they believed in the scientifically planned environment.

Post–World War I advocates of the regional middle landscape had to take more formal account of the proliferation of cities and suburbs. The vision of a regional landscape integrating cities, suburbs, towns, and farms within a scrupulously planned, well-tended landscape was best articulated by the Regional Planning Association of America (RPAA), a group of conservationists, planners, architects, economists, and social philosophers who met regularly between 1923 and 1933. In its planning of regional populations, economies, and institutions, the RPAA tried to avoid the extremes of either centralized urbanization or decentralized suburbanization. Following Olmsted, it also sought to satisfy citizens' social and psychological needs, not merely their physical and financial requirements. It was also sensitive to the value of regional diversity and so refrained from advocating a single scheme for all regions, this despite its members' admiration for the garden city. In its commitment to diversity, the RPAA strove as much to preserve as to establish worthy buildings and communities. It saw no conflict between these aesthetic and humane concerns and its equally strong concern for efficiency, which it pursued through detailed cost analyses of all its proposals.[28]

Although on several grounds it hardly meets the RPAA's standards of proper regionalism, the Tennessee Valley Authority (TVA) represents the nation's foremost example of regional planning. Created by President Roosevelt in 1933, it was seized on from its inception by proponents and opponents alike as the symbol of government intervention in economic affairs. So intense was the opposition that neither Roosevelt nor Arthur Morgan, whom he appointed TVA's chairman, was able to implement political, social, and cultural reforms alongside the economic improvements. Yet if the TVA thus did not produce grass-roots democracy and cooperative communitarianism, it did produce numerous technical achievements such as dam construction, flood control, land reclamation, and cheap electrical power. These advances surpassed those of the "Progressive" conservationists Hays describes. More important, TVA altered and improved a considerable portion of the southern landscape and did so, as the RPAA wished, scientifically.[29]

The culmination of the regional middle landscape is the "megalopolis"—a massive urban-suburban tract that leaves scant untouched landscape in its wake. The term "megalopolis" was coined in 1961 by Jean Gottmann in his book *Megalopolis: The Urbanized Northeastern Seaboard of the United States*.[30] Since then, other areas of the country have been similarly categorized. For Sam Bass Warner, as of the early 1970s, Los Angeles, the hub of the "Californian megalopolis" and the archetypal "fragmented metropolis," possessed the vast amount of room, urban-suburban decentralization, and therefore flexibility he believed necessary to achieve racial and economic justice, adequate public housing, and other social ends.[31] Whether, given the problems that have plagued Los Angeles in the past two decades, Warner or anyone else still believes this would be interesting to learn.

If more and more areas of the United States have become megalopolises, numerous utopian and reform-minded writers of the late nineteenth and early twentieth centuries envisioned the whole nation as a series of megalopolises, and they saw it as the perfect—or at least as a most desirable—organization of society. John Thomas has provided an illuminating analysis of the "model of the good society as a composite of city and country" held in common by utopians Henry George, Edward Bellamy, and Henry Demarest Lloyd. All three were forced by unchecked industrialization, urbanization, and other problems of the "real" world to move the locus of their ideal societies from the small towns in which they were raised to an "urban-rural continuum" of fully regional proportions, where overcrowded cities could be depopulated, sparsely settled countrysides repopulated, and traditional "neighborhoods" restored.[32]

Other utopians whom Thomas does not consider held comparable visions of America as a series of regional units. These visionaries included the twenty-five technological utopians whom I discussed in my *Technological Utopianism in American Culture*. Their envisioned megalopolises constituted what one utopian, Henry Olerich, called *A Cityless and Countryless World* (1893).[33] As another such utopian, Albert Howard, described the new America:

All cities are now circular in form the radii of which is [sic] one hundred miles, with an approximate circumference of seven hundred miles. . . . In all there are about twenty cities. . . . Indeed, by the all potent power of electricity, man is now able to convert an entire continent into a tropical garden at his pleasure.[34]

All of these utopian visions exemplify what Marx, citing Smith, contends has been "the cardinal image of American aspirations" since Jefferson's day: "a well-ordered green garden magnified to continental size."[35]

The four versions of the middle landscape described here barely introduce either the concept itself or its myriad manifestations in America, much less in Europe.[36] They merely sketch past and present attempts to meet threats to the ideal of the middle landscape, to achieve a synthesis in the "dialectical conflict between a pastoral ideal and a technological reality"[37] that Marx to this day still believes is impossible to achieve. Numerous other examples of such attempts are to be found in works by, among others, William Bowers, Don Kirschner, James Machor, Peter Schmitt, Reynold Wik, and, most recently, Peter Rowe.[38]

Clearly the middle landscape concept is applicable beyond Marx's restricted use of it, but I suggest four cautions in extending it. First, and least important, none of the persons studied by either Marx or me used the term "middle landscape," not that our respective uses of it to describe their efforts misrepresent them. Second, and more important, the concept is imprecise insofar as Marx sees technology as dynamic and destructive and nature as static and constructive rather than both as in fact being partly static and partly dynamic, partly constructive and partly destructive—depending on the particular circumstances. Third, and still more important, the concept may apply to Europe as well and so not be as peculiarly American as Marx suggests. Finally, and most important, the concept may ironically prove *too* useful, may explain so much of American history that it explains very little specifically.

Whatever the concept's ultimate utility, Marx's statement back in 1964 that the middle landscape had passed from the American scene a century earlier was unduly gloomy. Neither the yearning for the middle landscape nor the striving to realize it has ceased. Only the form in which it could be realized has changed. As Marx himself conceded in 1978:

One shortcoming of that book, soon made evident by events, had been my failure to recognize adequately the political basis for the continuing appeal of the pastoral world-view to Americans.

Nothing in my discussion of the subject could have prepared readers for the resurgence of native pastoralism, or the widespread dissemination of the fatalistic view of technology it fostered, during the explosion of protest incited by the Vietnam War. On the contrary, I had meant to leave the impression that our national susceptibility to pastoral idealism had been the product of largely transient circumstances, and that it therefore could have been expected to wane in the era of high technology. A few weeks after the book was published, however, Mario Savio, a graduate student at the University of California at Berkeley, told a mass sit-in of students, faculty, and others that the time had come for them to throw their bodies on "the machine," if need be, in order to stop it. That demonstration marked a critical point in the emergence of the radical student movement, and Savio's speech helped to popularize a metaphor that epitomizes much of the radical thinking of the 1960s.[39]

Here as in other writings since *The Machine in the Garden* appeared Marx has discussed the political dimensions of the issues his book treats in a largely nonpolitical context. Indeed, the book ends with the provocative but bare statement that "The machine's sudden entrance into the garden presents a problem that ultimately belongs not to art but to politics."[40] By contrast, Raymond Williams's complementary *The Country and the City* (1973), which concentrates on European literature and history, is avowedly political in its analysis. This is not to suggest that Marx was ever apolitical, for politics has always been a principal concern for him,[41] but to note the more explicit presence of politics in his later writings as he has been forced to acknowledge, however reluctantly, the persistence of at least some Americans' quest for the middle landscape.

In fact, where later in the 1978 essay quoted above Marx dismissed the likely political appeal of pastoralism and so the middle landscape to more than a tiny minority of Americans, by 1986 he could argue that "pastoralism, so far from being an anachronism in the era of high technology, may be particularly well suited to the ideological needs of a large, educated, relatively affluent, mobile, yet morally and spiritually troubled segment of the white middle class." Moreover, Marx here still claims that the pastoral ideal has long been and continues to be "used to define the meaning of America."[42]

These significant qualifications of his 1964 position lend support to my overall contention that the persistent quest for the middle landscape has been no forlorn exercise in nostalgia but a quite realistic and deliberate effort to reconcile phenomena—country and city, machine and garden—that we too often teach and are taught are irreconcilable. It is Leo Marx's achievement to have offered a more attractive and more accurate account of their early relationship.[43] I have in turn explored the continuation rather than disappearance of that relationship in later periods of American history. The clear persistence of the middle landscape in the four versions outlined here provides an opportunity to place American technology in a different historical perspective and to rethink the "meaning of America" for countless Americans. Insofar as Americans' quest for the middle landscape continues today, this historical perspective also illuminates contemporary discussions of American urban and suburban culture and crises.

3

. . . .

Like many other developments in American technology, the automobile has frequently been treated as either altogether good or altogether evil. The following two quotations are representative.

It is often said that a civilization may be measured by its facilities of locomotion. If this is true, as seems abundantly proved by present facts and the testimony of history, the new civilization that is rolling in with the horseless carriage will be a higher civilization than the one we now enjoy (Editorial, "The Horseless Age," inaugural issue of *The Horseless Age: A Monthly Journal Devoted to the Interests of the Motor Vehicle Industry* 1 [November 1895]: 7).

The ending of the age of automobility undoubtedly marks a significant turning point in American historical development. For automobility has had a more profound impact on Americans in the twentieth century than even Frederick Jackson Turner's frontier had on our nineteenth-century forebears. The question for the future is whether the new era of American history that is dawning will continue to develop as the age of the superstate serving the supercorporation, with self-interest, greed, and waste being its cardinal, and ultimately self-destructive, values. An alternative future characterized by true community and expanded democracy, free from the privatism, materialism, escapism, and exploitation that the automobile culture encouraged, is also within our grasp (James J. Flink, *The Car Culture* [Cambridge: MIT Press, 1975], 233).

As the quotation from *The Horseless Age* suggests, such treatment of the auto as being either good or evil dates back to its initial appearance in America in the 1890s. And as the quotation from *The Car Culture* indicates, such treatment persists today amid pervasive disillusionment with the auto, for reasons too familiar to detail here. One might therefore consider the auto as a prime example, a case study, of only contemporary concerns for the fate of our avowedly "technological society": that is, a society in which technology has become not just the material basis for society but in a real sense its social and ideological model. More specifically, one might consider the present criticisms of the auto as reflecting a profound change merely in recent decades in the attitudes of many Americans toward technology as a whole: from technology as a solution to all problems to technology as both a social and a technical problem in itself.

Yet reducing the issue of the auto's contribution to American society and culture to a question of good or evil is simplistic. Indeed, such an intellectual strategy actually distorts the past. Although some Americans of every generation from 1900 to the present *have* viewed the auto as either good or evil, a majority of twentieth-century Americans, I submit, have had more complex opinions. They have been overwhelmingly favorable toward the auto, at least until the early 1970s, but they have not been uncritical. They have valued the auto as a means of progress—and often as an embodiment of progress—but they have not been oblivious to the prices paid for such "progress."[1] Ironically, the severest critics of modern technology have rarely refused to dispense with the auto, among other technological devices, and have invariably depended upon it (and the train and airplane, etc.) to spread their message of modern technology's alleged evils.

In this chapter I will probe further several related dimensions of these more complex "mainstream" attitudes toward the auto and in turn toward technology as a whole. In particular, I will examine the extent to which the auto has been—and might again be—perceived and utilized as a principal means of reconciling phenomena ordinarily deemed irreconcilable: country and city, agriculture and industry, and most important for our time, "antitechnology" and "protechnology" ideologies.

From the beginnings of America's industrial revolution in the early nineteenth century until the present, citizens have routinely been taught that wilderness and civilization—or, in the terms most pertinent here, nature and technology—are permanently irreconcilable. The industrialization and urbanization of America inevitably meant the destruction of large portions of the American wilderness, the story goes, and the contemporary clashes between "environmentalists" and "developers" are merely another stage in that traditional conflict. Any serious reconciliation between nature and technology would seem improbable.

To be sure, these conflicts have existed, persist, and almost surely will continue. Yet in practice, if not in theory, throughout American history countless attempts have been made to mediate between nature and technology, as outlined in the previous chapter on the "middle landscape." A comprehensive history of those attempted mediations would constitute little less than a new history of the United States. Moreover, relatively few Americans at any time in our history have preferred either untouched nature or unadulterated technological advance. Whatever their particular prospects for realizing it, they have more often than not sought "the best of both worlds."

All three of the newer middle landscapes discussed in chapter 2— the urban, the suburban, and the regional—arose before the auto did, and all three at least initially depended upon other forms of transportation. Yet the auto was certainly important to each one and was crucial to the growth—and the appeal—of the suburban version after 1900. The automobile enabled millions to work in the city and live in the country, the "country" being of various distances from the city and taking various forms. The need for special tracks or wires or, for that matter, horses had limited the distance and the location of those earlier forms of transportation and so the flexibility and mobility of their (potential) patrons. Moreover, the use of horses meant a lack of cleanliness and a threat of disease which especially irritated "respectable" commuters. Meanwhile the use of public transportation of whatever variety meant additional irritation to them in the form of inevitable mingling with less respectable citizens. By contrast, as highways sprouted across America, the auto provided not only much more flexibility and mobility but also much more individual and family privacy and independence, at comparatively lower costs. Those many Americans who could afford an auto but not a suburban residence could still experience the country through periodic drives beyond the city limits.[2]

The attraction of the auto in this regard, it should be emphasized, was not restricted to inhabitants of older eastern and midwestern cities. Western and southern cities often favored the auto as a means of bridging country and city even (or especially) when, by virtue of either their youth or their industrial "underdevelopment," those cities had escaped many of the ills of their elder and more industrialized counterparts. And in the West and South, as in the East and Midwest, those able and willing to live outside the city nevertheless sought regular and easy access to it by auto.[3] Nor, for that matter, was the appeal of the auto restricted to urban and suburban folk. As Reynold Wik has demonstrated, farmers were as receptive to Ford's autos as to his tractors.[4] Far from viewing technology in these instances as an intrusion on their cherished agrarian ideal, they saw it as enhancing that ideal—and not simply because Ford himself hailed from a farming background and boasted of his origins. The auto and the tractor reduced the farmer's social and cultural isolation—"the idiocy of rural life," as Karl Marx called it; reduced the labor required to grow, harvest, and transport crops; and in turn increased access to markets, and thus profits.

In all these cases, then, and in others too numerous to cite here, not conflict but reconciliation between nature and technology was the principal objective. The significance of this point for an understanding of American culture as a whole, I suggest, can hardly be overemphasized.

Despite its appeal to consumers from so many segments of American society, the auto did not lack for critics. By the early 1920s Americans were beginning to pay a considerable price for what historian James Flink has properly called our "car culture": greater urban and suburban congestion, deteriorating central business and residential districts, disappearing public transportation systems, consolidation of small farms into larger ones, mechanical breakdowns, increasing traffic accidents and fatalities, and growing family and community dispersal. In fact, nearly all of the principal arguments commonly offered in favor of the auto had countering arguments.

In light of these earlier criticisms of the auto, it is necessary to confirm yet refine the point made tentatively at the outset about American attitudes toward technology as a whole in the twentieth century. If, as in the significant case of the auto, modern technology solved a number of problems, social as well as technical, from the outset it simultaneously bred or helped breed several others, social and technical alike. Equally important, relatively soon after its development as a product for mass consumption, not simply in recent decades, the auto was widely perceived as having both these positive and negative tendencies. Consequently, contemporary critiques of the car culture, whether justified or not, do have historical antecedents—contrary to what some of those critics assume.

Nevertheless, more research needs to be conducted on the role of the auto as a prime example of what I would term the characteristic American *accommodation* to technological development. By "accommodation" I mean the gradual acceptance of technological change, whether happily or not, as contrasted with the fierce opposition to such change symbolized by the English Luddites, or "machine breakers," of the early nineteenth century. The contribution of the auto to the promotion of the middle landscape is surely a revealing example of such accommodation. But as already indicated, it hardly exhausts the possibilities, several of which are suggested by the research of other historians of the auto on topics ranging from motels to gas stations.[5]

Americans' characteristic accommodation to technological change reflects what I would call their characteristic and complex conservative notion of progress through technology. This issue can likewise merely be sketched here. But suffice it to say that technological advances of various kinds have invariably been promoted, if not always universally accepted, as allowing Americans to achieve various changes without fundamentally altering their basic institutions and values. The promotion of the auto as enhancing Americans' existing individuality, mobility, privacy, and so democratic freedom is only one of countless examples of this orientation toward the future. It is for precisely this reason that the history of American technology is properly understood as reflecting more than shaping the society and culture from which it derives. The same holds true for all other societies, contrary to common notions of technology itself molding every society to varying degrees.[6]

The logical finale of this orientation toward the future is the long-standing and pervasive reliance on technological advances to fulfill America's alleged millennial—or, in secularized fashion, its utopian—potential. Technology was widely deemed a principal means of bridging the gap between the premillennium and the millennium or between preutopia and utopia. No less important but less often perceived, the transition via technological progress was usually expected to be evolutionary, gradual, and fairly smooth.[7] Consequently, the millennial or utopian ideal sought commonly represented the extension rather than the antithesis of the existing society. The new world would usually grow directly out of the existing world, not atop its ruins. Hence another reason to modulate the protest against the negative economic and social consequences of technological change; the alleged benefits were in the offing. And hence the seeming paradox of conservatism in the very name of radicalism—but a complex conservatism. Such complex conservatism is epitomized in the various attempted mediations between nature and technology outlined earlier,[8] those quests for "the best of both worlds." It is epitomized as well in the technological utopian fiction and nonfiction of Edward Bellamy, author of *Looking Backward* (1888), and his contemporaries, as detailed in chapter 8. The existence of this complex conservatism explains how so many Americans in so many different generations and situations could see the auto—an otherwise revolutionary invention—as a means of enhancing as opposed to undermining their particular circumstances; and why those same Americans were willing to bear the considerable burdens noted above for it.

In view of all this, Flink's delight over the impending demise of the car culture, much like Leo Marx's lament over the disappearance of the middle landscape after the Civil War, appears ahistorical and premature. Whatever the fate of the veritable American "culture" surrounding the auto which has admittedly developed, the auto per se is likely to survive in this country for the foreseeable future. Obviously its size, style, and power source will change drastically, as might its role in daily life. But the decline of the car culture need not, contrary to Flink and others, mean the virtual elimination of the auto or the transformation of the larger culture. Just as contemporary critiques of the auto ought to be tempered by the recognition that they are not unprecedented, so ought their accompanying apocalyptic visions of the auto's doom be humbled by the knowledge that earlier prophecies, hopeful and pessimistic alike, invariably failed to anticipate the future accurately.[9]

It is surely revealing that Flink's latest book, *The Automobile Age* (1988), qualifies his 1975 obituary for the car culture. He continues to contend that as a force for progress, the automobile industry and the culture surrounding it have been dead for decades. As economic and social forces in America and elsewhere, however, they may yet thrive into the next century—aided by various technological advances ironically developed by other industries. If anything, *The Automobile Age* is favorably disposed toward at least the automobile industry insofar as it has finally produced smaller, safer, less polluting, more fuel-efficient vehicles that can compete successfully with foreign imports. Flink's reasonable and persuasive revisionist positions reflect the intellectual attitudes concerning technology advocated here.[10]

Still, Americans' enthusiasm for the auto as an instrument, let alone an embodiment, of progress *has* certainly subsided. The current Japanese challenge to traditional American supremacy in the auto industry worldwide can be blamed—and praised—for many things, but not this. Meanwhile the ideal of the suburban middle landscape, prevalent in theory just as the post–World War II suburban explosion of cheap, partial imitations nullified it in practice, has faded as well. In turn, the handful of prewar American "garden cities," communities painstakingly designed to accommodate the auto in handsome settings, have with few exceptions become conventional suburbs. Nor have the visionary "cities of tomorrow" of the 1930s and 1940s, with their skyscrapers and superhighways planned for the suburban commuter, fared much better; if anything, the dreams of Norman Bel Geddes and other industrial designers and architects seem either passé or merely banal today.[11]

What, then, *is* the auto's future place in American culture? It is at once a necessary and valued yet problematic part of our individual and collective lives. At the risk of sounding unduly abstract, I propose that the persistence of the auto in whatever form be recognized as part of a de facto ongoing movement in America and elsewhere toward what I would term a technological plateau. By "technological plateau" I mean a society in which technology has become sufficiently advanced and widespread that equivalent attention can be given to achieving equally vital nontechnological improvements: social, economic, cultural, political, and so forth.[12] As in the case of the auto, technological progress has not necessarily meant stagnation or regression in the nontechnological realm, but progress in the two domains has rarely been equal, not least in the United States. That in turn is not to suggest the technological determinism in American history denied above but rather to suggest that American society and culture will in fact continue to shape American technology precisely as Americans' values and expectations change and evolve. It is also to propose that beyond a certain level of affluence for increasing numbers of citizens—a level, I concede, hardly yet reached by millions of Americans and others—further technological advances are less and less important and less and less appreciated.

Instead, other objectives—such as avoiding boredom, institutionalizing diversity at both work and leisure, extending democracy, and preserving the remaining natural environment—gradually become paramount.

Doubtless there are a number of exceptions to this generalization even among the very affluent persons to whom it most applies: for example, the seemingly endless benefits of computers (albeit with their own drawbacks, as discussed in chapter 7). Yet the growing indifference—or hostility—of numerous intelligent Americans to such one-time technological wonders as television, space flight, nuclear power, and, for that matter, large autos is indicative of the movement I outline. So too is the persistent popularity of such notions as "small is beautiful" and "appropriate technology."

These notions, however, like that of the technological plateau, are not mindlessly "antitechnology." This must be made emphatic to those contemporary technological utopians who would otherwise dismiss them as a priori impractical or reactionary. Rather, they seek—or presume—a mediation between technology and society akin to that of the middle landscape in all four of its earlier versions. In a sense, they are yet another version of the middle landscape. They apply directly to the auto as its own technology becomes, in effect, smaller and more appropriate to conditions of limited natural resources and of environmental hazards.

Lewis Mumford, whose critique of modern technology is explored in chapter 11, wrote repeatedly about slowing the pace of technological advance and creating a "technical plateau" in highly technological societies like the United States. In 1938, for example, he argued that

> Our problem in America, unlike that of our comrades in Soviet Russia, is to reduce the tempo of industrialism. We must turn society from its feverish preoccupation with money-making inventions, goods, profits, salesmanship, symbolic representations of wealth to the deliberate promotion of the more humane functions of life.[13]

Four years earlier, in fact, he had described the beginning of a new "dynamic equilibrium,"[14] an ongoing stage in the successful quest for balance and wholeness to be sought through critical utopianism, regionalism, and decentralization. As he put it in 1934, "The temporary fact of increasing acceleration, which seemed so notable to Henry Adams when he surveyed the progress from twelfth-century unity to twentieth-century multiplicity . . . will no longer characterize our society." Instead, "once we have generally reached a new technical plateau we may remain on that level with very minor ups and downs for thousands of years."[15] Here Mumford was clearly hopeful.

By 1970, however, he had become much less optimistic about this prospect, just as he had about technological advance overall. By then, he demanded such "a slowing down of tempo" precisely to resist what he now called the "megamachine." As he argued, "Nothing could be more damaging to the myth of the machine, and to the dehumanized social order it has brought into existence, than a steady withdrawal of interest . . . a stoppage of senseless routines and mindless acts."[16] Still, Mumford did not completely despair of the possibility of a technological plateau.

Whether a technological plateau will become a conscious goal of a majority of Americans instead of a de facto development among a minority of them cannot be predicted. Certainly the resurgence of technological utopianism during and after the 1991 Persian Gulf War has tempered my earlier, already qualified optimism. So, too, for that matter, has the apparent failure of most Americans to see the Japanese challenge to American technological supremacy as as much an opportunity to rethink our long-term nontechnological objectives as a purely economic crisis. In any event, among the key indicators of the prospects for a genuine technological plateau will be the fate of the auto and its future role within American society and culture.[17]

4

ALEXIS DE TOCQUEVILLE

AND THE DILEMMAS

OF MODERNIZATION

· ·

"The Los Angeles Alexis de Tocqueville Society will honor former President Ronald Reagan, and his wife, Nancy, with Lifetime Achievement Awards in Pasadena, California, on September 11, 1991." So appeared a notice in the August 26, 1991, *New York Times*. That the master of ceremonies for this "black-tie tribute" was to be comedian Bob Hope did not indicate its lack of seriousness. The Society, according to the *Times* notice, is "made up of individuals who have given at least $10,000 to United Way, the umbrella charity." Why the Society invokes Tocqueville's name is nevertheless curious, but, reports the *Times*, it honors "the French historian and political theorist whose influential nineteenth-century studies of American democracy cited instances of American generosity."[1]

That Tocqueville's illustrious name and writings should be invoked even here, in an area (charity) not immediately associated with him—as opposed to, say, the areas of democracy or revolution or liberty or equality—is wonderfully revealing of his persistent hold on Americans' self-image; of Americans' enduring need to compare Tocqueville's observations, analyses, and predictions with actual developments ever since.

Indeed, of the countless commentators upon the American scene since the nation's founding, Tocqueville (1805–1859) has undoubtedly enjoyed the widest and longest acclaim. The principal source of his enduring popularity has, of course, been his two-volume *Democracy*

in America (1835, 1840). His later works on France and on England—
most notably, *The Old Regime and the French Revolution* (1856) and
its uncompleted sequel, *The European Revolution* (published post-
humously)—have not, however, suffered neglect, especially among
Europeans. This undiminished interest in all of Tocqueville's work has,
in fact, turned Tocquevillian scholarship into a flourishing academic
industry.[2]

My concern here is with only one portion of Tocqueville's work and
with only that portion of Tocquevillian scholarship bearing upon it: that
pertaining to "modernization." By "modernization" I mean the evolution of supposedly "underdeveloped" societies into "developed" ones,
especially through technological advances either welcomed by or im-
posed upon the native populace by their leaders (elected or not), by
outside nations, or by both. "Modernization" was an enormously popular concept—and ideology—in the 1950s and 1960s as the British,
French, and other colonial empires gradually granted independence to
so many former territories in Africa and Asia. An avowed replacement
for imperialism, by then a largely discredited concept, modernization
held out the prospect, in the eyes of its generally American and Western
European proponents, of peacefully transforming those (former) colonial territories into functioning industrialized democracies led by able
native political and technical elites. Equally important, modernization
Western-style was a clear and attractive alternative to communism in
the height of the Cold War, though modernization Soviet-style also
flourished as a model.

Like the technological utopians whom I wrote about in my first
book, these anticommunist modernization proponents believed that
sufficient technological advances could in turn bring about the nontechnological advances they sought: a higher standard of living, greater
equality and equality of opportunity, greater social mobility, expanded
mass political participation, and improved education and technical
training. Like the technological utopians, too, they steadily reduced the
time needed to achieve those improvements from whole centuries to
mere decades. And like the technological utopians as well, they did not
appreciate (modern) technology's mixed blessings. Unlike the technological utopians, whose principal if not sole concern was the United
States, the modernization proponents obviously had to deal with foreign cultures not necessarily eager for these changes, though the native
populace's interests and concerns were either too often ignored or

naively assumed to be identical with those of their leaders (a situation not dissimilar to imperialism).

Significantly, as Susan Matarese has noted, Edward Bellamy's *Looking Backward* (1888), discussed in chapter 8, and nearly all the many other American utopian works that appeared in the late nineteenth and early twentieth centuries embodied "a messianic outlook which tends to see the United States as a paradigm for others, a chosen people destined to redeem the world through their example and guidance."[3] This attitude naturally grew out of the nation's self-image as a potential utopia, a self-image originating with European discoverers and early settlers. And this attitude accounts for both the limited specifics about the rest of the world in *Looking Backward* and most of the other utopian writings of its day and the blatant prejudices against foreigners and foreign-born Americans (and, for that matter, non-WASPs altogether) found in so many of these utopian works. The modernization proponents of the 1950s and 1960s conveyed abroad a similar (if less prejudiced) vision of the United States as a veritable utopia as they tried to steer "developing" nations toward capitalism and democracy and away from communism and tyranny.

Tocqueville was hardly a utopian, and he did not use the term "modernization" or any equivalent.[4] Yet he was certainly concerned with social change—and its absence—in the United States and Western Europe alike, and in recent decades this has allowed some of Tocqueville's most zealous scholarly interpreters to link his observations, analyses, and predictions to the concept of modernization and actually to deem Tocqueville's work a pioneering theory of modernization in its own right.

In contemporary political jargon, most of these academic admirers would be classified as "neoconservatives." Their ranks include such distinguished scholars as Raymond Aron, Reinhard Bendix, Louis Hartz, Seymour Martin Lipset, and Robert Nisbet. Since the beginning of the Cold War they have sought suitable ideological alternatives to Marxism, and in Tocqueville's work they claim to have found them—just as other neoconservative intellectuals have embraced Ronald Reagan as their political patron saint and have honored him as a de facto Tocquevillian. For all of these admirers, Tocqueville, rather than Marx, is the true prophet of the age. They contend that Western society has on the one hand preserved "liberalism" and avoided Marxian socialism and has on the other hand absorbed large-scale changes—democratization, industrialization, urbanization, and so on—and avoided revolution.

In another sense, a genuine revolution *has* occurred, but contrary to Marx it has been nonviolent and democratic in nature, and its product has been the peace and prosperity the West now enjoys. This situation is made all the more attractive when compared with the economic, political, and social conditions of so many former communist societies. Although none of these academic admirers of Tocqueville would label themselves utopians—a term of derision for them all—many would endorse the historic self-image of the United States as a nation qualitatively superior to any other and, with the demise of communism, once more a model for other nations. Whether "developing" nations will experience such restrained revolutionary transformation is, of course, less certain, given that numerous initial expectations in the 1950s and 1960s of such a pleasant fate for those nations have hardly been met. Yet the very accuracy of Tocqueville's famous prediction, at the conclusion of the first volume of *Democracy in America*, that the United States and Russia, then "underdeveloped" themselves, were "marked out by the will of Heaven to sway the destinies of half the globe,"[5] has bolstered the faith of his advocates in the overall accuracy of his observations, analyses, and predictions.

In the absence, however, of anything resembling a concept of modernization in Tocqueville's work, the only way to proceed is by reconstructing his view of social change and by suggesting how his would-be contemporary disciples might apply it today. In the process one must keep in mind the conclusion of historian Seymour Drescher, a leading Tocqueville scholar, that underlying virtually all of Tocqueville's analyses of America and of Europe are several, if not outright contradictions, then definite "tensions." These tensions were powerful enough to force him eventually to modify parts of his general understanding of social change in order to accommodate changes in contemporary society, but not so powerful as to force him to abandon that understanding altogether. Insofar as Tocqueville's work does speak to the process of modernization, these tensions—between liberty and equality, centralization and decentralization, and stability and instability—cannot be ignored.

In his foreword to *The Old Regime*, Tocqueville wrote, "No nation had ever before embarked on so resolute an attempt as that of the

French in 1789 to break with the past . . . to create an unbridgeable gulf between all they had hitherto been and all they now aspired to be." The attempt ultimately failed, and those who would have completed that break instead found themselves using "the debris of the old order for building up the new."[6] The failure did not surprise Tocqueville, for he conceived the transition from one era to another to be necessarily gradual, not abrupt. Civilization, he noted in *Democracy*, "is the result of a long social process, which takes place in the same spot and is handed down from one generation to another, each one profiting by the experience of the last."[7] The term "civilization" was apparently left undefined, save as the idea of social process. As Tocqueville used it here and elsewhere, "social process" implied social change, or as he put it elsewhere, a change in "social condition": "the ensemble of facts whose conjunction forms the situation of a people at a given period."[8]

Tocqueville was primarily concerned, however, not with social change in general but with one change in particular: the expansion of equality resulting from the recent and ongoing expansion of democracy in the United States and Western Europe. "The more I advanced in the study of American society," he wrote in *Democracy*, "the more I perceived that this equality of condition is the fundamental fact from which all others seem to be derived and the central point at which all my observations constantly terminated." Yet because the progress of democracy differed in each country, generalizations about even this social change were hazardous. Thus for Tocqueville the United States was uniquely fortunate in having "arrived at a state of democracy without having [had] to endure a democratic revolution," in having been "born equal instead of becoming so."[9] Less fortunate, Western Europe had to break with feudalism, sometimes violently, in order to create the proper conditions for democracy.

Wherever it took root in the West, democratization was a complex social process, not always comprehensible to those directly involved. Democracy had come to France, for instance, without the foreknowledge and certainly without the consent of the incumbent government. Democracy in France, he wrote, "has consequently been abandoned to its wild instincts, and it has grown up like those children who have no parental guidance, who receive their education in the public streets, and who are acquainted only with the vices and wretchedness of society." Government neither there nor elsewhere could stem the revolutionary tide and in fact in France was itself a partial cause of revolution.

Democratization, moreover, was not reducible to government fiat since it took the form of changes less in laws than in "ideas, customs, and morals."[10]

An emphasis on ideas, customs, and morals characterizes Tocqueville's overall understanding of social change. Though he respected the power and influence of institutions and other concrete phenomena, he believed that people's minds were ultimately swayed by intangible instruments. Thus in explaining the apparent triumph of democracy in America he ranked laws above geography as a causative factor and customs above them both.[11]

Social change depended above all, however, on human character itself, and Tocqueville normally analyzed customs as well as laws, institutions, and geography in terms of their influence on human character, especially on human habits. Yet he was convinced that even customs did not directly determine human character itself but rather indirectly affected habits. He insisted, therefore, that the expected triumph of democracy in the West would result principally from the habit of a "mature and reflecting preference for freedom."[12]

Given Tocqueville's reliance upon such intangible instruments and such imprecise indicators of social change as ideas, customs, morals, habits, and above all human character, it is hardly surprising that he formulated no detailed vision of the kind of society democratization might ideally produce (and so in turn no detailed vision of a "modernized" society). Drescher must therefore extract from a variety of passages to provide his pithy summary that such a society would likely guarantee "a maximum of individual liberty and collective participation in decision making, a maximum of social activity through nonrevolutionary channels, and a maximum of permissible dissent and creativity within the confines of a plebiscitarian framework."[13] Tocqueville confessed that "in America I saw more than America"—he saw "the image of democracy itself."[14] He did so, he admitted, not because America represented the final, let alone the perfect, form of democracy, but because it represented a huge experiment conducted in a giant laboratory, an experiment in which elements of the coming democratic revolution could be tested.

Why America? Because "The great privilege of the Americans does not consist in being more enlightened than other nations, but in being able to repair the faults they may commit" through a flexible and responsive political system. The flexibility of that system might not have given the people the most administratively efficient government, but it did produce "what the ablest governments are frequently unable to create: namely, an all-pervading and restless activity, a superabundant force, and an energy which is inseparable from it and which may . . . produce wonders."[15]

This energy found fulfillment in the activities of what Tocqueville termed "associations." In the first volume of *Democracy* energetic individuals formed associations "to promote the public safety, commerce, industry, morality, . . . religion" and politics. Associations served a dual purpose: they united heretofore isolated individuals in the pursuit of numerous causes, but by their very numbers and diversity of causes prevented large blocs of those same individuals from banding together to impose particular designs upon society as a whole. For of all the possible consequences of democracy, Tocqueville, like the Founding Fathers, most feared the tyranny of the majority: "If ever the free institutions of America are destroyed," he wrote in the first volume of *Democracy*, "that event may be attributed to the omnipotence of the majority, which may at some future time urge the minorities to desperation and oblige them to have recourse to physical force. Anarchy will then be the result, but it will have been brought about by despotism."[16]

In the second volume of *Democracy* the locus of tyranny shifted from the citizenry to the government itself. As Tocqueville had admitted in the first volume, "In democratic republics the power that directs society is not stable, for it often changes hands and assumes a new direction. But whichever way it turns, its force is almost irresistible." It had by now turned away from decentralized local associations and toward a centralized national bureaucracy. The individual citizen was now nearly helpless before an omnipotent government, his freedom and maybe his identity lost in a kind of Emersonian universe: "When the inhabitant of a democratic country compares himself individually with all those about him, he feels with pride that he is the equal of any one of them; but when he comes to survey the totality of his fellows and to place himself in contrast with so huge a body, he is instantly overwhelmed by the sense of his own insignificance and weakness."[17] Here lay the product of alleged excessive egalitarianism, perverted individualism, and unrestrained democratic government.

Tocqueville had a clear explanation for these changes. He held responsible first, institutions (the decline of associations and of agrarianism); then, customs and morals (the decline of class harmony and of public spirit); but most of all human habits (the periodic resurgence of sheer greed). Greed not only separated individuals formerly united in civic enterprises but also prompted them to turn their efforts from merely making a living through agriculture—which Tocqueville, like Jefferson, deemed crucial to the health of any democracy—to making a profit through commerce and industry. These changes in turn allowed the national government to exercise unprecedented power as long as it did not disturb those greedy individuals. [18]

Tocqueville consequently ended the second volume of *Democracy* more pessimistic about the future of democracy than when he had begun the first. His pessimism carried over into both *The Old Regime* and *The European Revolution*. It intensified as he, an ambitious politician, observed firsthand the renewed political and class conflicts at home. The tensions submerged within *Democracy* surfaced in these later works, for it was about the fate of France that Tocqueville, understandably, cared most.

In brief, Tocqueville argued that the French Revolution did not so much transform French society as accelerate changes already underway amidst the decline of French feudalism. Why, then, did the Revolution occur in 1789? Because the relative political and economic progress that had recently come about—an unprecedented degree of democratization and prosperity—had made the French "masses" increasingly rather than, as one might suppose, decreasingly conscious of a still seemingly unbridgeable gap between the objectives the Old Regime publicly proclaimed and those it had actually achieved. [19] As Tocqueville had warned in the first volume of *Democracy*, "Men are not corrupted by the exercise of power or debased by the habit of obedience, but by the exercise of a power which they believe to be illegitimate, and by obedience to a rule which they consider to be usurped and oppressive." For Tocqueville, then, the triggering mechanism of revolution was what Sasha Weitman terms the "radicalization of public opinion." [20]

The French Revolution did not, of course, yield anything resembling democracy. The masses soon wearied of pursuing Tocqueville's supreme value, liberty, and turned instead to that lesser good, equality. [21] Equality was hardly unimportant, but where equality could flourish under either dictatorship or democracy, liberty could do so only under democracy. And where, as in France, liberty and equality conflicted, liberty usually lost.

Notwithstanding the adverse social changes lamented in *Democ-*

racy, The Old Regime, and *The European Revolution,* Tocqueville remained fairly confident until the 1850s that genuine democracy could eventually and peacefully be achieved throughout the West. Only then, when he saw no apparent end to the upheavals regularly plaguing at least France (by now his principal index of mankind's social progress), did he begin to question that assumption. And only then did he begin to question the complementary assumption of continuous social change, and in turn the virtue of such change.[22] Left unresolved, because still intrinsic to social change as he understood it, were the now seemingly perpetual tensions between liberty and equality, centralization and decentralization, and stability and instability. Not that Tocqueville necessarily wished them resolved, for their likely resolution—toward greater equality, centralization, and instability—would threaten not only individual liberty but also any remaining prospects for genuine democratization.

As indicated earlier, many of those scholars claiming the closest ideological affinities with the master have not adequately appreciated these tensions within his work. They have not done so either because those tensions have not been apparent to them or because their acknowledgment of them would have undermined the most literal applicability of his work to theirs. Whatever the reasons, it is evident that, given the uncertainties of his times and his career, he at no point actually envisioned the "postindustrial" liberal democracy that allegedly now prevails in the West. (Its existence is, of course, frequently questioned despite the growth of the service sector of Western economies and the shrinkage of the manufacturing sector.) Moreover, given those same uncertainties, he finally declined to predict any further social changes at all save for increasing friction between the propertied and the propertyless.[23] Those who would cite Tocqueville for their purpose thus impose on the subtleties and ambiguities of his thought and character a more simplistic understanding of social change than he himself ever entertained. In so doing they ironically reduce his overall intellectual stature. The very use of such terms as "liberal democracy" confuses rather than clarifies, insofar as those terms have clearly changed in meaning since Tocqueville's day.

In order to place Tocqueville's work in proper contemporary as well as historical perspective, let us reconsider it in light of the argument provided by political scientist Samuel Huntington in 1957. Asserting that "conservatism" per se represents not a particular ideological stance but rather a reaction against some variety of change, Huntington, himself a "neoconservative," contends that "no conservative ideal exists to serve as the standard of judgment." Instead, "the lack of a [single] conservative ideal necessarily vitiates the autonomous definition of conservatism."[24] The real problem, he suggests, is *what* to conserve. The argument applies to Tocqueville, whatever the contemporary ideological categorization of his work. Tocqueville had initially hoped that his supreme value of individual liberty could be best preserved and perhaps strengthened under democracy. He was thus willing to forego the aristocratic privileges and monarchical rule which, given his background and status, he might otherwise have preferred. Later, when faced with the possibility and, near the end of his life, the probability that neither democracy nor any other known political system could guarantee liberty or other cherished values, such as association and agrarianism, he turned "conservative" in precisely the way Huntington describes:

> No one is born to conservatism in the way in which Mill is born to utilitarianism. The impulse to conservatism comes from the social challenge before the theorist, not the intellectual tradition behind him. Men [and women] are driven to conservatism by the shock of events, by the horrible feeling that a society or institution which . they have approved or taken for granted and with which they have been intimately connected may suddenly cease to exist. The conservative thinkers of one age, consequently, have little influence on those of the next.[25]

Just as Huntington in 1957 urged his contemporaries to conserve their then "liberal" values and institutions against the threat of communism, so Tocqueville a century earlier had in effect urged his contemporaries to conserve their own then "liberal" values and institutions against the threat of excessive democracy and unchecked revolution. That Tocqueville obviously has had considerable influence upon succeeding generations of thinkers, and especially supposedly "conservative" thinkers, reflects the misreading both of his complex thoughts as "mere" conservatism and of "conservatism" itself as monolithic and eternal. Yet if, as Huntington concludes, conservatism per se consequently fails to ask ultimate questions or provide final answers, it does remind people of the "institutional prerequisites of social order."[26] And by the 1850s it was, in a general sense, social order, not social change, that Tocqueville sought most.

If the need for a sizable dosage of "order" is granted in presumably all "modernized" or "modernizing" societies, Tocqueville indeed speaks to the present. This of course endears him to those who, like Huntington and other academic Tocqueville admirers, seek nonrevolutionary routes to mature or maturing postindustrial capitalist democracies throughout the world. But obviously any number of other respected theorists both before and after Tocqueville have also demanded "order." Why, then, necessarily worship at Tocqueville's intellectual shrine? More important, why necessarily assume the superiority of "order" over "change" and of the inevitability of the one rather than the other? Why not consider the possibility, as did Tocqueville himself for much of his life, of their reconciliation—of "ordered change"?

When, near the end of his life, Tocqueville retreated from the basic assumption that social change is *continuous*—not necessarily smooth or straight, but simply unceasing—his observations, analyses, and predictions proved most seriously flawed. Yet the basis of Tocqueville's appeal to many of his contemporary academic admirers is precisely the notion that social change need no longer be continuous, now that the postrevolutionary stage of "modernization" either has been reached or shortly will be; and that the arrival at that stage can henceforth be accurately measured and predicted. Given the similarities in their visions of America and the rest of the world between the turn-of-the-century utopian writers and the post–World War II proponents of modernization, it is not surprising that both routinely fail to consider what happens once the ideal society is finally achieved; both naively assume that the new social order will be at once permanent and free of significant upheavals.

To persist in these assumptions is to lay the trap into which these academic admirers of Tocqueville have in recent years regularly fallen. This is because the vast majority of "modernizing" or "developing" nations have deviated from the expected Western route to modernization, if they have contemplated such a route at all. In fact, the very concept of modernization, together with its accompanying ideal types of "tradition" and "modernity," has itself been critically questioned and in some quarters wholly abandoned.[27] Likewise have the most sophisticated theorists of modernization, such as Huntington himself and S. N. Eisenstadt, recognized these dilemmas and conceded what Eisenstadt terms the possible "breakdown" of the modernization process.[28] The fall of communism may temporarily revive the modernization proponents as they celebrate the presumed triumph of Western capitalist democracies over what President Reagan once called "the evil empire." But it would be premature, to say the least, to anticipate wholesale conversions to the modernization model anywhere. By this point it should be painfully clear that the exportation of Western technology to Africa, Asia, Latin America, and Eastern Europe does not necessarily translate into Western democratic values, institutions, and practices.[29]

Ironically, as two other Tocqueville scholars have argued, Tocqueville was at best indifferent and at worst hostile to industrial workers and to the industrial cities which drew them away from farms and villages. As historian Arthur Kaledin has noted, except to study prison labor, Tocqueville failed to visit American factories and workshops. When he was in Boston he was interested in neither Lowell nor Waltham. And as historian Edgar Newman has elaborated, Tocqueville "despised the Industrial Revolution and abhorred the misery it produced."[30] Yet he never thought that workers should unionize to protect their interests and was as unsympathetic toward industrial labor as he was toward urbanization overall. His model for France was an envisioned pastoral, democratic America, and his solution to problems in France's industrial cities was depopulation and wholesale retreat to the countryside. So much, then, for excessive reliance on this French aristocrat to provide the basis for any serious model of modernization, itself premised upon industrialization and other technological advances.[31]

What has not been so readily recognized or conceded is the historical context in which the concepts of modernization, tradition, and modernity originated—or more precisely, the fact that they originated in particular historical contexts and have not always been a part of our vocabulary. As historian Richard D. Brown concedes in a pioneering study of the modernization of American life between 1600 and 1865, the concept of modernization "may prove to be merely one more in the succession of scholarly fashions."[32] That Tocqueville (and his contemporaries) did not employ such concepts reflected not so much his innocence regarding the status of American and other Western societies as his knowledge, or shrewd conjecture, about the then transitional nature of those societies; this is reflected in the tensions that run throughout his profoundest writings.

It hardly follows that all eras are transitional at heart or that scholarly efforts to chart the stages of societal development are inherently flawed. What does follow is that all such stages run along a historical continuum the end of which is not yet in sight—contrary to recent suggestions of an "end of history" amid communism's demise.[33] Hence whatever the precise proportion of "order" and "disorder" in any society at any period, the probability of further social change, and of the unpredictability of such change, must be taken for granted. This does not, of course, preclude the possibility of a technological plateau of some kind, for such a development presumes continuous nontechnological social change.[34] Those who would still attempt to apply Tocqueville's work to their own ought therefore to appreciate the deepest lesson that can be learned from his work and from the fate of his work: caution, even humility, in the face of complicated social change, lest convenient logic be retained at the expense of historical truth.

II

TECHNOLOGICAL
MUSEUMS
REVISITED

5

THE MACHINE SHOP

IN AMERICAN SOCIETY

AND CULTURE

. . . .

In 1982 the Armington and Sims Machine Shop and Foundry reopened at Greenfield Village in Dearborn, Michigan.[1] Its reconstruction after thirty years of inactivity is a notable achievement, and not just for this tourist mecca founded by Henry Ford in the late 1920s. It pays tribute to an institution that has been sadly neglected amid Americans' enthusiasm for more glamorous components of our industrial revolution such as the steam engine, the steamboat, the railroad, the automobile, and the assembly line. Yet the machine shop was a keystone of that transformation of the United States in the nineteenth and early twentieth centuries from a predominantly agrarian to a predominantly industrial society and in turn from a second- to a first-rate world power.

The industrial revolution that so changed the United States began in Great Britain in the mid-eighteenth century. Prominent British engineers commonly passed on their expertise and their inventions to their American counterparts, who eventually surpassed them in most areas. In both countries the growth of textiles, the first industry to be revolutionized, directly spurred the growth of the machine shop. The development in the late eighteenth and early nineteenth centuries of large, complex, and accurate spinning and weaving machines required ever more accurately shaped metal parts, repair services, and machines themselves. Because completed machinery was often unwieldy to transport, the earliest machine shops were usually adjuncts to the major textile mills, as was the Essex Company of Lawrence, Massachusetts, the forerunner of the Armington and Sims Engine Company. Indeed, initially machine shops were frequently placed in the basements of new mills so that mechanics could build machines while carpenters and masons completed the buildings' structures. Although these shops were founded to fulfill the needs of their parent companies, as means of transportation improved, and as the textile industry expanded in the 1820s, they began to sell a wide variety of machines to other mills and to general customers (having earlier at most traded or leased them to competitors only). By about 1850 the parent companies started divesting themselves of these shops and the latter began to operate independently and in separate quarters. This happened with the Essex Company, which spun off the Lawrence Machine Shop in 1852. In addition to textile machinery, these shops produced such diversified products as steam engines, locomotives, and machine tools. Some of the newly independent shops became highly successful; others, such as the Lawrence Machine Shop, failed in the face of stiff competition both from one another and from wholly independent shops—the latter having begun outside the textile industry in the early nineteenth century.

At first, most establishments like the Lawrence Machine Shop did custom work to order. They could turn out a variety of products. However, increasing demand for such items as engines or machine tools led to specialization, especially around the time of the Civil War. The J. C. Hoadley Company, which (along with the Merrimack Machine Shop) succeeded the Lawrence Machine Shop—and was succeeded in turn by Armington and Sims—is a good example of a more specialized shop; it primarily made portable steam engines. Further distinctions began to appear as certain shops concentrated on repair work and ceased to manufacture new products, while others moved in the direction of mass production of specific items. Still other shops focused on custom work and became prototypical "job shops" similar to the Armington and Sims Shop.

A repair or job shop would often consist of a single room with several lathes and perhaps a small planer, a tool chest filled with assorted hammers, chisels, and files, and a small foundry. By contrast, a production shop would likely encompass dozens of lathes, several planers, other tools such as shapers, boring, drilling, milling, and grinding machines, a separate erecting and assembling room, a large foundry, a blacksmith shop, a drafting room, and an office. Equally important, where the repair or job shop relied primarily on hand and foot power, the production shop relied heavily on water and steam power.

A May 1851 *Harper's New Monthly Magazine* article by Jacob Abbott on the Novelty Iron Works in New York City, manufacturer of steam engines for large ships, provided the layman with a vivid sense of the enormous size and complexity of a typical production shop and the awesome power of its machines. As Abbott described it in part:

> Perhaps no one of those vast movements which are now going forward among mankind, and which mark so strikingly the industrial power and genius of the present age, is watched with more earnest interest by thinking men, than the successive steps of the progress by which the mechanical power of steam and machinery is gradually advancing in its contest for the dominion of the seas. . . . The armories in which the ordnance and ammunition for this warfare are prepared, consist, so far as this country is concerned, of certain establishments, vast in their extent and capacity, though unpretending in external appearance, which are situated in the upper part of the city of New York, on the shores of the East River. . . . The entrance to the enclosure is by a great gateway, through which the visitor on approaching it, will very probably see an enormous truck or car issuing, drawn by a long team of horses, and bearing some ponderous piece of machinery suspended beneath it by means of levers and chains. . . . Beyond the entrance, and just within the enclosure may be seen a great crane used for receiving or delivering the vast masses of metal, the shafts, the cylinders, the boilers, the vacuum pans, and other ponderous formations which are continually coming and going to and from the yard. . . . This central engine, since it carries all the machinery of the works, by means of which everything is formed and fashioned, is the life and soul of the establishment—the mother, in fact, of all the monsters which issue from it; and it is impossible to look upon her, as she toils on industriously in her daily duty, and think of her Titanic progeny, scattered now over every ocean on the globe, without a certain feeling of respect and even of admiration.[2]

Ironically, these factorylike enterprises contributed to the decline of the traditional machine shop not simply by their greater output but also by their reduction of much labor to repetitive routine work requiring fewer skills than those possessed by traditional machine shop workers. This in turn contributed to the rise of technical and professional schools for training what became known in the 1850s as mechanical engineers—an addition to the existing professions of civil and military engineering.

Yet what about the inner workings of that traditional machine shop? As historian Monte Calvert has argued, there existed a "shop culture" throughout the heyday of the machine shop in the years between 1820 and 1890.[3] By "culture" Calvert properly means certain values, regulations, behavior patterns—in short, a way of life. To be sure, the role of the machine shop in training aspiring machinists and engineers as well as in producing machines is familiar. Yet Calvert shows how this was as much a process of socialization as of technical training.

Calvert demonstrates that this "shop culture" at once derived from and nurtured a self-perpetuating social and technical elite of well-bred and well-to-do citizens, all of them males. Predominantly WASP in origin and located primarily in the Northeast, these machine shop owners and operators rigorously controlled the entry of apprentices and understandably catered to their social and economic peers. Their shops were usually organized as limited partnerships with fewer than one hundred employees in all, as was true of the Armington and Sims Engine Company. They provided close supervision of their young charges and were consequently deemed quite respectable workplaces by their apprentices' families.

This was particularly important in light of the progressive deterioration in America (from the nation's founding on) of the traditional rigid apprenticeship system that flourished for centuries in Europe and that, in the case of Britain, partly accounted for its leadership in the industrial revolution of the mid-eighteenth century. As W. J. Rorabaugh has shown, apprenticeship in this country was undermined from the very start by factors ranging from the democratic ethos to social and geographic mobility, and by the Civil War had become a moribund institution.[4]

Contrary to the appealing image of upward social mobility for everyone, which they promoted, few shop owners and operators were of humble origin. Like the workplaces of many other American businessmen, the often dirty and noisy conditions of the shops contrasted with the cleanliness and quiet of their proprietors' respectable homes—the upkeep of which was generally the responsibility of their wives and daughters. The belief in the dignity of manual labor on the part of this avowed social elite also contrasted with their family backgrounds.

Competition for business among the shops was strikingly modest. Successful shops established close, lasting commercial and social relations with their customers, and they willingly exchanged useful information with "rival" shops. Thus the machine shop was fundamentally a gentlemanly enterprise. Its ideals, generally realized in practice, were dignity, sobriety, self-restraint, and dedication to work.

The ethos of the machine shop (and often that network of personal relations) extended to related enterprises, particularly the newer railroad shops and naval engineering firms. All eschewed the crass materialism that accompanied the industrial revolution in America as elsewhere. Rather, they sought a respectable profit, not a grand fortune, and they relished the intellectual challenge of their work above its financial opportunities. Some even considered their shops as *de facto* laboratories advancing American science and technology. Ironically, though, the machine shop itself, along with the prosperous middle-class home, was seen as a kind of moral and psychic sanctuary from the very technological society its owners, operators, and workers were simultaneously creating. Daily life outside the machine shop and the bourgeois home could often be harsh and immoral. Few if any machine shop owners and operators—and their wives and daughters—saw an inconsistency here. It was the supposedly natural way the workplace and the home were to function.

After 1865, however, this shop culture was challenged by the rise of what Calvert calls "school culture," or formal educational institutions for training certified professional engineers. These institutions stressed abstract, theoretical, codified knowledge derived from books rather than more practical, more intuitive information obtained from actual job experience; pure science with mathematical roots instead of applied science; and standardized examinations and other objective measurements of ability and performance in place of subjective judgments based on class and status. Not a social and economic elite but the growing middle class was their intended source of students. Not extraordinary, but merely competent, engineers was their goal. And not the old-line machine shop but the new bureaucratic corporation was their students' intended employer.

Gradually the engineering school replaced the machine shop as the principal vehicle for training mechanical and other engineers. Mechanical engineers with full-fledged degrees were mostly from humbler origins than their informally certified predecessors had been, and they were being successfully placed in those large corporations. Yet the shop culture fought vigorously to retain its domination and won some battles before losing the war. Only by about 1905 was the outcome clear.

By then the American Society of Mechanical Engineers, founded by the leaders of the shop culture in 1880 partly to ward off threats from the emerging school culture (though partly also simply to establish their professional identity), had been taken over by the latter forces. The indifference of the shop culture leaders to the emerging issue of what professionalization now meant—thanks ironically to their persistent assumption of already being a professional elite—had given way to intense concern on the part of formally educated mechanical engineers and their students.

For obvious reasons the machine shop was frequently characterized by these educators as stagnant, even reactionary. Yet not only were machine shop owners, operators, and employees hardly opposed to scientific and technological advance per se, they themselves contributed repeatedly to such advances through improvements in their own production processes. The impersonal moving assembly line and the reduction of skilled workers' tasks to simple, repetitive motions were both made possible, ironically, by the kind of precision machinery originating in the machine shop. Most ironically, it was a diehard shop man, Frederick W. Taylor, who, early in the twentieth century, developed what became known as Scientific Management—a management strategy generally associated with highly bureaucratic corporations, government agencies, schools, and so forth. Paradoxically, Taylor was inspired, at least in part, by a keen desire to preserve decision-making by engineers as opposed to managers and financial experts and to retain the machine shops' close ties to industry. Only the late 1910s and 1920s, after Taylor's death and the initial failures of portions of his scheme— symbolized by stopwatches and time and motion studies—did more refined and more effective forms of management come to permeate the large corporations and related bureaucratic institutions. Scientific Management did little for shop culture.

In other, subtler ways the machine shop contributed to the maturation of American society and culture. Along with factories, public schools, churches, and additional communal institutions, it instilled in its members a number of traits deemed critical to the survival of the young republic at a time when government at all levels was widely perceived as both fragile and remote. The high ideals and practices of shop culture were carried over to life outside the workplace. If, as historian John Kasson has persuasively argued, model antebellum factory towns like Lowell, Massachusetts, were avowed republican communities,[5] so, more implicitly, were model machine shops. Where the owners and operators of Lowell and other such towns had to contend with workers from poorer backgrounds than their own and later with immigrants with radically different values and views, those in command of the typical machine shop were frequently dealing with their social and economic peers. The machine shop was thus a society and a culture in miniature.

The machine shop further functioned as an institution with its own aesthetic values. Contrary to the still popular notion of art and technology as wholly separate realms, technology in many respects is, of course, an art form. Without suggesting that life in the machine shop consisted to any degree of formal discussions about aesthetics, it is clear from many sources that Americans, like Europeans, thought seriously about whether or not to decorate their machines. For a long time it was nevertheless assumed that most Americans, unlike most Europeans, left their machines undecorated, in the manner of the "plain style" associated with the Puritans. In an influential study, *Made in America: The Arts in Modern Civilization* (1948), cultural critic John Kouwenhoven took this assumption to its logical extreme and contended, with considerable success, that there had in fact developed an American aesthetic based on simplicity and functionalism—a "vernacular" style, as contrasted with the "cultivated" style of European art.[6]

Kouwenhoven's argument about American aesthetics overall does not, however, extend to machines, as the research of Kasson and curator John Bowditch, among others, has made clear.[7] Americans characteristically favored complex designs for and ornamentation of machinery and, no less important, regarded both as high art. Even the elite engineers in the machine shops and elsewhere, those supposedly most resistant to decoration, frequently relented in order to distinguish their machinery from that of others and so not only express pride in their work but also sell their products. Notwithstanding traditional republican dislike of the luxury, frivolity, and debauchery commonly associated with high art of any kind, most Americans saw machine decoration as the genuine republican art form.

Finally, the machine shop ought to be understood as a system in miniature, and in a broadly social as much as in a narrowly technical sense. Contrary to another popular contemporary notion, "system" as denoting a coherent integrated order of some kind is not a recent invention. Americans, among others, used the term in just this way throughout the nineteenth century.[8] The initial application of the term in this country was, appropriately enough, to a technological achievement: the so-called "American System of Manufacturing" of precision instruments, interchangeable parts, mass production, and the like. The term was coined by some admiring British officials in the 1850s to describe what they believed to be typical American manufacturing techniques; by this point American technology had definitely come of age and posed serious challenges to traditional British supremacy. (That uniform rather than literally interchangeable parts were, for financial as well as technical reasons, the common practice among American manufacturers until the late nineteenth century hardly mattered to those at home and abroad who sang the American System's praises.) There, too, "system" encompassed, besides machinery, the relevant functions of government, of management, of labor, and of culture. In fact, the ability to conceive of a system as such is itself a notable achievement. Without exaggerating the dimensions or the complexity of the machine shop, that institution, as a key part of the "American System of Manufacturing," was a de facto system in this extended sense. Hence once more the appropriateness of a shop culture—a way of life integrating people, machines, values, and socializing processes. As the distinguished MIT historian of technology Robert Woodbury put it in the preface to his *Studies in the History of Machine Tools*, "One can hardly say that the machine tool was a sufficient condition for the Industrial Revolution, but we may be certain that it was a necessary condition for the development of the industrial society in which we live."[9]

Kurt Vonnegut's *Player Piano* (1952), as detailed in chapter 10, examines through fiction the fate of skilled machine shop workers whose jobs are eliminated by automated tools and machines, all operated by computers. Vonnegut's novel is futuristic, and its predictions were largely fantasies when it appeared. Yet the machine shop, which survived the professionalization of mechanical engineering, has in recent years in reality been challenged by computers, particularly CAD/CAM (Computer-Aided Design/Computer-Aided Manufacturing). Now engineers can design ever more sophisticated equipment to produce ever more items with ever less human intervention. The new skills machine shop workers are being forced to learn in situations where their jobs are not simply eliminated are invariably computer-related: programming, interactive graphics, and adaptive controls, for example. Paradoxically, these very skills may prove to be the salvation of the machine shop insofar as they may attract new and younger talent to an industry that many outsiders deem old-fashioned, dull, lacking in status, and unresponsive to technological change. This was the conclusion of *The Machine Tool Task Force Report* of 1980, the most comprehensive report of its kind in the industry's history.[10] Prepared by a large group of prominent machine tool builders, users, researchers, and academicians, the report anticipated new jobs for properly skilled and, if necessary, retrained machine shop workers. The report also advocated closer ties between the industry and academia and more instruction in colleges and universities in necessary courses as well as improvements in academia's own machine shops—an ironic reversal of the nineteenth-century shop culture's attitude toward the school culture.[11]

This and other recent reports, including the National Academy of Engineering (NAE)'s 1983 *The Competitive Status of the U.S. Machine Tool Industry,* have cited the now-familiar litany of problems plaguing American industry overall: failure to attract more women and minorities, failure to devise a practical contemporary apprenticeship system, failure to listen to the criticisms of employees, failure to reduce or eliminate workplace hazards, and failure to make reliable, efficient, competitively priced products vis-à-vis Western Europe and especially Japan.[12] By 1978, the United States, once the world's leader in manufacturing the tools and machines used almost everywhere, imported more than it sold abroad. That the decline was particularly apparent in advanced machine tools for nondefense industries reflected America's growing dependence on the Pentagon to buy its defense products at virtually any cost and with little if any competition and no incentive for efficiency. For this reason the 1983 NAE report urged no Defense Department (or other major government) subsidies or purchases because they ultimately were self-defeating for the industry.

If these problems were systematically addressed, the American machine shop would be an even more integral part of "high-tech" manufacturing than at present and might in turn be associated once again with the cutting edge (no pun intended) of American technology. That would surely be a most ironic reversal of the nineteenth-century shop culture's fate.

Ironic as well would be a (partial) return to the smaller-scale machine shops of the industry's early days. As mechanical components in machine design become both lighter and smaller, and as computer-aided decentralization of decision-making becomes increasingly common, such a prospect is not unrealistic.[13] Indeed, that 1983 NAE report characterized the industry as being comprised of small companies. Over 65 percent of them employ fewer than twenty workers and are primarily family owned, allowing little opportunity for the mergers or acquisitions that would concentrate industry.[14]

Significantly, too, machine shops are still categorized as job, repair, and production shops, with production shops as in the nineteenth century generally much larger in size and in number of employees than the other two varieties.[15] A 1991 Associated Press story describes the persistence of a family-owned and -operated blacksmith shop in Baltimore occupying a building where such a shop has existed since 1810! The shop specializes in ornamental ironwork and now employs twelve workers, versus thirty in its heyday in the late nineteenth century, when iron ornamentation was more common on gates and windows. Contemporary electric arc welders and electric grinders are somehow integrated with nineteenth-century anvils, molds, and patterns. The shop is not yet computerized but may soon be. As one employee puts it, "there are some people today who believe in doing it the eighteenth-century way without electricity, using bellows. We just can't do that here. You cannot make a living without a little bit of [modern] technology."[16] This shop is surely unusual, but it is hardly unique in American technology. In any case, the future of the American machine shop and of its workers may not then be as bleak as commonly assumed.

Whatever the machine shop's future, it would be mistaken to wax too nostalgic over the disappearance of the traditional shop as represented by Armington and Sims. For all its contributions to American technology, it was outdated by the late nineteenth century in both its equipment and its method of instruction. And for all its contributions to American culture, it was a closed society in terms of class, ethnicity, gender, and race. The professional engineering schools that largely replaced it were hardly perfect, but they were far more up-to-date technologically and were considerably more accessible to men at least from different economic and social backgrounds. Where, by contrast, British machine shops and their rigid apprenticeship system refused to give way, insisting that professional engineering schools were unnecessary, that nation's technological and economic hegemony was undermined in the long run, and the United States, along with Germany, surpassed Britain in the early twentieth century as the leaders of the industrialized world.

Yet the feelings invariably generated by tourist visits to Armington and Sims and similar old machine shops are wonderfully revealing of Americans' characteristic ambivalence about their technological past. How much better was the past, so many conclude, in the sense of smaller, more personal, and more congenial workplaces; but how primitive were those same workplaces, and how far have we advanced since then.[17] With technology as with so much else, one must be careful to limit one's nostalgia without necessarily eliminating it altogether. This requires a firm grasp of what really took place in "the good old days." *Player Piano* achieves such a balance in fiction. Armington and Sims and its counterparts can do likewise in fact if exhibited properly. As the following chapter contends, seeing tools and machines in person and in historical context greatly enhances one's appreciation for the technological past and present and for the connections between them.

6

ON TECHNOLOGICAL MUSEUMS: A PROFESSOR'S PERSPECTIVE

. . . .

For many academics outside art and art history, museums and historic sites are alien territory, pedagogically speaking, staffed by alleged intellectual inferiors who supposedly couldn't make it in the professorial big leagues. Historians of technology who teach at colleges and universities are less guilty of this assumption than most other professors, but are by no means free of unjustified condescension toward curators, archivists, and other museum and historic site professionals. Such attitudes are unfortunate and harmful.

Since beginning to teach the history of technology more than fifteen years ago, I have regularly taken classes to pertinent nearby museums and historic sites. I have done so not because of any prior expertise in material culture but because of a simple desire to complement and enhance class readings, lectures, and discussions. Even at the outset of my career, it seemed to me that seeing structures and machines first-hand and, if possible, in operation made more sense than merely reading about them or seeing pictures or slides. Despite the financial and organizational problems of such ventures, I have never regretted those class outings. Indeed, many of my students at the University of Michigan, at Harvard, and more recently at the University of Maine have rated them among the highlights of my courses. By requiring my students to write papers about their experiences, I have, I believe, raised their visual literacy as well as enhanced their understanding of technology's past—this at a time of allegedly declining technological literacy. As one student wrote of her experience at the Maine State Museum, "I honestly believe that I gained more from this museum visit than any others [here or elsewhere] simply because I approached the visit with a purpose other than entertainment."

Before visiting any of these museums or historic sites, my students are required to read two provocative and perceptive articles: George Basalla's "Museums and Technological Utopianism," and Larry Lankton's "Reading History from the Hardware."[1] Both authors are historians of technology concerned about technological museums' intellectual and ideological functions. The first article raises important questions about the display of technology in museums and historic sites and about the overt and covert messages given to usually unknowing visitors—above all the alleged equation between technological progress and social progress—and the frequent accompanying endorsement of the various industries and companies manufacturing or donating the items on display. The second article raises equally significant questions about how much visitors to these institutions can really learn, depending on both their existing knowledge, values, and perspectives and their understandable attraction to objects that already mean something to them. The two readings better prepare my students to evaluate these and any other exhibits in technology, science, and even art that they may someday see.

I wish to examine here, as a representative case study, the Maine State Museum (MSM), which opened in 1971 near the capitol building in Augusta as New England's only state museum. I have taken several classes to the museum and have had them focus on the "Made in Maine" exhibition, which is about nineteenth-century manufacturing in a state usually associated with forests, potatoes, seacoasts, and tourists. The exhibit represents the museum's biggest effort to date, in terms of construction, organization, research, collection, display, and interpretation.

Most of my students are from Maine, and some had gone as children to the museum. But the 1983 construction and 1985 opening of the "Made in Maine" exhibition so transformed the institution that it no longer represents what those who visited it earlier recall. This is unfortunate insofar as it is always interesting to have students make such comparisons—particularly if the institution has remained basically the same for years—but it is surely a small price to pay for the changes that were necessary to make the museum the exciting and enlightening place it has since become.

In brief, "Made in Maine" consists of displays illuminating four work environments: home, shop, mill, and factory. These rather vague if not outdated categories derive from Victor Clark's classic *History of Manufactures in the United States* (1929). Most visitors ignore the categories anyway and concentrate on the specific displays themselves. In addition to an introductory display of artifacts and historical images reflecting manufacturing in Maine, there are reconstructions of a dozen period-room work environments plus several cases filled with Maine-made goods. Visitors use several ramps to get from one display to another. Home is represented by spinning yarn in an 1820 kitchen and by sewing clothes in an 1880 parlor (all dates are circa). Shop is represented by an 1815 gun shop, an 1820 furniture shop, an 1850 shoe shop, an 1870 blacksmith (small machine) shop, and a 1900 fishing rod shop. Mill is represented by an 1830 wool fulling and finishing mill and an 1890 cupola furnace from a stove foundry. Finally, factory is represented by carding and spinning wool and by weaving wool in parts of 1850 and 1890 factories respectively. Bridging shop, mill, and factory is an 1850 waterpowered woodworking operation that rises through all three levels of the exhibition. Using water released from a turbine placed well below the lowest floor level (with the aid of hidden electric motors and pumps), it manufactures barrel staves, shingles, and wheelbarrows. Last but hardly least, there is an excellent (and free) visitor's guide to "Made in Maine," something often missing from other technological museums. Students are urged to read it both during and after their visit and to use it as the starting point for their papers.

Not all of my students have uncritically praised the exhibition. Yet no student, as far as I can tell, has found it boring or uninformative. Their likes and dislikes about the exhibition fall into three major categories: the displays themselves; the relationship between those displays and their personal and familial experiences as Mainers and as New Englanders; and the messages about technological and social progress and about the nature of industrialization in Maine conveyed by those displays. These categories, like the comments themselves, are applicable to all technological museums that ask visitors to take them seriously.

To begin with, my students have, like me, uniformly appreciated seeing structures and machines in person, in context, and in some cases

Overview of working conditions in nineteenth-century Maine shops, mills, and factories, "Made in Maine" exhibition, Maine State Museum (*Photo courtesy Maine State Museum*)

in operation, as compared with merely reading about them or viewing pictures or slides. As with the reconstructed Armington and Sims machine shop, so here, nothing substitutes for the hardware itself. As one student wrote, "For my nonmechanical mind, written description of a machine such as a lathe or a mill with belts powered by water does not evoke images. Instead, I am left with a blank mental template. After seeing the hardware personally, I have images in my mind that will not fade because I can associate them with the exhibition." And as another student put it, "I felt like I was looking through a time machine into the past."

Equally important, my students have generally appreciated the specific displays—above all the three-story waterpowered woodworking mill, easily the largest and most impressive part of the exhibition. As one student observed about it and the other reconstructed work environments, "One of the more pleasing aspects was the attention to detail—the snow on the floor of one display, the frost on the window of another, and something as seemingly minute as saw marks on a board." Or as another student put it, "All of the shops had such an authentic look it was eerie."

What has troubled a number of students about the displays can be summarized as follows: (1) insufficient signs to direct visitors to exhibitions—for there are other museum exhibitions besides this one on topics ranging from agriculture to ice harvesting to shipbuilding—and the absence of a numbering system for the components of "Made in Maine" itself (though the exhibition does use logos to identify the four work environments it describes and does have small plaques accompanying each display); (2) insufficient labels for the displays apart from the visitor's guide and insufficient lighting by which to read the guide (perhaps justified by the deliberate attempt to re-create the lighting of past working conditions); (3) too few or too many re-created (taped) workplace sounds (students differed considerably here); (4) the insufficient number of structures and machines in operation (perhaps justified by the deterioration this often produces and the potential loss of the artifacts themselves)—"Make looms weave, engines produce power, and clocks ring," one student pleaded; (5) the insufficient number of mannequins (though at least one student appreciated their absence "because it allowed some imagination; the curators and designers did not do all the work for us"); (6) the absence of actors and actresses portraying historical figures (perhaps justified by the distraction they invariably create from the artifacts themselves); (7) the absence of any personal recollections and interviews, whether in print or on tape, accompanying the hardware; (8) the absence of films and videos to supplement the displays themselves and to illuminate the work process itself; (9) the absence of displays of papermaking, Maine's biggest industry, because of both the huge size of the actual machinery and the museum's decision, for the sake of authenticity, not to substitute smaller-scale models; (10) the absence of displays of shoemaking, Maine's second biggest industry, because the machinery involved wasn't made in Maine but was instead rented out to Maine shoemakers; (11) the absence, for whatever reasons, of displays of such other major Maine industries as potatoes and maple sugar, and the consequent exhibit of wool, merely the third largest Maine industry, as a substitute for and representative of these others; (12) the seemingly artificial separation of "Made in Maine" products from the other items in the museum, most of which are also Maine products—as one student suggested, the exhibition should be retitled "The Industrialization of Maine"; (13) the related problem of including in the "Made in Maine" exhibition tools and machines used to produce Maine products but themselves made elsewhere (looms, for instance); and finally, (14) the further related problem of displaying items also made elsewhere in New England and in some cases in the United States overall, and the consequently diminished luster of "Made in Maine" items. As one student asked, "Doesn't most every town in New England have a mill or a blacksmith? I am from a small Massachusetts town, and we are also proud of our traditional industries."

Criticisms similar to these have been made by other students of mine about other technological museums, and most are valid points that deserve attention. Hence the representativeness of the MSM example for rethinking the educational role and value of all technological museums.

Beyond these reactions to the displays themselves, many of my students have made connections to their existing knowledge of Maine history, to their feelings about the state, and to personal or familial experiences or locations. These connections reinforce the technical materials and information being provided, but are equally important in and of themselves. If nothing else, my students have uniformly appreciated the exhibition's recognition of the sheer number and variety of items manufactured in nineteenth-century Maine. As then MSM Director Paul Rivard observes in the catalog accompanying the exhibition, "Made in Maine" treats "the history of the vast majority of Mainers who were not lumberjacks, not lighthouse keepers, not the captains of tall ships."[2] This recognition has in turn inspired or renewed pride on the part of numerous students in their state. As a prospective high school social studies teacher wrote, "It was nice to see that Maine's history is comparable with our whole nation's. I have always thought of Maine as a backward state, never adapting to advances of technology until absolutely necessary."

On a more personal level, as one student noted, "My rural background helped me to appreciate this exhibition more since some of the items on display are like the antiques found in my parents' home, for example, the treadle sewing machine which still gets an occasional workout by my mother." And as another student recalled about a trip hammer used in flattening metal and making ax heads, "I was suddenly

A display of various and sometimes unexpected "Made in Maine" items, Maine State Museum (*Photo courtesy Maine State Museum*)

excited to find that it was used in a mill in my hometown. I thought it was great that my hometown offered nations a world-class product." And as a third student wrote, "The shoe shop was particularly interesting for me because I have worked part time in a shoe shop for the past five years. I understand the skill and craftsmanship it takes to make just one pair of shoes, and likewise the benefits of structures and machines."

A wool-spinning "jack," a mid-nineteenth-century machine found in early woolen factories, "Made in Maine" exhibition, Maine State Museum (*Photo courtesy Maine State Museum*)

Not all such personal responses, however, were positive. Several students criticized the insufficient number of northern Maine items exhibited, reflecting the so-called two Maines and students' frequent identification with one or the other. Here as elsewhere the poorer, less populous North resents the booming, more populous South. As one disappointed northerner argued, "Contrary to popular belief, northern Maine is rich with technological history." (That northern Maine, for reasons such as a smaller population and less wealth, produces fewer "museum quality" items than southern Maine hardly satisfies such critics.) Several other students, and not only women, criticized the exhibition as sexist. One female student lamented, "The overwhelming message is that technology in Maine was invented and used mostly by men" (though any accurate portrayal of the nineteenth-century workplace has to reflect, if not necessarily endorse, this state of affairs).

Finally, following their readings of the Basalla and Lankton articles as well as of other course materials, my students found in the exhibition varying messages about technological and social progress and about the nature of industrialization in Maine. Virtually all appreciated the exhibition's sense of sheer technological—if not necessarily social—progress in the development of ever more powerful, efficient, and complex tools and machines. Likewise nearly all appreciated the absence, despite that sense of development, both of what I earlier called Whiggism regarding technological progress as allegedly equal to social progress and of the kind of shameless promotion of industries and companies manufacturing or donating tools and machines that Basalla properly condemns. Furthermore, nearly all appreciated the absence of the presentation of "Made in Maine" products in the form of a cornucopia, to use one of Basalla's three categories. A cornucopia would have suggested a false sense of endless abundance in the state at that time, though parts of the exhibition do imply a pervasive prosperity in industrial Maine. In the words of one student, "All the shelves were full, pots were filled, and barrels were overflowing with items." But this in itself is hardly the excess Basalla rightly rejects.

By contrast, a number of students saw in the exhibition the presentation of "Made in Maine" products in the form of Basalla's other two categories, those of aesthetic object and of romantic or sentimental object. As one student noted, the engines and turbines especially fit the aesthetic category: "They are placed on individual pedestals for one to view, and one feels as if one is in an art museum. Many finished products are displayed in this fashion too. Guns, clocks, stoneware vessels, glassware, and tools are hung up on walls and enclosed in glass cases." Some students even thought (erroneously) that the glass partitions before all displays were there not only to protect and preserve the items within but also to "glorify priceless artifacts," removing them from their everyday contexts. Equally important, as another student put it, "The sentiments you get from these displays are how great the good old days were, yet how much better we are today, and how far we have come from how other people have lived." As with the Armington and Sims Machine Shop, so with "Made in Maine," these mixed feelings about the past and the present are common to most technology museum exhibitions. Yet few such exhibitions ask visitors to reflect upon the significance of this ambivalence, and "Made in Maine" could certainly do more here. Individual and collective recognition of Americans' true feelings about their technological heritage could have profound effects upon their attitudes toward contemporary and future technological developments.

In addition, many students faulted the exhibition for insufficient attention to the actual processes of manufacturing the items exhibited, to the changes in those processes over time, to the social implications of the technologies displayed, to the time, pay, pressures, and hazards for the workers involved, and to the long-term fate of the industries and workers alike. As one student asked, "What was it like working in a rifle shop all day? Did someone working in a woolen factory make decent wages? What were the people who used the displayed machinery like?" And as another student complained, "We are not shown the profit-maximizing mill owners moving to the South or outside the U.S. because cheaper wages and so higher profits can be found there. Nor are we shown the new processes that lowered costs and made better products, in turn putting many small craftsmen out of business."

To the extent that these last criticisms are fair, and I believe they are, they are particularly telling, insofar as the exhibition's principal claim of originality, in addition to the recognition of "Made in Maine" products, is, in Rivard's own words, "social integration in a complex nineteenth-century story. . . . In an analysis of the American story that the nation's history museums tell today, we find pathetically little attention directed to the history of work in nineteenth-century factories and life in urban cities in relation to their social, economic, and technological significance."[3] If, as Rivard properly maintains, the museum's core is its collection, the artifacts, alas, do not necessarily speak for themselves. As Lankton's article makes clear, technological museums can take little for granted regarding visitors' prior knowledge, much less whatever they learn through their visits. Hence the need for more historical and social context at MSM and elsewhere. And this applies still more to the nonstudent general public, as does everything else discussed here.

Despite the criticisms I have enumerated—not all of which I myself share—most of my students have liked the exhibition. No less important, nearly all have come to appreciate the often misunderstood human dimensions of museums and historic sites, from the varying expectations of those outside the institution (whether public officials or donors or scholars or ordinary visitors) to the difficulties of mounting exhibitions (from finding desired objects to obtaining and then displaying them) to the challenge of educating without overwhelming or boring visitors with limited attention spans to that ambivalence such exhibitions invariably evoke about the alleged "good old days" of a century or two ago. The refreshing candor of Rivard in acknowledging both these factors and the consequent periodic need to rethink the exhibition and the museum overall has reinforced this healthy perspective. His informal talks to students, lectures to fellow professionals, and related publications might well serve to guide others. Far from resting on the exhibition's laurels, he and his staff and their successors have begun addressing some of the criticisms raised by my students and other visitors and have been considering, for example, enlarging the exhibition's introductory and concluding areas to create greater structure and coherence, increasing the number, information on, and readability of object display labels, and using headsets to provide different perspectives on the same objects and displays. Also contemplated is the display of more Maine-built steam (and gasoline) engines, small machines, boats, and automobiles.

In the meantime in 1991 the museum opened another major, permanent, and complementary exhibition entitled "12,000 Years in Maine," spanning prehistoric times to the period just before "Made in Maine" begins. Containing over 2,400 artifacts and specimens, this exhibition includes many examples of preindustrial objects fashioned by prehistoric peoples of the state, by Maine Indians, and by European explorers and settlers. Ideally, "12,000 Years in Maine" will demonstrate that technology has been an integral part of human existence since civilization began and is anything but a recent phenomenon. This surely is or ought to be a principal lesson of any serious history of technology course, whatever its particular chronological boundaries.

As I tell my students during our postvisit class discussion of the exhibition, their very ability to recognize problems in the exhibition is a positive indication of their new degree of visual literacy. If only the general public visiting museums could be equally alert! Like other forms of technology, those in "Made in Maine" have not come to us like manna from heaven but are instead the results of avowedly human efforts. My students' gradual, sometimes painful, recognition of this fact justifies for me the value of all such class ventures.

7

. . . .

The greatest challenge facing any technological museum is not financial or organizational or even artifactual, but intellectual. It is the dual challenge of explaining to lay people how structures and machines work and what functions they perform and of re-creating an image of the past that accurately illuminates their historical and social significance. No technological museum, however large and well funded, can ever alone convey the true complexity of technology's past, just as no book(s) can do so either. As the prior chapter suggests, museums require both the artifacts themselves and adequate written materials about them. Yet this is no guarantee of success, given such obstacles as competing images of technology's past on the part of visitors, donors, trustees, etc., and those same persons' frequent desire for sensory as much as cerebral experiences at technological museums—such as ruminating on the "good old days," as at the Armington and Sims Machine Shop or the "Made in Maine" exhibition.

These obstacles are hard enough to surmount when the structures and machines being exhibited are comparatively old and comparatively easy to fathom, as with Armington and Sims and "Made in Maine." But when the artifacts are much newer and much harder to grasp, those dual intellectual challenges arise at the very outset, at the point of conceptualization. Indeed, at first glance, computers and museums, the focus of this essay, seem wholly incompatible. Museums ordinarily house objects of some lineage, and computers, so relatively recent in origin, hardly appear to qualify.[1] Moreover, the very pervasiveness of computers today, combined with the rapid improvements in each computer "generation," would appear to make older varieties unworthy of display. What would be the point?

Equally important, even in their earliest representations, computers were never primitive or simple in the manner of, say, waterwheels or lathes, and their remarkable accessibility to nonexperts in recent years has not made their actual operations any more understandable. For many, they are the ultimate "black boxes." Where laypeople can see a waterwheel or a lathe or, for that matter, a steam engine at work and quickly grasp its structure and function, the same does not hold for computers. The computer's inside, as well as its outside, is not "visually revealing, even to an expert . . . because the heart of the machine, or better, its brain, is for all intents and purposes invisible."[2] The programming code that goes into the software and that determines the computer's function(s) is not illuminated in the software itself. Moreover, how does one explain the extremely complex mathematics and physics that govern computer operations? How does one convey the extraordinary speed of contemporary computer calculations on the order of a nanosecond (one billionth of a second)? Unlike many other machines, such as waterwheels or steam engines, computers are not particularly interesting, much less beautiful, to look at when at work, unless the tasks being performed are themselves of some interest to the viewer. Yet computers must be viewed in operation if museum visitors are to begin to grasp their structure and functions.

These intellectual challenges have not, however, stopped a number of computer aficionados from establishing in Boston and Washington, D.C., respectively, an entire museum and a major museum gallery devoted to the celebration—and, to varying extents, the history and social significance—of modern computers. These enthusiasts include computer company executives, computer engineers, and professional curators and historians. Eventually these pioneering exhibits will be supplemented by others at different institutions; and Boston's Computer Museum itself has recently been transformed radically. For now, though, it is useful to see what to date has been accomplished at both the Computer Museum and the National Air and Space Museum ("Beyond the Limits: Flight Enters the Computer Age") and then to suggest what remains to be done. The issues raised here naturally apply far beyond the particular exhibitions themselves.

The Computer Museum opened at its present location in November 1984 in a century-old warehouse on Boston's waterfront, where it shares space with the popular Children's Museum. Some of the computers displayed had been at the museum's original site, opened in 1979, at Marlboro, Massachusetts, headquarters of Digital Equipment Corporation (DEC), a leading computer manufacturer. The company's top executives had been spurred to start a museum in order to save from the scrapheap a famous early computer on which they had worked years before. To that end, and to serve the general public, the museum was incorporated as a nonprofit enterprise in 1982. By law, it had to leave DEC. Now relocated, it bills itself as the world's only museum "devoted solely to computers and their impact on society" and boasts of having "the most comprehensive collections and exhibitions on this subject in the world."[3] Approximately 150,000 persons a year visit.

By contrast, the National Air and Space Museum (NASM) opened in 1976 in a huge building of its own and soon became the most popular of the Smithsonian Institution's many museums and one of America's most visited museums (approximately nine million persons annually). Its twenty-three exhibition areas house artifacts ranging from the Wright Brothers' original 1903 *Kitty Hawk Flyer* and Lindbergh's *Spirit of St. Louis* to the Apollo 11 capsule that landed on the moon. Dozens of airplanes, rockets, engines, propellers, models, instruments, uniforms, medals, and insignia are on display. Despite these impressive exhibitions, scholars have long criticized NASM for its lack of attention to historical and social context, for its separation of air and space from related technologies, for its substitution of famous vehicles for serious illumination of the nation's aviation past, and for its questionable Whiggish endorsement of that past as inevitably leading to current and future progress.[4] Significantly, the chairman of the Computer Museum's board of directors is quoted in a 1988 museum newsletter as looking to NASM as a "superb 'role model'"[5] for his own institution—this despite the Computer Museum's avowed concern for computers' "impact on society" and NASM's traditional neglect of contextual issues. Yet what makes "Beyond the Limits" unusual for NASM is its interest in genuine historical and social context. The exhibition opened in May 1989, replacing a smaller exhibition on flight technology housed in one of the museum's original galleries.

At present, the Computer Museum's public displays occupy much of the six-story building's top two floors and a bit of the first floor. A large glass-enclosed elevator takes visitors to the top floor and in the process offers an excellent view of both the Boston skyline and its waterfront. Of the current permanent exhibitions summarized below, few have been there since the museum's 1984 opening.

(1) "The Walk-Through Computer" illuminates how computers work. Visitors interact with a two-story working replica of a desktop computer blown up fifty times normal size. They use a giant trackball and keyboard to find, as a common problem computers solve, the shortest land route between any two major cities on any one continent. A 108-square-foot computer screen pinpointing the two cities also shows interesting sights along the way. Visitors then walk inside the computer, where they see a huge spinning disk drive retrieve data, peer inside banks of random access memory chips, and walk past ceiling-high interface boards to view the microprocessor. Pulsing neon lights simulate data flowing through the computer, while an animated computer video explains how software drives hardware.

(2) "People and Computers: Milestones of a Revolution" illuminates computers' fifty-year evolution from a few expensive electronic behemoths in the 1940s to the millions of desktop computers and microprocessors used today. Each of the nine milestones re-creates a life-size computer environment typical of its era and complements each display with "time tunnels" highlighting other major historical developments of the period. Each milestone also incorporates interactive computer stations, films, and videotapes. Among the famous computers shown are (portions of) MIT's Whirlwind (1940s), a pioneering vacuum-tube computer whose rescue from the scrapheap spurred the museum's founding; Remington Rand's UNIVAC 1 (Universal Automatic Computer) (1951), America's first business computer; and Control Data Corporation's 6600 (1976), a pioneering "supercomputer."

(3) "Smart Machines" illuminates robots, artificial intelligence, and the degree to which they mirror or exceed human intelligence and physical prowess. Numerous robots and computers perform various activities, many of them requiring visitor participation.

(4) "The Computer and the Image" illuminates computer-aided image building and processing, graphic technology, design simulation, and animation (including a theater showing computer-generated films). Complementing it are periodic temporary displays of computer-based works of art.

(5) "Tools and Toys: The Amazing Personal Computer" illuminates

The Walk-Through Computer, The Computer Museum, Boston (*Photo by Jack McWilliams*)

its many contemporary and future uses in work, play, learning, and communications, inviting visitor participation in thirty-five different interactive stations. Video and music making, graphic designing, game playing, writing, and desktop publishing are among the activities included.

(6) "The Learning Center" demonstrates the efficacy of computers as educational tools and offers computer programs on architecture, geography, history, and other subjects.

(7) Smaller displays focus on integrated circuits or chips; on the NASA Apollo Program Guidance Computer; on the 1805 Jacquard Loom, a precursor of computers using holes punched in cards to translate mechanically stored information into an image; and on the 1890 Hollerith Tabulator, another precursor of computers also employing punch cards and utilized by the Census Bureau in that year to count the entire American population mechanically for the first time.

(8) Finally, the first floor houses a display of the Digital VAX 6310 super minicomputer used by the museum for admissions, accounting, appointments, word processing, information storage, and messages (electronic mail). Next to it, as one enters the museum, is a store carrying computer-related books, videos, slides, postcards, games, jewelry, and chocolate "chips."

Missing from the store as from the rest of the museum is a catalog of the permanent exhibitions. Although one may eventually be published, at present there is only a two-page (free) guide and floor plan, which is helpful but inadequate. Most of the exhibitions, especially the newer "Smart Machines," "The Walk-Through Computer," "People and Computers," and "Tools and Toys," do have ample labels (and videos) with sufficient information for interested visitors, but the kind of detailed guide available for "Made in Maine" would be welcome here.

The Computer Museum deserves considerable praise not merely for its sheer existence (collecting computers and computer-related materials that might otherwise have gone to the scrapheap) but also for demonstrating that computers do have a past. That computers' true history is barely fifty years hardly diminishes the need to document their past. If anything, given the rapid obsolescence of each computer "generation," it is ever more imperative not to lose that history. Moreover, the attempt to cover both the history of and the contemporary developments in computers in a comparatively small space (53,000 square feet, including office, storage, and work space) is highly com-

mendable. Not surprisingly, the museum's founders and major support-
ers are current or former computer industry executives and technical
experts with a vested interest in putting a predominantly positive
face—or screen—on their industry and on computers' impact on society. Without their material and financial contributions, the museum
would not exist. The critical issue is the orientation of the professional
staff and, in turn, its exhibitions.

The history of computers over the past half-century or so undeni-
ably confirms unceasing—and amazing—technical progress: from vacuum tubes to transistors to integrated circuits to microprocessors, from
plugboards and paper tapes to magnetic storage tapes to hard and floppy
disks and diskettes, from computers the size of whole buildings to the
size of large rooms to the size of small refrigerators. The several as-
tounding contrasts that the museum provides between old and new
computers regarding comparative size, power, efficiency, and appearance confirm the value of seeing technology in person rather than
merely reading or hearing about it. Such firsthand comparisons rightly
question the traditional assumption in the history of technology that
bigger is better (as do, less explicitly and less dramatically, both the
Armington and Sims Machine Shop and "Made in Maine"). Ironically,
the museum thus needed to create a giant replica of an ordinary desktop
computer in order to show how smaller has become better.

Nevertheless, until the opening in 1990 and 1991 respectively
of "The Walk-Through Computer" and "People and Computers," the
Computer Museum had generally failed to meet the two major intellectual challenges of explaining how computers work and what they do and
of illuminating computers' history and social significance. In addition,
until then, the museum's overall atmosphere, from its color schemes to
its furniture selections to the absence of human figures from its exhibitions, was sterile and antiseptic rather than warm and inviting (if perhaps in keeping with the impersonality associated with computers,
fairly or not). Only the display of the transistor computer IBM 1401, re-
creating a 1965 Travelers Insurance Company data processing office,
showed any signs of real life, with its crumpled printouts, empty Coke
bottles left on a programmer's desk, and single mannequin. And the display's value was undermined in part by its explicit promotion through
contemporary advertising materials of the wonders of both IBM and
Travelers Insurance, the worst such examples of corporate advertising
in the entire museum—if characteristic of technological museums, as

George Basalla's critique makes painfully clear. Happily, the museum's overall atmosphere has warmed up considerably. Incorporating a revamped Travelers office, its "People and Computers" exhibition has numerous mannequins (including some women and blacks), and its corporate advertising there and elsewhere has been toned down to appropriate levels.

Until recently as well, the museum's layout lacked sufficient direction and order. Unaware of the logic governing the placement of many exhibitions, visitors hardly knew where to go once they stepped off the sixth- (or fifth-) floor elevator. This is partially remedied by the two-page guide, an improvement on previous briefer ones. With several permanent exhibitions now open, visitors have a far easier time making sense of the museum's layout and going from one exhibition to another. Yet visitors still encounter too many undefined technical terms. Persons unfamiliar with computer jargon, such as some of the many Harvard University students I have brought to the museum, do not know, for example, what core memory, bits, 4K words, arithmetic control units, and magnetic drums mean. Such confusion reinforces their anxieties about computers. Given the museum's mission, that is a most unwelcome reaction. Moreover, few of the historical computers noted above are ever in operation, unlike all of the modern computers. Although finances as well as potential deterioration are admittedly key factors in this policy, inactive computers appear especially like "black boxes." In "People and Computers" this dilemma is partially resolved by video presentations of several historical computers in operation.

Like so many other technological museums—not least, NASM—the Computer Museum initially presented the Whig Theory of the history of technology. Sheer technological progress, however impressive, was automatically equated with more complex social progress. And that technological progress in turn was presented as an inevitable triumph by certified individual heroes, without recognition of the failures, missteps, accidents, coincidences, choices, and group efforts that actually occurred and that in fact account for the ultimate decisions and developments. Until recently, too, the museum's presentation of computers' social consequences was equally one-sided. Nowhere, for instance, were there any indications of such fundamental by-products of computers as technological unemployment, dehumanization of many remaining tasks, danger of excessive exposure to VDT screens, invasion of privacy, information overload, loss of data through computer viruses, and, above all, threat of accidental nuclear war. Instead, along with the computer industry, the military establishment largely responsible for the computer's development was heavily praised in an atmosphere reminiscent of the height of the Cold War. Academia's ties to the computer portion of the so-called military-industrial complex were likewise celebrated, never questioned.

To its considerable credit, the "People and Computers" exhibition has qualified this excessive Whiggism and has provided a more balanced—and more accurate—version of computers' evolution and of their mixed blessings for society. At the exhibition's very entrance, for example, where eighteen video monitors form an archway while a ninety-second video conveys both the passage of time and computers' evolution since 1935, "progress has its price" is stated explicitly. That theme is found throughout the exhibit, beginning with the first of the nine Milestones, "The 1930s: Mechanizing Names and Numbers." Along with praising the Social Security system and the punch-card machinery (the ancestors of computers) that made it practical, the display asks what it is to "feel like a number" and to "mechanize information." In Milestone Two, "The 1940s: The Computer Is Born," a case displays memory units for seven early computers that for various reasons proved unsuccessful. "Innovations rarely happen overnight," the label rightly states. "Usually they are the result of lengthy experimentation. The computer had to wait for information to emerge from the memory." Meanwhile, "reliability was a problem." Similarly, in Milestone Four, "The Late 1950s: Programming," photos depict various computers, each of which followed a different set of instructions. Only the creation of programming languages—especially FORTRAN, used for scientific computing, and COBOL, used for business data processing—"allowed computers to obey commands more familiar to people and made it possible for programs written on one computer to run on another," according to the display's label. Here too, then, technological progress was hardly without setbacks and detours and was anything but inevitable, contrary to Whiggism.

Also in Milestone Two is a discussion about how Whirlwind, begun under a contract to develop a flight simulator for the U.S. Navy, eventually became the prototype for the air defense computer system in use until 1983. Here is a superb example, in the accompanying label's words, "of how technology research often leads to unexpected results." This recognition is a complementary way out of Whiggism, which

Introductory video archway, "People and Computers" exhibition, The Computer Museum, Boston (*Photo courtesy The Computer Museum*)

concedes as little to unanticipated positive developments as it does to unexpected negative ones. But the exhibition needs to say more about this issue.

Other social and economic problems related to the proliferation of computers are addressed in other Milestones. In Milestone Three, "The Early 1950s: Computers for Sale," there are mounted copies of several newspaper stories and advertisements regarding computers and automation. As the accompanying label properly says, "Machines that seemed to think and work tirelessly were viewed with both hope and despair. . . . New technologies often give rise to such debates. How would you feel if one of your relatives lost a job to a robot?" Regarding computers and privacy, Milestone Five, "The 1960s: Computing Means Business," addresses this persistent concern. "Your life on file?" asks one label. "During the 1960s, governments and big corporations used computer tape drives and disk drives to stockpile huge amounts of information. . . . Do you have any control over how these records about you are used?" No answer is given, but at least the question is clearly posed. Regarding supercomputers and the unprecedented ability to communicate internationally, Milestone Seven, "The Late 1970s: Supercomputers," concedes in a sign that "a small world still has big problems." For example, this display implies that, as helpful as super-computers are in simulating conditions of global weather and war, thereby altering how humans solve problems, they cannot solve all problems, contrary to the expectations past and present of some computer enthusiasts.

Finally, regarding the future of computers, in Milestone Nine, "The 1990s: Computers, Computers Everywhere," a computerized mannequin or "animation" asks visitors both to reflect on what they've seen (and perhaps experienced themselves) and to predict the future. "Is this what they call progress? What do you think?" So goes one sign. "You are the future," says another. "But these changes are only the beginning," the accompanying label adds. "Figuring out how to use computers in ways that benefit people around the world will be a challenge for you and future generations." Here again, but more ex-plicitly than anywhere else in either "People and Computers" or the museum overall, the excessive Whiggism that once characterized the entire institution is thankfully put in its place.

Similarly, as the Cold War has ended, so, too, has the museum's un-critical endorsement of the military-industrial complex. Gone, perhaps for good, is the former exhibition of portions of the IBM AN/FSQ-7 (1958), the largest computer ever built. Weighing 175 tons, requiring over 25,000 vacuum tubes (subject to frequent replacement), and occu-pying a four-story building, it was used by the U.S. Air Force to monitor North American skies for enemy aircraft from 1958 until 1983. Yet a modern personal computer (PC) is more powerful than this, as was made clear in the earlier exhibition with a contemporary PC placed beside those portions of the huge AN/FSQ-7. The loss of such a graphic comparison is admittedly unfortunate, but perhaps that exhibition could be redone elsewhere in the museum in a post–Cold War atmo-sphere.

Gone, too, also perhaps permanently, is the re-created and deadly serious SAGE (Semi-Automatic Ground Environment) Air Force "Blue Room," which was one of twenty-four across North America, all of them using the AN/FSQ-7 computer. Contrary to the Cold War propaganda film *SAGE: In Your Defense*, formerly shown in conjunction with this model air-defense direction center (and now excerpted for the video accompanying Milestone Three), the endless watching and waiting for

The pioneering 1940s Whirlwind Computer on display in the "People and Computers" exhibition, The Computer Museum, Boston (*Photo by Doug Baker*)

the Soviet attacks that never came apparently proved less than thrilling for some. Graffiti was discovered by museum staff on the knobs of the interceptor and command consoles. Some scribbles complained of how boring the job was; others were said to be less polite. In either case, the graffiti illuminated the realities of daily life with computers—and in turn the nature of computer culture—better than the hardware itself and applied to the civilian sector as well, as many civilian computer operators have come to know. If space is available, it would be helpful to redo at least part of the Blue Room exhibition in order to illuminate this important point and to combine it with the old AN/FSQ-7–PC physical comparison.

In the absence of these Cold War exhibitions it is certainly appropriate for Milestone Two to include, next to displays about the 1940s Whirlwind computer, a photograph of a Patriot missile being fired. The label reads: "The work begun on Whirlwind still affects you today.

How? In 1991, this computer-guided Patriot missile played an important role in the Gulf War. The use of computers for tracking and intercepting planes and missiles in flight dates back to work done on the Whirlwind." The already noted immediate impact of the Gulf War in reviving so many Americans' declining faith in unadulterated technological progress is, of course, another matter, one the museum need not treat.

Despite "The Walk-Through Computer" and "People and Computers" exhibitions, visitors of all ages and backgrounds, including many of my students, alas, remain more intrigued by the admittedly entertaining exhibitions on computer games and computer graphics in "Smart Machines" and "The Computer and the Image" respectively. Here the museum moves from computer reverence to computer revelry. Even the display of the first video game (MIT's *Space War,* 1962) is given insufficient attention as a historical phenomenon. In fact, within the "Smart Machines" exhibition itself visitors are invariably lured away from the serious displays to those with computers that play chess, checkers, and tic-tac-toe; that compose music from jazz to rock and plot the musical notes then being played; that draw pictures and color maps by voice commands; that check for and correct writing errors; that bargain for groceries; and that ask and promptly answer questions about visitors' heights, food and wine preferences, geographical destinations, and medical and psychological conditions. At times the atmosphere is strikingly akin to a high-tech amusement arcade. Who would not be enticed?

Also in the "Smart Machines" exhibition are impressive videotaped displays of twenty-five historic robots from the 1960s on, including NASA's Mars Rover and underwater Sea Rover. Other robots on the video—plus a few actually displayed below the monitors—handle various industrial tasks that illuminate robot arms and robot vision. Still other robots on the video perform various wonderful humanitarian activities, from turning pages and providing artificial limbs for the handicapped to acting as nightwatchmen for the otherwise unprotected with whom they talk and respond like living entities. As one display panel states, all these robots in "Smart Machines" "perform jobs that are too dangerous, difficult, or plain boring for humans." That sounds perfectly reasonable, but is it? Who determines this? Are boring tasks as necessary to be performed by robots as dangerous or difficult tasks? And do the growing number of workers losing their (dangerous, difficult, or boring) jobs to industrial robots thus have no right to complain? Ironically, this same video claims that "robots cannot mirror human behavior," that they merely do what our computers program them to do, and that any fear of robots threatening or replacing people is "needless." Such reassurance is surely misplaced if not insulting.

A still more unsettling display here is the "Frankenstein set," which originated for an advertising photograph. Robot doctors "Igor" and "Max" construct a "robot child" in a dungeonlike operating room by inserting into their child the "robotic spark of life," the disk bearing the software. "Are robots *really* smart enough to create other robots?" the display label asks. "No, not yet, but come on in and see just *how* smart today's machines can be," it continues. This conscious perversion of Mary Shelley's disturbing novel, in which self-promoting scientist Victor Frankenstein secretly creates and immediately abandons a grotesque-looking creature, is too blatant to ignore.

To be sure, a small part of the "Smart Machines" exhibit discusses the origins and initial twentieth-century debates over the possible dangers of robots and, more generally, artificial intelligence (A.I.) gone beyond human control. Recently expanded a bit and updated to 1990, this section briefly discusses the contributions of such A.I. luminaries as Alan Turing, John McCarthy, Marvin Minsky, Seymour Papert, and Joseph Weizenbaum. But as with the museum's treatment of the technical problems and limitations of early computers prior to the installation of "People and Computers," visitors are still given the distinct impression that all of A.I.'s potential errors have been corrected, that future potential is unlimited, and perhaps most important, that mankind remains in firm, full command of this technology—all questionable assertions. In fact, this section's updating emphasizes the merger in the 1980s of A.I. and robotics into "smart machines" and the incorporation of A.I. into the undergraduate curriculum and personal computers alike. As with robotics alone, social concerns are largely neglected and then dismissed.

Curiously, the "Smart Machines" exhibition on both robots and A.I. provides little sense of the reverence shown in the 1950s and early 1960s toward "electronic brains," as computers then were commonly called. The awe of early computers is particularly apparent in both the Whirlwind and UNIVAC exhibitions—formerly separate, now two parts of "People and Computers"—as revealed in the accompanying 1952 television videotapes of Edward R. Murrow posing mathematical problems to Whirlwind and Charles Collingwood asking UNIVAC to predict the outcome of that year's presidential election. These broadcasts were also many Americans' first look at computers. As John Kasson has shown about Corliss engines, steam locomotives, and other nineteenth-century machines, awe in the face of large-scale technology did not necessarily mean fear; it could equally mean worship. What it always meant was a sense of new, overwhelming power.[6] A similar awe characterized the huge early computers, as indicated by the responses of both those hard-nosed, ordinarily unsentimental television journalists. By contrast, the feelings generated by the "Smart Machines" exhibition are far less passionate and border on a smug satisfaction that computers have developed as expected and that all is well in the world. As the museum's press release on "Smart Machines" puts it, "This major exhibit shows how machines are becoming more like ourselves."[7] Perhaps this is the inevitable result of computers' simultaneous proliferation and miniaturization, yet, as the museum's professional staff concedes, some visitors will be neither pleased nor complacent over this development.

All is obviously not well in our computerized world, and the dilemma posed by the reliance on contemporary computers to call national, state, and local elections is a perfect example of computers' mixed blessings. Compare this to 1952, when, as the UNIVAC exhibition television tape makes clear, computers provoked sufficient anxiety—the other side of the awe toward them—that Collingwood praised rather than criticized UNIVAC for apparently "refusing" to predict the winner of the Eisenhower-Stevenson presidential contest. Momentarily flustered by the computer's surprising failure to respond to his question, Collingwood quickly concluded that UNIVAC was probably being more honest than most professional pollsters and didn't really know the outcome either. In truth, as was later revealed, UNIVAC had accurately predicted that Eisenhower would win by a landslide, but UNIVAC's operators could not believe it or at least were too afraid of being wrong to allow the computer's prediction to be made public. How different is the now-general practice of predicting elections on the basis of scattered representative returns, despite the possibility not only of computer error but also of influencing other potential voters. The UNIVAC exhibit might, then, make some visitors concerned rather than satisfied over computers' current role in the American electoral process. As the museum's professional staff also concedes, that could be a healthy development that would thereby enhance the museum's educational mission.

Admittedly, any museum seeking a predominantly lay audience cannot focus on the negative, or even the serious, but must also entertain. One of the most successful ways in which the Computer Museum balances education and entertainment is through, of all things, a short film of early computer programming. Formerly shown intact in a now defunct "communications theater," it has been incorporated in abbreviated form into "People and Computers" as one of the many short videos available to those who wish to pursue particular topics further. Its audience will thus likely be smaller than before. A Stanford University student production, the film humorously depicts the difficulties of computer programming in the 1960s, including long waits to have programs run, punch cards getting bent and shuffled out of order, and subsequent dismay when the computer finds many program errors. Here the museum readily admits the unreliability, slowness, and frustrations of early computers but implicitly contrasts those problems with their seeming absence in contemporary computers. Except for occasional indications in "People and Computers," one would never guess that the latter, through either human error or disk failure, also suffer from system crashes, software bugs, and lost data. Despite these recent significant qualifications, computers at the museum are still too often presented as objects to be laughed at in their initial forms and worshiped in their current ones.

Curiously, according to the museum's own label, the AN/FSQ-7 had an average "down time" (or malfunctioning period) of under four hours annually, surely a favorable comparison with contemporary air traffic control and other often unreliable large-scale computer systems. This important point, which could be read as qualifying the museum's overall praise for newer computers, is likely lost on most visitors overwhelmed with the explicit old-versus-new comparisons.

As part of its good humor, the Stanford film deliberately plays on the stereotype of computer programmers as "nerds." In the process the film illuminates what most of the museum's presentations neglect, the culture of computers and computer operators. Other parts of "People and Computers" now address this, especially brief videos of computer pioneers, of their workplaces, and, to a lesser extent, of their unhailed associates. An early 1950s film of workers at Philadelphia's UNIVAC Remington Rand facilities describes them as under thirty-five, "perfectly normal" except for their high IQs, and hardly "mad professors." The film's defensiveness is amusing and revealing.

Equally important, "People and Computers" treats computers in the context of popular culture without reducing them to the fun and games of "Smart Machines" and "The Computer and the Image." This is another major advance in the museum's evolution. Most of the videos accompanying each of the nine milestones have selections on computers in popular culture: commercial films, television shows, and television ads. The museum claims that its assortment of videos on these and other aspects of the history of computers is the world's largest. Several milestones have mounted related newspaper articles and print ads as well. These examples not only complement the more general historical displays found at each milestone—capsule summaries of the Great Depression, World War II, the 1950s and 1960s, etc.—but also illuminate the growing degree to which computers have replaced clocks, looms, lathes, steam engines, assembly lines, and other earlier structures and machines as the dominant metaphors and models of our culture. It is unfortunate that more is not made of this profound intellectual and psychic as well as material change. My favorite example is the otherwise unmemorable 1982 Disney movie *Tron*, which Milestone Seven mentions as having pioneered the use of computer-controlled special visual effects for films. There is a photo from *Tron*, but nothing is said about its presenting the world as itself a giant computer akin to earlier societies' "clockwork universe," for instance. The latter is really much more important than any visual effects and should be noted explicitly.

Before the installation of "People and Computers," the museum failed to utilize a sufficient number of these easy-to-use videos to present (its then more Whiggish version of) computers' historical development and contemporary impact. More generally, the museum previously lacked sufficient interactive displays and sufficient imagination to employ them successfully. The museum's proficiency in interactive exhibitions has now become so pronounced that it has recently begun recreating nine of its most popular and effective ones into affordable kits to distribute to museums and science centers around the world—another form of decentralized technology made possible by computers. All the interested museum or science center needs is the computer equipment to run the program.

One of the most impressive early interactive videos was—and still is—the display of the Apollo Guidance Computer used on America's early spacecraft and lunar landing missions through the early 1970s, which is placed alongside a contemporary touch-screen-activated PC. The PC is programmed to perform the same tasks as the astronauts once did and thereby to give visitors a better feel for operating an older computer, one admittedly outmoded once NASA's Apollo program ended. In so doing, however, the museum inevitably risks offering the false message of computers' alleged simplicity. Punching a few keys on already programmed machines or pressure-sensitive pads on preprogrammed robots or giving voice commands to either is a superficial interaction, regardless of the information obtained and the accompanying sense of achievement. There is no hint of the physical and especially mental labor associated with the computer, both to serve it and to make use of its results. Ironically, the display has been altered slightly to state that "real space travel is not like a video game" and to demonstrate the differences. Save in part, however, for the revamped Travelers Insurance Company–IBM exhibition and other parts of "People and Computers," visitors are shown neither what ordinary computer operators do (or have done) nor the boredom and repetition of such work— loading and unloading punch cards or tapes or disks, folding and sorting endless reams of computer printouts, coding and debugging programs. Instead, visitors are still too frequently led to believe that virtually every activity that the computer has performed has come about by plugging the machine in and letting it run. To this extent, the Whig theory of the history of technology yet prevails, though again far less than before.

Despite its impressive "Walk-Through Computer" and "People and Computers" exhibitions, and contrary to its self-proclaimed educational mission, the Computer Museum may still best serve those already familiar with computers. It is too early to know for sure, but if this continues to be true, the museum would hardly be unique—or deserving of further criticism. As noted concerning "Made in Maine," and as applies to all museums, not merely technological ones, visitors' existing knowledge, values, and perspectives, and their understandable attraction to those objects that already mean something to them, govern their experiences. Because complex artifacts such as computers are clearly more difficult for laypeople to understand, the institution introduced various pamphlets for teachers and pre-college students in 1988. In simplified language, these materials cover the initial major exhibits and

Entrance to "Beyond the Limits: Flight Enters the Computer Age," National Air and Space Museum (*Photo courtesy National Air and Space Museum, Smithsonian Institution*)

discuss, for example, the history of electronic computers and how computers work. They are a useful supplement especially to "People and Computers" and "The Walk-Through Computer."

Similar educational materials for NASM's "Beyond the Limits: Flight Enters the Computer Age" have been available from the start. Indeed, the two sets of materials could form the basis for the guides both institutions presently lack. In the case of "Beyond the Limits," however, the exhibition's curator, historian Paul Ceruzzi, has written a book with the same title (MIT Press, 1989) for those interested in pursuing further the topics his exhibition covers. Valuable though it is, the book is simply too large to be carried about as an unofficial guide.

Despite the absence of a guide, the exhibition is so compact and well laid out that its overall message is effectively conveyed throughout: the simultaneous growth of the aerospace and computer industries in the United States and the reciprocal relationship that has evolved between them over the past half-century. As an exhibition label puts it, "They have so influenced each other that it is difficult to separate their histories." As post–World War II jet airplanes approached the speed of sound and as ballistic rockets were being developed simultaneously, calculations for stress analysis, for aerodynamics, and for trajectories were required in unprecedented number and complexity. Yet the 1940s typical "computer system" consisted of a room full of men and women using mechanical calculators, slide rules, paper, and pencil. "Computers" then referred to the persons doing calculations, not to their instruments. Hence the aerospace industry's strong support of the fledgling computer industry. The electronic computers developed since then have found ever more applications in the aerospace industry as they have become smaller, lighter, more reliable, and more powerful. Equally important, the growth of computer graphics since 1961—when Ivan Sutherland devised a program in which line drawings could be created, erased, moved around, and manipulated—has revolutionized aircraft and spacecraft design.

By concentrating on just these (albeit highly significant) aspects of computers, the exhibition automatically avoids many of the problems—and opportunities—confronting the far more ambitious and comprehensive Computer Museum (which, in its computer graphics display, has a small section on "Designing the Aircraft Wing"). And by placing the exhibition amidst other NASM second-floor galleries it likewise automatically provides a larger context for the items displayed, though NASM's uncritical endorsement of technological progress is part of that context.

"Beyond the Limits" is divided into seven sections, each clearly marked and logically connected to one another: design, aerodynamics, manufacturing, flight testing, air operations, simulators, and space operations. There is none of the earlier uncertainty of the Computer

Museum about where to go next or why a display is located one place rather than another.

"Beyond the Limits" is as successful as the Computer Museum in showing how computers have evolved, how they function, and what exactly they do—thus it meets one of any computer exhibition's two major objectives. It provides as lucid, if briefer, an overview as its Boston counterpart of the transition from vacuum tubes to transistors to integrated circuits to microprocessors, and from computers the size of whole buildings to the size of large rooms to the size of small refrigerators. And it clearly shows how crucial it was for the aerospace industry to have simultaneous shrinkage in size and growth in power of computers that could then fit inside aircraft as well as help to design and control them on the ground. "Beyond the Limits" also has portions of the Whirlwind computer, its own partial SAGE installation, and its own exposed Control Data supercomputer; these make such comparisons with the Computer Museum more meaningful. The exhibition's contrasting historic photographs of scores of engineers, draftsmen, and human "computers" working on full-scale drawings of airplanes and spacecraft under design with the far smaller staffs needed for computer-aided design today is more effective than the Computer Museum's initial heavy reliance on hardware alone to make the same point. In "Beyond the Limits" the same photographic comparison is also nicely made of the number of persons needed for the 1969 Apollo Launch Control versus those needed for the 1981 space shuttle counterpart, thanks to advanced computerization. As with the Computer Museum, however, there is no discussion here about the number of workers whose jobs were thereby eliminated.

"Beyond the Limits" also displays and adequately identifies hundreds of other artifacts. These range from old slide rules to portions of an F-16 fighter's tail to a complete Mariner 10 spacecraft (whose guidance and communications systems used computers).

Each of the seven sections has at least one interactive display, clearly identified by different symbols. All video screens are in duplicate: one placed low enough for children, the other high enough for adults. These are NASM's first extensive interactive displays and provide some of the historical and social context missing from the artifact-based exhibitions that dominate the museum—just as do the interactive displays in "People and Computers." Several of the displays define terms presented on glossary screens; others provide "bio-blocks" for learning more about the people and stories behind the displays; still others enable visitors to explore the computer's capabilities by themselves and to try mechanical "hands-on" displays such as designing a rocket ship and piloting a Stealth bomber. Here, too, the gallery is similar to the revamped Computer Museum, though it likewise risks conveying that false message of computers' alleged simplicity through overreliance on preprogrammed, easy-to-use interactive devices.[8]

Similar to the Computer Museum as well, the corporate sponsors of "Beyond the Limits" are identified and praised—without them there would be no exhibit—as are, more so than in the current Computer Museum, the historic ties between the computer and aerospace industries and between them and government and academia. The familiar message of unadulterated technological progress is more pervasive here than in the present Computer Museum and is as pervasive as elsewhere in NASM. The critical questions noted above concerning computers' negative social effects are largely ignored here as they once were in Boston. Thus the admittedly factual statement early in the gallery that "the military has been the main underwriter of research in the computing field" is likely to be read by visitors as a wholly positive condition, reflective of NASM's overall worship of the American military. The enormous profits that surely motivated the defense contractors here as elsewhere are ignored. Moreover, given the distance between most visitors and the aerospace industry, except as airline passengers, far less personal experience is brought to bear upon what one sees than is the case in Boston, where the overwhelming majority of visitors can relate to at least personal computers and their often mixed blessings.[9] In these respects "Beyond the Limits" only partly succeeds in meeting any computer exhibition's other major objective: illuminating computers' history and social significance.

Nevertheless, "Beyond the Limits" is superior even to the revamped Computer Museum in its refusal to adopt a Whiggish attitude. Instead, it acknowledges both that computers have developed in unanticipated ways rather than through an inevitable progression and that computers have not (yet) replaced human beings in fundamental decision making. As a label at the beginning of the exhibition concedes, "no one . . . had predicted how compact and powerful computers in space [as in aircraft] would become." The same point has been elaborated by

Exposed portion of Cray-1 1976 "Supercomputer," "Beyond the Limits" exhibition, National Air and Space Museum. A similar display is at the Computer Museum, Boston. (*Photo courtesy National Air and Space Museum, Smithsonian Institution*)

curator Ceruzzi in an essay on computers in general.[10] As he argues there, none of the computer's inventors expected the advent of small, portable, personal computers accessible to laymen without extensive programming skills. Instead, these pioneers commonly assumed that a mere half-dozen giant computers would suffice for the entire world and would perform complicated calculations for only the largest governmental, business, and academic institutions under the direction of an elite of professional programmers. (As detailed in chapter 10, this is more or less the situation in Kurt Vonnegut's *Player Piano* [1952], which describes the entire United States as operating on one huge computer and implies similar conditions elsewhere in the world.) Consequently, those pioneers did not anticipate, much less fear, the reliance on computers for so many decisions in our contemporary world. This superb example of the characteristic inability on the part of even the most brilliant scientists and engineers to forecast technology's future is as significant a point as computers' remarkable evolution over the past half-century, the point emphasized in the Computer Museum's "People and Computers."

"Beyond the Limits" includes several refreshing reminders of the persistent human element amidst computerization. A label in the design states that "computers help sift through the complex options, but the final choices remain with people." And a label in the aerodynamics section regarding wind tunnels notes that they "could not predict perfectly—no design was proven until flown by a human being."

However, that same latter label goes on to say that "some computers have become test pilots themselves." This development is epitomized in the full-scale model of the Grumman X-29 experimental fighter that dominates the gallery. This aircraft is so deliberately unstable that it requires three identical computers to keep it flying—in return for extraordinary maneuverability, albeit with vastly reduced human pilot control. Should all three computers fail, a possibility the exhibition ignores, the pilot would be unable to control the X-29, which would crash. Yet near the end of the gallery is a tribute to computers as "unsung heroes" for their automatically shutting down for safety reasons (as well as for their launching of) various contemporary space vehicles— a point elaborated upon in Ceruzzi's book regarding the unblemished role of computers in the 1986 *Challenger* space shuttle disaster.

The exhibition and book do, however, concede that computers are also prone to false alarms and that human beings must be ultimately responsible for these decisions and for the consequences of computer failure. (In a perverse but useful way, the inclusion of references to computer hackers confirms this same point; they are also mentioned in "People and Computers.") The exhibition concludes, "As we enter the twenty-first century, we see a world made at once smaller and more complex by the development of computers in flight. The choices we make—technological, political, and social—in where these computers will go and what tasks they will perform may be the most important challenge facing humankind." The degree to which visitors come away with an awareness of choices that still need to be made cannot be known, but to the extent that "Beyond the Limits" succeeds here it will mitigate the sense of technological determinism all too readily espoused elsewhere in NASM. This may well be its most important contribution to visitors' understanding of modern technology.

Yet both "Beyond the Limits" and the Computer Museum must go further in illuminating computers' human dimensions. Much more needs to be added about, first, unsung ordinary workers' contributions to computers' development; second, the specialized computer jobs held by these workers that have evolved simultaneously (data-entry operators, data-base administrators, system analysts, system managers, and word processors); and third, the various conditions, favorable or not, in which they work. In addition, much more needs to be added to what already exists in each institution about important non-American computers and developers. Too many visitors in each case come away with the impression that computers are an exclusively American invention and achievement.

Both the Computer Museum and "Beyond the Limits" deserve praise for being pioneering introductions to computers and de facto contributors to the technological literacy crusade discussed in chapter 12. Their mixed successes in meeting the methodological and interpretive challenges analyzed here reflect as much traditional museum approaches to displaying technology as they do these institutions' particular orientations, values, and biases. They also reflect the varying, sometimes conflicting, visions of museum professionals, their superiors, and their audiences. Yet these limitations hardly excuse their respective failings. In this light it is notable that the Computer Museum has systematically embarked upon a five-year exhibition plan that, when completed, will transform virtually the entire institution and address most of the criticisms raised in its first several years of operation. All of the original exhibitions excluding "Smart Machines" will be changed, while an additional five thousand square feet of space will be opened. The success of both "The Walk-Through Computer" and "People and Computers" provides hope for the successful completion of a permanent exhibition illuminating the large-scale computer-based systems that underlie contemporary society, including telephone, banking, airline, utility, communications, manufacturing, and retail networks. It is also notable that NASM is currently rethinking its overall orientation as well and is intending to provide a more critical, more social and cultural, and so more balanced perspective for many of its exhibitions, though specific plans have not yet been formulated.[11] For now, suffice it to conclude that more accurate, more comprehensive, and more contextual portrayals of computers, however difficult to organize and mount, and however painful for computer enthusiasts to concede, in the long run will be in the best interest of both museums and their visitors.[12]

III

FOUR

TECHNOLOGICAL

VISIONS

REEXAMINED

8

EDWARD BELLAMY

AND TECHNOLOGY:

RECONCILING

CENTRALIZATION AND

DECENTRALIZATION

. . . .

In 1988 Americans and others observed the one-hundredth anniversary of the publication of Edward Bellamy's *Looking Backward: 2000–1887*. This remains the most popular utopian novel ever published in the United States and is available today in no fewer than six different paperback editions. An avowedly utopian picture of life in America in the year 2000, *Looking Backward* continues to be read, discussed, and debated, long after most of its predictions have either been realized or, more often, have come about only in part, if at all. Each year, thousands of persons here and abroad are transported along with Julian West, a young Bostonian, from the crowding, competition, disease, greed, and corruption of late nineteenth-century industrial America to a society of full employment, material abundance, technological progress, and social harmony. In the process, they join Julian in his quest for understanding how utopia came about without bloodshed, much less revolution, and how this transformed America apparently fulfills the varying needs and desires of every citizen. That hundreds of other utopian novels and nonfiction writings published in the late nineteenth and early twentieth centuries have faded into obscurity makes *Looking Backward*'s enduring popularity all the more striking.

Often overlooked or minimized in trying to account for that enduring popularity is the fact that *Looking Backward* is at least as much about technology and its use and abuse as it is about cooperation, corruption, and socialism. Technology was then and obviously still is a topic of almost universal interest and concern. No less important, the role of technology in *Looking Backward*, which this chapter will try to illuminate, is complex and subtle, revealing new dimensions of Bellamy's scheme and possible sources of the book's appeal.

Technology is at once a principal cause of and solution to the problems Bellamy identifies throughout the book: inefficiency (overproduction and underproduction, idle capital and labor, excessive competition, mismanagement); inequality (of opportunity and of income); immorality (greed, monopoly, exploitation); and urban blight (slums, crowding, disease, poverty, child labor). The purposeful, positive use of technology—from improved factories and offices to new highways and electric lighting systems to innovative pneumatic tubes, electronic broadcasts, and credit cards—is, in fact, critical to the predicted transformation of the United States from a living hell to a heaven on earth. Although these technological marvels were clearly realized in whole or in part long before the year 2000, they were surely "state-of-the-art" for turn-of-the-century America.

More specifically, the United States of the year 2000 is very much a technological utopia: an allegedly ideal society not simply dependent upon structures and machines, or even worshipful of them, but outright modeled after them. In some respects the citizens of Bellamy's paradise seem to be quite willing cogs in the new industrial order, and their carefully regimented lives seem happily to emulate the mechanized processes that have helped to create their world.

Bellamy, however, believed he was describing a society in which greater freedom and creativity (and spirituality) would exist than was possible in his own society—itself an example of "bad" management and moral disorder. As his fictional spokesman, Mr. Smith, replies to a skeptical "lover of freedom" in a Bellamy essay defending his Nationalist scheme:

> Well, aren't we parts of a great industrial machine now. The only difference is that the present machine is a bungling and misconstructed one, which grinds up the bodies and souls of those who work in it, and turns out poverty, prostitution, insanity and suicide as its finished products, while the new machine will be scientifically constructed, with an equal view to the comfort of the workers and the increase of the product.[1]

Indeed, the continuous "scientific" management of all citizens from birth till death is as critical to utopian society's well-being as are the structures and machines that surround them. Management of people, as epitomized by the industrial army, is as much an integral part of modern technology as the "hardware" itself. That bureaucracies in highly technological societies like our own epitomize *mis*management and *in*efficiency should not obscure their place in Bellamy's day as exemplars of the very opposite trend: a new civic and industrial order leading ultimately to utopia.

As Bellamy understood to a limited degree, technological societies do not have to be identical in design, appearance, shape, or size. Instead, it is a hallmark of especially twentieth-century technology to provide choices in these matters. Consequently, alternatives can and, by now, do exist. Principal among such alternatives are those of centralization versus decentralization. Where in Bellamy's day and long after it was commonly assumed that modern technology requires ever greater centralization of both facilities and personnel, recent critics—above all the late E. F. Schumacher and his disciples—have argued otherwise.[2] They have demonstrated that modern technology can and ought to be made "appropriate" to different economic, social, cultural, and political contexts. Much of their work has dealt with "underdeveloped" countries; but the general notion of appropriate technology has international applications. It is a relative term with varied meanings.

Moreover, any number of enthusiasts for computers, word processors, electronic mail, video display terminals, and other components of the current "information revolution" have claimed decentralization as their own position. For them, however, the key is not so much the smaller scale of operations, as with Schumacher, as the ability to work in or near one's home and to make decisions far away from the central office. The vision of an "electronic cottage" in Alvin Toffler's work, as elaborated in the final chapter, is nevertheless every bit as utopian as any of the schemes in Schumacher's writings.[3] In both cases decentralization is deemed a positive development if not an outright panacea. This would have intrigued yet also probably perplexed Bellamy.

Decentralization, then, is a multifaceted term. Any one of its manifestations, however, does not necessarily translate into another: spatial separation, for example, may be large or small in scale and may be democratic or nondemocratic in operation. This explains the recent concern for the welfare of geographically isolated but often closely monitored workers in "electronic cottages"—whether their own homes or small offices or factories—who may be exploited as much as were workers centuries ago in the original cottage industries in England and elsewhere. Likewise, small-scale appropriate technology projects may not be havens of democracy in decision-making either. The same instruments that have created the information revolution and that in turn have made decentralization a reality can thus be used to enslave as well as to liberate—just as with so many prior technological devices, including those in *Looking Backward*.

Consequently, the values and practices of decentralization in one sense of the term or in one situation may nowadays conflict with those in another sense or in another situation. Put differently, the current image of pure decentralization may conceal lingering centralization, with some of the ills associated with it. How does this relate to *Looking Backward?*

Throughout the book are subtle tensions between technology-based centralization and decentralization akin to those contemporary ones. The situations are not, of course, identical, and the tensions in *Looking Backward* do not produce overt conflict, whereas those of our time probably will. If anything, in Bellamy's scheme, these tensions are the (almost) inevitable result of his attempt to create, administer, protect, and refine a huge utopian community of national dimensions supposedly catering to the needs and desires of its millions of individual citizens as well as to those of society in general. Bellamy was certainly familiar with the communitarians of the antebellum period and was sympathetic toward their crusades. As he observed retrospectively in 1892, "In a broad sense of the word the Nationalist movement did arise fifty years ago" in the form of "the Brook Farm Colony and a score of phalansteries for communistic [communal] experiments." But then the overriding concern for ending slavery redirected the energies of "these humane enthusiasts."[4] The time for such small-scale enterprises had, for better or for worse, passed. Although their avowedly decentralized schemes were not wholly outdated, they nonetheless had to take new forms amid the changes that had occurred since their heyday.

On the one hand, then, technology as depicted in *Looking Backward* has led to centralization in the form of the overall administration of society (the industrial army); of society's decision-making processes (the president of the United States and the other top administrators of the industrial army's "ten great departments");[5] of its production, distribution, and consumption facilities (its department stores and warehouses); of its domestic enterprises (cooking, dining, laundering, and tailoring); and of its large urban apartment complexes. But on the other hand, technology has led to decentralization in the form of widely separated towns and villages; of smaller-scale department stores and warehouses near them; of electronic broadcasting systems (through music from music halls and sermons from churches in each city wired to home telephones); and of dining facilities within individual apartments (for meals other than dinner).

Technology, then, has spurred centralization and decentralization alike. Moreover, several of these developments in themselves mix centralizing and decentralizing tendencies. Whatever tensions might result from such a mixture would be a modest price to pay for the perfection of Bellamy's overall scheme. And those tensions would be minimized by technology as well. Without the various technological devices and accompanying social arrangements summarized above, his scenarios would have been far less realistic and, presumably, far less appealing.

Using technology in these and other forms, Bellamy also sought a balance—and a minimal tension—between collectivism and individualism, homogeneity and heterogeneity, wholesale equality and equality of opportunity, industrialism and agrarianism, cities and towns/villages, and population concentration and dispersal. Bellamy and his contemporaries Henry George and Henry Demarest Lloyd had as "their working model of the good society . . . a composite of city and country," or a "vision of an urban-rural continuum running from village neighborhoods to gateway cities."[6] In this as in other respects Bellamy's ideals were not unique. More than a score of other prophets of technological utopia published their visions between 1883 and 1933 and were frequently influenced by *Looking Backward*'s themes and, no less important, by its exceptional popularity. All agreed on the basic values, design, and organization of future society.[7]

Why should Bellamy have attained fame and influence while his fellow technological utopians endured obscurity? Or why was *Looking Backward*, as Burton Bledstein puts it, "a seminal document that was itself an historical event in the ideological formation of . . . an urban, industrial middle-class cultural movement in the social revolutionary 1880s"?[8] One possible explanation is that Bellamy, a seasoned author, simply wrote better. A second explanation is that he wrote just at the onset of what has been termed the late nineteenth-century crisis of confidence in America, where all but one of the rest of the technological utopians wrote during or after its peak. A third and complementary explanation is that imitations of *Looking Backward,* or unauthorized sequels to it, as were most of these works, could hardly generate the enthusiasm of the original. A final and deeper explanation, which excludes none of the other three, is that the emphasis of *Looking Backward* on cooperation and community as well as on technological advance offered a more balanced and more appealing vision than the strictly materialist focus of nearly all the other works. That this balance would be socially engineered and technologically based is exactly my point.

More broadly, *Looking Backward* may now be seen as a pioneering attempt to offer an alternative to the increasingly urban, industrialized, and—yes, centralized—America emerging in Bellamy's day. His was not, however, a conventional conservative critique calling for a wholesale return to farms and to agrarian values. Neither was it a conventional radical critique, seeking unadulterated socialism and workers' control. (It is indicative of the book's appeal that reputable scholars a century later can argue passionately on behalf of one or the other of those interpretations.)[9] Instead, Bellamy provided a middle ground between these and the other "extremes" noted earlier and repeatedly used what was then modern (or even futuristic) technology—as, again, both hardware and management—to try to effect it. Insofar as the course of modern technology in America and elsewhere has, with few exceptions, led routinely toward centralization of structure and decision-making and toward ever larger scale and size, Bellamy's overall scheme may be more pertinent today than most of his otherwise outdated particulars would suggest.

The design and layout of Bellamy's utopia embodies and illuminates these objectives. The envisioned domestication of both technology and nature will resolve the tension that Leo Marx, among others, has deemed irresolvable: the tension between the industrial and the agrarian orders, between the machine and the garden, a tension that Marx believes lies at the heart of the American experience. Bellamy (and the other technological utopians) would resolve the tension by the modernization rather than abandonment of the garden, by transporting it out of the wilderness and relocating it in the city—a city itself to be transformed from a lethal chaos into a healthy order. As time-traveler Julian West describes the Boston of 2000:

> At my feet lay a great city. Miles of broad streets, shaded by trees and lined with fine buildings, for the most part not in continuous blocks but set in larger or smaller enclosures, stretched in every direction. Every quarter contained large open squares filled with trees, along which statues glistened and fountains flashed in the late-afternoon sun. Public buildings of a colossal size and architectural grandeur unparalleled in my day raised their stately piles on every side. Surely I had never seen this city nor one comparable to it before. Raising my eyes at last toward the horizon, I looked westward. That blue ribbon winding away to the sunset—was it not the sinuous Charles? I looked east—Boston harbor stretched before me within its headlands, not one of its green islets missing.[10]

The new "industrialized garden" does not, then, take the form of Marx's "middle landscape" or of Jefferson's ideal of an agrarian-based yet technologically proficient yeoman republic. Rather, it consists of a series of what have since been termed megalopolises: massive combinations of urban and suburban tracts covering vast areas. These are the extreme examples of what I call the regional middle landscape. As West recounts in *Equality* (1897), Bellamy's sequel to *Looking Backward:*

> Still we swept on mile after mile, league after league, toward the interior, and still the surface below presented the same parklike aspect that had marked the immediate environs of the city. Every natural feature appeared to have been idealized and all its latent meaning brought out by the loving skill of some consummate landscape artist, the works of man blending with the face of Nature in perfect harmony. . . . "How far does this park extend?" I demanded at last. "There seems no end to it." "It extends to the Pacific Ocean," said the doctor. "Do you mean that the whole United States is laid out in this way?" "Not precisely in this way by any means, but in a hundred different ways according to the natural suggestions of the face of the country and the most effective way of co-operating with them."[11]

The megalopolises are tributes not only to philosophical ingenuity, which reconciles machine to garden, and centralization to decentralization, but also to the scientific planning of which Bellamy (and the other technological utopians) are so proud. Here millions of persons live, learn, work, and play in perfect comfort, contentment, and happiness, ever free of dirt, noise, chaos, want, and insecurity. As Bellamy wrote in his Postscript to the second edition of *Looking Backward*, the work, "although in form a fanciful romance, is intended, in all seriousness, as a forecast, in accordance with the principles of evolution, of the next stage in the industrial and social development of humanity."[12]

Such scientific planning is not, of course, limited to the physical environment but also extends to the administration of society and to the rest of the social and cultural environment. As West confesses with envy to Dr. Leete, his guide through utopia, "nowadays everybody is a part of a system with a distinct place and function. I am outside the system, and don't see how I can get in."[13] West's sense of alienation is, of course, temporary, and his subsequent visit to a huge city warehouse confirms the practicality of a society that balances centralization and decentralization, collective and individual needs and desires, in this as in most other areas: "It is like a gigantic mill, into the hopper of which goods are being constantly poured by the trainload and shipload, to issue at the other end in packages of pounds and ounces, yards and inches, pints and gallons, corresponding to the infinitely complex personal needs of half a million people."[14]

I do not wish to ignore Bellamy's repeated emphasis on solidarity, on virtually forced cooperation, and on militarylike discipline. Lines like the following are still chilling to read despite so much of the book being overly sentimental and contrived:

> Well now, Mr. West, the organization of the industry of the nation under a single control, so that all its processes interlock, has multiplied the total product over the utmost that could be done under the former system. . . . The effectiveness of the working force of a nation, under the myriad-headed leadership of private capital, even if the leaders were not mutual enemies, as compared with that which it attains under a single head, may be likened to the military efficiency of a mob, or a horde of barbarians with a thousand petty chiefs, as compared with that of a disciplined army under one general—such a fighting machine, for example, as the German army in the time of Von Moltke.[15]

Yet *Looking Backward* cannot be reduced to an early totalitarian utopia on the order of George Orwell's *1984* (1949) or Eugene Zamiatin's *We* (1920), notwithstanding Arthur Lipow's suggestive study.[16] An avowed democratic socialist and severe critic of the bureaucratic stultification of much of modern socialism, Lipow reads *Looking Backward* as a literary blueprint for what he calls authoritarian socialism and sees the Nationalist movement as its political embodiment. He treats the technocratic hostility toward politics, the envisioned industrial army, the distrust of workers and undisciplined masses, and the obsession with submerging individuality into a mystical whole as antecedents of twentieth-century communism and fascism alike. Surely such an interpretation at once exaggerates these American visionaries' hidden agenda and gives them considerably greater foresight and influence upon genuine authoritarians than they deserve.

Still, Bellamy and his fellow Nationalists were not simply well-meaning democratic reformers who blended easily into the Populist and Progressive crusades, which are themselves, of course, the subjects of periodic revisionist historical analysis. Their traditional image as genteel middle-class reformers frightened by contemporary crowding, corruption, strikes, disorder, and other social ills does not account for the particular spatial, organizational, and cultural dimensions of *Looking Backward* and related utopian writings of the same era. Nor does it put their crusade into proper historical perspective.

Without claiming to account for all of these dimensions of *Looking Backward*, Bledstein has illuminated several by a provocative analysis of what "looking" meant to Bellamy's predominantly middle-class readership. It meant that they could temporarily become tourists not just in utopia, as was inevitable, but, equally important, in contemporary preutopia as well. Readers could simultaneously "distance themselves from and cope with what most deeply distressed them" about late nineteenth-century urban industrial America. Contrary to so many conventional interpretations of the book—or, for that matter, the plot itself—this touristlike stance meant not sheer escapism from those contemporary social ills but rather a middle ground, yet another balance, between escapism and engagement, between pleasant fantasy and dismal reality. That in turn instilled greater confidence in the nation's future and a greater ability to adjust to everyday life prior to utopia's arrival. Ironically, Bledstein contends, Bellamy's very "silence about anger, controversy, conflicting agendas, and contested relations in the new public structures of a technological civilization spoke boisterously." For "Beneath the cool surface, Bellamy was stirring a hot book, not without signals to the reader of the author's prowling passion. . . ." But such passion was kept covert and respectable (or "cool"), and ultimately *Looking Backward*'s very ordinariness and orderliness "came across as truthful to the appearances of a civilized life that the middle class for a century now has preferred to imagine looking at: . . . the new, clean, electrified, post-industrial Boston"[17] and other American cities.

In the final chapter of his *Alternative America*, John L. Thomas has outlined what he aptly terms "the legacy" of Bellamy, George, and Lloyd. Their individual and collective influence ranged from Scientific Management and Technocracy to regionalism and the Tennessee Valley Authority (TVA), from elitist to grass-roots economic and social planning, and from right-wing to left-wing political schemes. Nearly all, however, either used or would have used technology to create a balance between centralization and decentralization in the manner described earlier. This "adversary tradition," as Thomas calls it, "was not simply an exercise in nostalgia but the climactic expression of an American 'third way'"[18] between geographical, economic, political, social, and cultural extremes. It was also, I suggest, a multifaceted and not always systematic attempt to accommodate preindustrial values and ways of life to emerging industrial "modern" society. *Looking Backward* may not have directly inspired all of these reformers, but, as the following case study will suggest, it certainly anticipated many of their later efforts.

Among the most interesting and explicit expressions of this phenomenon—and one with which Thomas does not deal—are the "village industry" experiments developed by automaker Henry Ford and his associates between 1918 and 1944. Ford is commonly associated with many diverse aspects of twentieth-century American life—from peace crusades to square dance revivals to eclectic museums—but large-scale, heavily centralized, predominantly urban systems of mass production are surely foremost among them. No American contributed more than Ford to the development of giant factories and assembly lines.

Yet Ford was a complex man whose cultural and social values frequently conflicted with and sometimes undermined his business practices. The farm boy whose mechanical skills led him into the manufacture of the very vehicles that threatened the agrarian way of life he cherished never resolved his mixed feelings about modernity. Above all, he disliked the heterogeneity, impersonality, and materialism of twentieth-century America's industrial cities. But rather than renounce outright either large cities or the large industries that helped bring them about, Ford devised various means of coping with these ills. His solutions ranged from periodic retreats to the countryside to the lifelong embrace of farmers (particularly those who had purchased Ford tractors), to the collection of innumerable agricultural as well as industrial artifacts at Dearborn beginning in the 1920s and, not least, to the establishment of nineteen "village industries" in southern Michigan to manufacture and assemble parts for cars.

When lumped together with those other odds and ends of Ford's colorful life, the village industries can easily be characterized as merely antiquarian and nostalgic efforts to "freeze" history, as flights from reality having no relevance to Ford's own time, much less to ours. But this is a gross simplification. Whatever Ford's other motives for their establishment may have been—whether, say, for profits or for public relations or for union busting—he intended the village industries as serious experiments: as small-scale, widely dispersed, frequently pastoral alternatives to the huge urban industrial systems characteristic of modern technological society, the very systems Ford himself had helped devise. More precisely, they represent pioneering experiments in decentralized technology and society going well beyond anything Bellamy conceived but reflecting the values of *Looking Backward*—a book, to be sure, Ford almost certainly never read and may not have known about.

Set along the often picturesque Rouge (7 sites), Raisin (5), Huron (4), Saline (2), and Clinton (1) rivers in southeastern Michigan—none of them more than sixty miles from Ford world headquarters in Dearborn—these communities were all either self-contained or adjuncts of nearby small communities. As William Simonds, a Ford publicist, described them in 1927, "Industrialism does not necessarily mean hideous factories of dirty brick, belching smoke stacks and grimy workmen crowded into ramshackle hovels." Instead, "The little Ford plants are placed in leafy bowers and surrounded with flowering shrubs, green bushes and trees. The spots you would select for a picnic Henry Ford has picked for factory sites."[19]

The village industries varied considerably not just in type of automobile part manufactured and assembled on the premises but also in building design and in size of work force. Some, like the first two, Northville (which began operations in 1920) and Nankin Mills (1921), were reconstructed nineteenth-century grist mills that had been abandoned. Others, however, like the next two, Phoenix (1922) and Plymouth (1923), had completely new, modern buildings, though sometimes on the site of former grist mills. Sharon Hollow (1939) had the smallest work force, under 20 employees; Ypsilanti (1932) had the largest, 1,500 at its peak. Most of these workers were men, but several locations had at least a few women, and Phoenix's work force was over 90 percent female.

Ford's dream was to employ exclusively farmers, craftsmen, and other rural folk who could either walk or quickly drive (their Fords!) to work. For the most part this aspect of his vision was realized, and relatively few urban dwellers, including city-bred workers in older Ford plants, were ever hired. Instead, the largely rural-bred workers in the nineteen sites were strongly encouraged to retain or to acquire a plot of land on which to grow crops for personal consumption in their spare time, that is, before and after working hours and during their days off. These full-time factory workers were, then, also part-time farmers and, Ford claimed, beneficiaries of the very modern technology at work and at home alike that allowed them the leisure to supplement their income.

Despite the clear differences between the village industries and conventional branch automobile plants, the former were nevertheless integral parts of the Ford Motor Company. All were directly linked, in terms of both production and transportation, to the huge Highland Park and Rouge complexes Ford had already created near Detroit. The raw materials and finished products therefore had to be small and light enough to be transported efficiently from Highland Park and Rouge to and from the village industries (and sometimes between the latter). Hence such items as gauges, horns, valves, regulators, switches, and taps were chosen for manufacture and assembly.

Ford's village industries did not come about in a vacuum, as the realization of one very rich and powerful man's unique fantasies. Rather, they were part of efforts elsewhere in America between the two world wars to alter the course of industrial urban life. Some reformers forsook large-scale industrialization and large cities altogether; these included Ralph Borsodi, Helen and Scott Nearing, and the Nashville Agrarians of *I'll Take My Stand* (1930) fame. Others, more akin to Bellamy, tried to balance modern technology with small-scale rural living and working conditions; these reformers included Arthur Morgan in the early days of the TVA, of which he was first chairman of the board of directors. Ford chose the latter course, and there are several parallels between his efforts in the private sector and those of Morgan in the public sector. In fact, the village industries themselves comprised a system that took on regional dimensions akin to TVA—but a system that Ford, like Morgan at TVA, hoped would inspire changes in the nation's predominantly large-scale urban systems. The 1930s and 1940s, moreover, were a period of extensive academic and public discussion about America as a nation composed of regions.

Just as TVA never resembled the "grass-roots democracy" described by its longtime director David Lilienthal,[20] so the village industries never resembled the bastions of yeoman purity described by Ford and his publicity agents. Like TVA, they were commercial enterprises as well as social experiments; and like nearly all else in the Ford empire, they were under the constant scrutiny of Ford himself. Yet the village industries did enjoy a measure of freedom. They were not conventional company towns, were not owned by the Ford Motor Company, and were comparatively free from the notorious Ford Sociological Department. The workers appear to have enjoyed their diversity of employment and the proximity of their residences to their workplaces. Not a few workers—and whole towns—were thereby saved from financial ruin during the Depression.

To this extent the village industries do represent pioneering examples of decentralized technology and society. As Ford argued, it was precisely small-scale, widely dispersed forms of the same modern technology already available in conventional large-scale, heavily urban automobile plants that made these rural enterprises possible—just as with the towns and villages, smaller department stores and warehouses, credit cards, home telephones, and other aspects of Bellamy's utopia. Yet physical location, scale, and size remain issues separate from decision-making, which continued under the firm control of Ford and his top subordinates. Moreover, Ford, like Morgan at TVA, resorted to a giant technical organization to create (or renew) semiagrarian small communities—much as Bellamy might have done in similar circumstances. Once again, then, decentralization is a complex, multifaceted phenomenon whose particular applications may be neither uniform nor complete.

It would be as easy to condemn Ford as a hypocrite as it would be to dismiss him as an eccentric. But this, too, would be a gross simplification. In his unsystematic, unorthodox way Ford understood a good deal more about the direction of modern technological society than did most of his seemingly sophisticated contemporaries. Like Bellamy, he sought a limitation on the ever greater size, scale, and impersonality of technological development and a concern for other aspects of the "good life." Yet the limits he would impose were clearly relative, not absolute—unlike, say, the Nashville Agrarians or the Nearings.

Nevertheless, most of these nineteen experiments were eventual failures. The Ford Motor Company sold nearly all of them in the years after Ford's death, though a few are, under different ownership, currently involved in "high-tech" enterprises. The rest have become county and municipal government offices, community centers, antique shops, and garages. One, at Willow Run (1941), has been abandoned and dismantled.

Still, decentralized technology is today more popular—and more practical—than ever before, thanks to computers, word processors, and other devices. Meanwhile the decentralization of society—whether of government, industry, schools, or other institutions—has become public policy in many quarters, and not just in the United States. Consequently, these largely forgotten and unexplored experiments are, like Bellamy's own vision, of more than antiquarian interest. They provide an alternative form of technological development that seeks a necessary balance between the all-too-common antitechnological and protechnological extremes. Such a new "middle landscape" or "middle way" may even be termed progressive.

Aldous Huxley had such a vision in mind when he wrote his new Foreword to the 1946 reprint of *Brave New World*—a book that, most ironically, uses Ford and Ford's large-scale, heavily centralized assembly lines as the focal point for its brilliant satire of future technological utopia or, more precisely, dystopia. As Huxley conceded about his 1932 work:

> [I]t seems worth while at least to mention the most serious defect in the story, which is this. The Savage is offered only two alternatives, an insane life in Utopia, or the life of a primitive in an Indian village, a life more human in some respects, but in others hardly less queer and abnormal. At the time the book was written this idea, that human beings are given free will in order to choose between insanity on the one hand and lunacy on the other, was one that I found amusing and regarded as quite possibly true. . . . If I were now to

rewrite the book, I would offer the Savage a third alternative. Between the utopian and the primitive horns of his dilemma would lie the possibility of sanity—a possibility already actualized, to some extent, in a community of exiles and refugees from the Brave New World, living within the borders of the Reservation. In this community economics would be decentralist and Henry-Georgian, politics Kropotkinesque co-operative. Science and technology would be used as though, like the Sabbath, they had been made for man, not (as at present and still more so in the Brave New World) as though man were to be adapted and enslaved to them.[21]

Huxley, then, might have approved of the village industries—about which he probably knew little or nothing—despite condemning the rest of the Ford ethos and empire. And Huxley might likewise have looked with a favorable eye on the decentralized components of Bellamy's utopia.

A decade before *Brave New World* initially appeared, and so thirty-four years after *Looking Backward*, Lewis Mumford published *The Story of Utopias*. As detailed in chapter 11, Mumford is a key bridge figure between the Western utopian tradition and the philosophical and practical proponents of decentralization ranging from Bellamy and Ford through Schumacher and Toffler. In this his first book Mumford, eventually to become a distinguished critic—and defender—of technology and utopias alike, saw decentralization as a means of balancing stability and change. Long before he had attacked the modern "megamachine," he had here shown that any future utopias—or any genuinely good societies—could use technological advance to preserve and improve local communities and that technological advance need not homogenize the United States or other nations in the name of progress. The focus on local community did not entail isolation or parochialism; modern transportation and communications networks allowed mobility and exchange of persons and ideas, but not at the expense of different local (and national) cultures. As Mumford put it regarding Eutopias (that is, authentic utopias),

> If the inhabitants of our Eutopias will conduct their daily affairs in a possibly more limited environment than that of the great metropolitan centers, their mental environment will not be localized or nationalized. For the first time perhaps in the history of the planet our advance in science and invention has made it possible for every

age and every community to contribute to the spiritual heritage of the local group. . . . Our eutopians will necessarily draw from this wider environment whatever can be assimilated by the local community; and they will thus add any elements that may be lacking in the natural situation.[22]

As Bledstein reminds us, *Looking Backward*'s considerably decentralized administration "featured . . . consumer control, private choice in the popular realms of cultural taste, leisure, and retirement activities"—with retirement at age forty-five to boot in most cases. Moreover, "Authors and journalists, for instance, were required to develop a local constituency for their product, or not be in business. No community was called upon to lose a vernacular language, deny foreign origins, or cease to practice ethnic customs. Only at the common level of the industrial public would mass literacy in an official language tied to careers and a shared body of book knowledge prevail."[23] This example of balance in Bellamy's scheme and of the considerable degree of freedom and creativity he allowed citizens surely enhanced the book's appeal.

The road from *Looking Backward* to *The Story of Utopias* to *Small Is Beautiful* is neither smooth nor straight. And it frequently detours in the direction of *Brave New World* or *The Third Wave* or other questionable schemes—questionable, that is, for those not enamored of shallow technocractic solutions to profound moral and social problems. Yet Bellamy's interesting and complex uses of technology, as toward both centralization and decentralization, make *Looking Backward* a less technocratic and so a more timely work than has long been assumed.

A product of America's peak of faith in technology as the solution to social problems, not just technical ones, *Looking Backward* nevertheless recognizes the need for economic and especially ethical constraints on otherwise unadulterated technological advance and unbounded materialism. No less important, it also provides for flexibility in the design, organization, and administration of an otherwise overly rigid technocratic regime. The particular mix of values and arrangements that Bellamy devised hardly appeals to us now as it did in his day, and his middle-of-the-road stance in this as in so much else—surely a key to the book's popularity—often makes for dull reading today. But Bellamy's anticipation of some basic dilemmas and solutions of our postindustrial society justifies a careful rereading and renewed appreciation of *Looking Backward* more than a century after its publication.

9

. . . .

Writing sympathetically in 1981 about the proliferation of serious utopian novels by and about women—including Ursula LeGuin's *The Left Hand of Darkness* (1969) and *The Dispossessed* (1974), Marge Piercy's *Woman on the Edge of Time* (1976), Joanna Russ's *The Female Man* (1975), and Mary Staton's *From the Legend of Biel* (1975)—sociologist Krishan Kumar observed "a certain paradox" about their physical and economic settings. These avowedly feminist visions of a supposedly perfect or at least radically better future world were "dominated and suffused by a rampant *primitivism* . . . clearly drawn from pre-industrial and non-industrial societies." That these tribal, pastoral, and peasant agricultural societies are ones in which women are or have been "most subordinated to men, to a degree going well beyond their position in present-day industrial societies," troubled Kumar. That modern women obviously wouldn't tolerate such arrangements didn't allay his concerns.[1]

Kumar recognized that feminist utopias were hardly new,[2] though he didn't address the orientations of earlier such works. Nor did he deny the legitimacy of LeGuin's, Piercy's, Russ's, Staton's, and others' respective overall critiques of male hegemony in the past and present alike. If anything, he appreciated this proper use of utopian writings as vehicles for social criticism. Yet he wondered why primitive settings were common to these fantasy realms "in which women have come triumphantly into their own, sometimes through the satisfying device of extinguishing the men."[3] Is this what women (if not men) should really seek? More specifically, are modern technology and modern civilization so antithetical to women and to their general values and customs that they should strive to be rid of them altogether? Are they so inextricably connected with male hegemony that their continuation precludes any female equality, much less supremacy?

A related question about utopian writing by men had been raised in 1979 by literary scholar Elaine Hoffman Baruch. If, she asked, "utopias for men are often dystopias for women . . . [m]ight it then be possible that dystopias for men are utopias for women?"[4] Baruch herself answered the question in the negative, though she did acknowledge an exception in Piercy's novel.

I have nonetheless come upon a nineteenth-century feminist utopia that has precisely the orientation toward women and toward technology that both Kumar and Baruch seek and that may stand as an undeservedly obscure precursor of the kind of contemporary feminist utopias they wish to inspire. *Mizora: A Prophecy* is a utopian novel written by one Mary E. Bradley Lane. Published under the pseudonym Princess Vera Zarovitch, it appeared in serialized form in the *Cincinnati Commercial* in 1880–1881 and, upon popular demand, in book form in 1890. In the years since I first read it, *Mizora* has been reprinted and has been increasingly cited by a number of feminist and utopian scholars. But the particular issues concerning technological and social progress that interested me initially and interest me still have generally been ignored.

Literally scores of utopian novels, short stories, and tracts were published in late nineteenth- and early twentieth-century America. Most were similarly written by unknown persons and were both literary and commercial failures. The great exception to this sad fate is, of course, Edward Bellamy's *Looking Backward* (1888). Yet Bellamy himself was hardly a prominent writer before that work appeared, despite his considerable earlier fiction and nonfiction publications. And the extraordinary popularity of *Looking Backward* hardly guaranteed the success of those utopian works which, unlike *Mizora*, appeared after it, or those which, like *Mizora*, were perhaps reprinted because of it.

Mizora not only is better written than most other utopian works of the day but also probes more deeply than most the nature and significance of utopian society. Nevertheless, beyond what *Commercial* editor Murat Halstead called "our limited literary world"[5] of presumably Cincinnati or the Ohio Valley, the novel apparently created no stir once it was reprinted. Few original copies survive, and Mary Lane remains a comparatively unfamiliar name to scholars of American history, literature, and feminism. In fact, given her preference for anonymity and, according to Halstead, her initial reluctance to publish *Mizora* as a book, one must seek evidence that she actually wrote the novel. The evidence consists of an 1889 copyright in the name of "Mary E. Bradley," the penciled addition of the name of "Mary E. Bradley Lane" to the Library of Congress copy of the original edition, and the listing of the latter name in Lyle H. Wright's definitive *American Fiction, 1876–1900*. Despite extensive research I have been unable to learn more about the author's background.[6]

Mary Lane's apparent decision to conceal her authorship from her husband as well as all other acquaintances is surely not unconnected to the content of the work. *Mizora* is principally about the envisioned dominant role of women in an allegedly ideal society—specifically, a "modern" technologically oriented society like our own. If Ann D. Wood's analysis of the motivation behind another, albeit truly popular, nineteenth-century American female novelist applies to others as well, then Mary Lane may have written in part simply to lessen the emotional and psychic oppression of contemporary domesticity. As for Wood's Sara Willis, so for Lane, writing may have provided "a way *out of* the home,"[7] a substitute for unattainable physical liberation. That Mary Lane sought anonymity is in a sense beside the point: in writing for a popular audience in the first place, and moreover in writing as a partial critic of male hegemony, she was, like Willis, already overstepping the boundaries of respectable Victorian womanhood. To have revealed her identity might, as with Willis, have been too bold a step.

The significance of *Mizora* for present-day readers, however, derives not from its author's identity but from her stance on the role of women in modern society, an issue no less controversial in her day than in ours. To be sure, other late nineteenth- and early twentieth-century Americans, men as well as women, wrote utopian fiction that dealt seriously with the role of women. But these works ordinarily envisioned simply greater equality for women than the wholesale inequality that existed at their time. This was the case with *Looking Backward*, which has a separate industrial army for women and a division of labor according to sex. Although roughly half of these utopias envisioned less than complete equality with men, that being too revolutionary even for self-professed visionaries, including some of the female writers, nearly every one of them advocated the right of women to attend high school and college, to work outside the home, to vote, and to hold political office—in short, to carve out some sphere of independence from men.[8] Such advances would still be significant if not quite revolutionary.

What makes *Mizora* unusual and—save for Charlotte Perkins Gilman's *Herland* (1915)[9]—probably unique among these utopian works is that its women have eliminated men altogether! True, they have done so only gradually, after many years of struggle against their once haughty and omnipotent oppressors. Moreover, they have in part succeeded just because large numbers of males had been killed in the numerous struggles for power—not only against fellow males but also against females—within Mizoran society. The women were then able to pass and to enforce legislation restricting male participation in government. That in turn finally secured a lasting peace. Not, however, until they had discovered "The Secret of Life," a modestly undetailed form of parthenogenesis (reproduction without male participation),[10] could they eliminate men completely. And not until they then practiced eugenics among themselves and their offspring could they produce the kind of Aryan women they sought. For three thousand years there have been no males in Mizora, and its uniformly blond, blue-eyed, beautiful, robust, intelligent, and cultivated inhabitants harbor absolutely no nostalgia for the "old days." Significantly, Mizoran men were dark-skinned and are said to have constituted a separate, inferior "race." The novel makes no (other) explicit mention of sex but hints that women in those earlier times found it degrading. Likewise the novel provides no dates, but utopia clearly takes place in the distant future.

Lest *Mizora* seem a familiar tale of physically superior Amazons completely eliminating their characteristically weak male countrymen, it should be emphasized that Lane does not conceive the Mizorans as Amazons. Despite their pride in their large waists and enormous lung power, the Mizorans are exceedingly refined. They would fit comfortably into the middle-class Victorian homes of late nineteenth-century America (and Britain) at least in this respect. And the Mizorans maintain single-family rather than communal homes, with each mother directly responsible for her young daughter's well-being.

More important here, the Mizorans are exceedingly advanced technologically, as their reproductive techniques attest. Technology for them "is the goddess who has led *us* out of ignorance and superstition;

out of degradation and every other wretchedness . . . humanity has known."[11] The society they inhabit combines a semiagrarian paradise with a highly industrialized and automated state. Menial labor is simply unknown, and leisure time is abundant. Their technology is, in contemporary parlance, ecologically conscious and appropriate for its natural and female-made surroundings. In addition, as in *Looking Backward*, their society boasts a full-scale, life-long meritocracy in which individual talent alone determines advancement in education, work, and government. Like the inhabitants of *Looking Backward*, everyone is comfortable economically and socially, but there are distinctions among citizens. For example, teachers have the highest salaries because education is Mizora's highest concern, and the government pays all student fees.

Like the advancement of women, the advancement of technology and of meritocracy is a familiar objective of both utopian and nonutopian reform writings of the nineteenth and twentieth centuries. For that matter, except for "The Secret of Life" (which Gilman adopts and may have taken from Lane), all the other inventions or discoveries found in *Mizora*—ranging from automobiles and airplanes to mechanical house-cleaning and synthetic foods to controlled weather and a public broadcasting system—are predicted by other visionaries as well. Yet practically none of these other works makes women the rulers of society, much less its sole inhabitants.[12] Rather, women here frequently take to extremes, in good utopian fashion, Victorian assumptions about the special goodness of women vis-à-vis men even when there is some surface gender equality. Women are put on still higher pedestals than in nonutopian writings. But they rarely exercise equal power with men. Moreover, the few utopian works that do make women the rulers of society are usually quite critical of their new role. Women are generally depicted either as true Amazons, and so too primitive and uneducated to rule a "civilized" society, or, where society is already civilized, as excessively vain, jealous, and frivolous and so likewise unfit to rule. Often an outsider, invariably a handsome and charismatic male, the antithesis of their native males, fortuitously appears to rescue society from barbarism or chaos.[13] By avoiding these female stereotypes, *Mizora* is, again, exceptional and, again save for *Herland*, perhaps unique.

Interestingly, recent research by feminist archeologists and folklorists has raised provocative questions as to the possible orientation of some of the earliest civilizations toward feminist values and mores and their eventual destruction by patriarchal invaders. One prominent archeologist, Marija Gimbutas, argues that during the Stone Age, "between 7000 B.C. and 3500 B.C., the people of Europe lived in sedentary agricultural societies that worshiped the Great Goddess, delighted in nature, shunned war, built comfortable settlements rather than forts, and crafted superb ceramics rather than weapons." In these societies, she contends, "Women headed clans or served as queen-priestesses. Men labored as hunters and builders. But neither men nor women dominated the other sex."[14] This peaceful "Old Europe," Gimbutas claims, was torn apart by Indo-European warriors on horseback between 4000 B.C. and 3500 B.C. Their deities dethroned this nurturing Goddess and replaced relative equality between the sexes with patriarchy and hierarchy. As difficult as this thesis is to prove, it has provided some historical perspective on *Mizora, Herland,* and other feminist utopias.

Lane may nevertheless not be endorsing the unisexual—and, in effect, asexual—society she describes. Her heroine and narrator, Vera Zarovitch, an exiled Russian princess, chances upon Mizora after being shipwrecked (as common a means of reaching utopia as *Looking Backward's* lengthy sleep). She eventually discards her Victorian assumptions about the supposed inferiority of women to men, but clings resolutely to the need for men as the equals, though no longer the superiors, of women. Nor can she fully accept the emotional restraint, the strict organization, and the non-Christian pantheism (Nature as "the Great Mother") of the Mizorans. Her female consciousness *has* been altered through her fifteen years in Mizora, but not so far as to embrace a world without men. Her heroism stems as much from her ability simply to survive exile, first in Siberia and then in Mizora, as from her willingness to discard a portion of her gender prejudices (though not her racial or religious biases) and to return to the Western world to attempt to secure equality for women.

Although Vera returns to the West and survives her ordeal, the novel's conclusion is anything but optimistic. She and her companion Wauna, daughter of the preceptress of Mizora's national university, fail to persuade Europeans or Americans to seek equality for all. Wauna then becomes depressed, takes ill, and finally dies before reaching Mizora. The princess's consequent grief is compounded by the discovery that both her long-lost husband and her only child are dead. "Life," she laments in the novel's closing lines, "is a tragedy even under the most favorable conditions."[15]

Whether this somber conclusion represents Mary Lane's own feelings about life or whether it represents only an accommodation to readers accustomed to a mixture of seriousness and sentimentality is unclear. Dee Garrison has shown how sixteen popular, though not utopian, female novelists of the same period, writing like Lane for a predominantly female audience, clothed subversive notions about female equality with men in conventional plots not dissimilar to *Mizora's*.[16] Of course, at least since the 1950s, with the publication of Helen Papashvily's *All the Happy Endings*—or certainly since the landmark publications in the late 1970s of Elaine Showalter and of Sandra Gilbert and Susan Gubar—feminist literary critics have been "reading against the grain" to find female anger at male dominance submerged subversively beneath orthodox plots.[17] Perhaps Lane's work should be interpreted in that same light.

In any case, the utopian quality of the novel is not diminished. For if many utopians such as Bellamy have described an alternative to existing society in anticipation of bridging the gap between nonutopia and utopia, an equal number, beginning with Plato, have composed theirs exactly to emphasize that the gap between the two can never be bridged. Both varieties of utopian writing have been potent vehicles of social criticism. Though hardly a classic utopia in the manner of either *Looking Backward* or *The Republic*, *Mizora* is a provocative picture of the future that clearly deserves a contemporary reading.

Mizora obviously fails to provide the "equality of androgyny" which Baruch explicitly seeks: "that is, an equality of interchangeable difference whereby temperaments and roles traditionally assigned to one sex or the other are open to both."[18] Ironically, early in her stay Vera had said to herself that Mizora "would be a paradise for man,"[19] given the appealing physical and intellectual nature of its female inhabitants and the assumption of male hegemony—indeed, of male presence—that she brought with her. Only *Herland*, written a quarter of a century later by a much more sophisticated social critic, offers the modest prospect of such equality. Still, both novels provide the biological as well as social engineering for humane purposes that Baruch and Kumar alike advocate—though without the decimation of either sex.

The liberation of women from domestic chores and other predominantly female jobs through technological advance has not, however, been so simple a process as both Baruch and Kumar imply. They make the common error of equating (greater) freedom from traditional manual labor with social and psychological freedom. If, as Kumar argues, "the advance of power-driven machinery has opened up to women thousands of jobs which were previously restricted to men by virtue of their heavier physique,"[20] that in itself has been a mixed blessing—just as the mechanization of manufacturing, as epitomized by the modern assembly line (with its gender-typing of numerous assembly line tasks), has been a mixed blessing for its male and female workers alike. As historian Ruth Schwartz Cowan, among others, has shown, the domestic industrial revolution of the twentieth century usually increased rather than diminished the workload of even well-to-do women by making available ever more household appliances and so encouraging ever more domestic tasks. That in turn raised ever higher the standards of cleanliness and comfort appropriate for respectable families.[21] Contemporary belief in the alleged ability of "high-tech" machinery like computers alone to liberate and equalize women is equally naive and misplaced.[22] It is akin to the questionable faith in technological decentralization as a virtual panacea.

These qualifications confirm all the more the wisdom of control over technology by women as well as men which both Baruch and Kumar properly seek.[23] Furthermore, they may confirm the wisdom of Mary Lane's reluctance to deem technology the solution to all of women's—and men's—problems. What is needed instead is some balance between antitechnological primitivism and uncritical technological utopianism, between unjustified nostalgia and equally unjustified optimism. Whether a more developed version of the feminist perspective on technology found in *Mizora*—one incorporating the maternal, nurturing, peaceful uses of technology the novel describes—could lead in this direction remains to be seen. Scholarly appreciation of not just feminist utopias old and new but also actual feminist approaches to technology is still at an early stage.[24]

But Kumar's dismissal of motherhood and the values and mores associated with it in the feminist utopias he treats as being at once primitive and antitechnological is highly questionable. Even Margaret Atwood's *The Handmaid's Tale* (1986), a recasting of George Orwell's dystopian *1984* from a woman's point of view, refuses to denounce motherhood despite its perversion by right-wing religious fanatics who have taken over the United States and who enslave all fertile women in order to offset the infertility plaguing most younger women. Nor does the novel denounce the computers and other high-tech gadgets used to enforce biblical beliefs and practices. Atwood recognizes both that motherhood is not intrinsically primitive or antitechnological and that modern technology can be gainfully employed by progressives and reactionaries alike.[25]

For these reasons and despite its weaknesses, *Mizora* cannot be so lightly dismissed either. Ironically, equating science with technology, *Mizora*'s narrator Vera claims to have written the novel "for the sole purpose of benefiting Science and giving encouragement to those progressive minds who have already added their mite of knowledge to the coming future of the race."[26] As literary scholar Carol Farley Kessler observes, "where United States Utopias by men stress as ends in themselves matters of public policy—be they political, economic, or technological—women's Utopias are more likely to include these matters as they provide *a means to the social end* of fully developed human capacity in all people."[27] Given my own criticism here and elsewhere of technological progress as an end in itself, a stance without doubt characteristically male, I could only endorse Kessler's implicit criticism of that position and her clear support of the feminist alternative.

Kumar concludes his essay by reference to the American Indians' Ghost Dance, "a millenarian ritual" in which they engaged when, by the late nineteenth century, they "had finally given up the hopeless struggle against their European conquerors." Kumar asks if "the growing literature of feminist utopianism [is] the ghost dance of the feminist movement?"[28] Obviously I disagree, but it is a wonderful coincidence that Kurt Vonnegut's *Player Piano*, discussed next, not only mentions this Indian ritual (and in more detail than Kumar) but also offers what I contend is a healthy balance between antitechnological primitivism and uncritical technological utopianism, albeit without sufficient concern for the past, present, and future roles of women. *Player Piano* thus complements *Mizora* in ways that at first glance are not evident but that should become apparent in due course.

10

KURT VONNEGUT'S PLAYER PIANO: AN AMBIGUOUS TECHNO- LOGICAL DYSTOPIA

. . . .

Kurt Vonnegut's *Player Piano* (1952) takes place at an unspecified future date in the town of Ilium, New York. The United States is now the dominant world power, without apparent rivals for international hegemony; it achieved this position through victory in a third world war ten years earlier.

That international conflict, however, had a second, no less important result: the domination of technology over mankind, at least in the United States. In order both to meet wartime production needs and to compensate for the drainage of manpower into the armed forces, automated machinery replaced most manual laborers and computers replaced most supervisors of those laborers. These changes remained in effect after the war, despite the return to America of millions of former or future workers and supervisors. The inevitable consequence of their return was "technological unemployment."

Yet at the time of the story, the United States is hardly an economically depressed society. Quite the opposite: its technology has made the country more prosperous than ever and has in fact made possible both cradle-to-grave medical care and a guaranteed annual wage for all citizens. The changes technology has brought about are so profound as to be termed the Second Industrial Revolution.

The United States of *Player Piano* is, in a sense, itself a giant automated machine, with millions of parts. Not only is life for all citizens overwhelmingly automated, but every citizen has an assigned part in the social mechanism. Moreover, one huge computer, named EPICAC XIV (i.e., thirteenth addition to the original model), makes the major decisions about national policy and so largely determines the fate of all citizens. True, technically trained human beings control EPICAC insofar as they built and continue to operate it in its Carlsbad Caverns home. But they always defer to its answers to their questions—as do, they make certain, all other citizens.

To the managerial and engineering elite who, if only in theory, nevertheless run the United States, the nation is a veritable technological utopia. Unlike such other, wholly static utopias as *Looking Backward*, American society will develop further, but its fundamental form is permanently established.

To most of Vonnegut's Americans, however, contemporary society is far from utopian; rather, it is a technological dystopia. They appreciate the material benefits of technology but resent their loss of meaningful labor and in turn of personal identity and social purpose. They also resent the paternalism and condescension of their technocratic leaders, whose lives are repeatedly portrayed on state-run television as difficult and trying, unlike the supposedly idyllic lives of ordinary citizens. It must be stressed that many adults do "work." But their work is menial and unsatisfying, contributing little to American society. It is restricted to three areas: (1) the army, which requires enlistments of twenty-five years but which is unarmed save for its occasional overseas duty—for fear of possible rebellion against the ruling elite and sabotage against its structures and machines; (2) the Reconstruction and Reclamation Corps (derisively called the "Reeks and Wrecks"), which apparently has shorter enlistment requirements but no more significant duties, being restricted to the infrequent road repairs for which automated structures and machines would be too expensive; and (3) the various forms of self-employment, running from bartender to barber to pool shark. The elite positions are restricted to those whose IQ's and vocational aptitudes— as measured in nationwide tests scored by computer—grant them opportunities for advanced education and then managerial and engineering positions. (Higher education itself is centered upon an engineering curriculum devoid of humanistic content, much less individual choice.) The overwhelming majority of citizens are excluded from childhood on from significant jobs.

In the case of Ilium and presumably other communities, these nationwide divisions between the elite and the masses are exacerbated by the separation of their places of residence. In Ilium, the elite live in a plush suburbanlike setting near the Ilium Works, the area's principal production unit. The Ilium Works manufactures "parts for baby carriages and bottle caps, motorcycles and refrigerators, television sets and tricycles,"[1] all by automated assembly lines. So few are the number of persons needed for the production process that the night shift at least can commute to and from work in a single station wagon. The masses live across the Iroquois River in a township of prefabricated dwellings called Homestead. Few of them have any association with the Works and most of them work, if at all, at the menial tasks already described. Once again, however, the masses do not suffer economic deprivation. Rather, they enjoy glass and steel houses whose amenities include microwave ovens, ultrasonic appliances such as dishwashers and clothes washers and dryers, automated ironers, and twenty-seven-inch color television sets. Yet their living conditions do not compensate for their working conditions and thus fail to eliminate their gnawing resentment and discontent. Homestead is therefore somewhat similar to the site after which it is named: the huge steel plant outside Pittsburgh operated by Andrew Carnegie and the scene of a violent clash in 1892 between labor and management. Ilium, however, is far from similar to the site after which it is named: Troy, home of the Trojans, captured by the Greeks through the use of the wooden horse and completely destroyed. The banality of the modern Ilium contrasts unfavorably with the grandeur of the original.[2]

Understanding *Player Piano*'s meaning and message requires drawing connections between its major and minor plots and certain developments in both Vonnegut's own life and American history. I do not contend that the novel is autobiographical, but do suggest several likely personal and historical sources that illuminate it. In that context, it is notable that between 1947 and 1950 Vonnegut worked for General Electric in Schenectady, New York, as a public relations specialist in a research laboratory. He has indicated his dislike of that job and, for that matter, of most jobs in modern large corporations. Despite the Ilium Works' employment of just a handful of workers, its impersonality is probably modeled after that of General Electric, as is probably the impersonality of industrial work as a whole in *Player Piano*. Ilium itself is almost certainly modeled after Schenectady. After observing the initial replacement of well-paid, highly skilled machinists by a computer-operated device rigged to cut rotor blades for gas turbines, Vonnegut quit his job at GE in order to write a novel in which, as Vonnegut later put it, machines "frequently got the best of it, as machines will."[3] *Player Piano*, he continues, "was my response to the implications of having everything run by little boxes. . . . To have a little clicking box make all the decisions wasn't a vicious thing to do. But it was too bad for the human beings who got their dignity from their jobs."[4]

The novel's central plot revolves around Dr. Paul Proteus, the thirty-five-year-old manager of the Ilium Works. His job is the most important and most prestigious in the entire community, but he is being seriously considered for a similar position at the larger and more important Pittsburgh Works. He actually is favored for the post, partly because of his own achievements to date but partly too because of the achievements of his late father, George. His father was "the nation's first National Industrial, Commercial, Communications, Foodstuffs, and Resources Director, a position approached in importance only by the presidency of the United States."[5] Indeed, the National Industrial Planning Board which grew out of his father's position has since become far more powerful than the presidency. (As in technological utopias like *Looking Backward,* so in this technological dystopia, conventional politicians are invariably either eliminated altogether or deprived of dominant power.)

Player Piano's National Industrial Planning Board at once resembles and takes to extremes the partly successful attempts during the New Deal to engage in national and regional planning. Taken for granted in *Player Piano,* large-scale planning has never been applied in real-world America to the extent that its foremost advocates have sought. Such New Deal federal government experiments as the Works Progress Administration and the Civilian Conservation Corps—both possible models for the novel's Reconstruction and Reclamation Corps—were frequently ridiculed as wasteful or condemned as socialist. The Technocracy movement of the same period, a private crusade taking to logical if extreme ends the same assumptions regarding the value of planning, was widely dismissed as fanatical and fascist. Yet planning, as much as structures and machines themselves, makes possible the conditions of *Player Piano.*[6]

Meanwhile Paul's prospects for the Pittsburgh post are further enhanced by his friendship with Dr. Anthony Kroner, the supreme manager of America's Eastern Division (which includes both Ilium and Pittsburgh) who will make the decision, and by Kroner's admiration for

Paul's father. Paul's prospects are also boosted by the aggressive efforts of his wife, Anita, to make her husband as socially appealing as possible through endless parties, gossip, pep talks, and other means of social climbing.

From the outset of the story, however, Paul appears vaguely discontented with life in general and, in the eyes of first Kroner and then Anita, insufficiently eager for the promotion to Pittsburgh. Paul's prospects are undermined more directly by Dr. Lawson Shepherd, a former college classmate but presently envious subordinate at the Ilium Works. Shepherd gossips that Paul is losing his nerves and so his competency. Even before learning of these rumors, Paul rightly calls Shepherd "Dog-Eat-Dog."

Whatever his reservations about his present or future position, Paul remains passive until prodded by others and by unforeseen events. The prodding begins at a dinner party given by the Ilium Works' Kroner, a party affording Paul an ideal opportunity to secure his promotion. To the party comes Ed Finnerty, Paul's eccentric old friend who left the Works for a major managerial post in Washington, D.C., still the nation's capital. Finnerty, however, has recently resigned from his post and has returned to denounce the entire "system"—much to the disgust of all at the party, save Paul. Though Paul fails to endorse Finnerty's critique, he is aroused by it and accompanies Finnerty on a drinking spree to Homestead. There they meet an equally outspoken critic of society, James Lasher, a sometime anthropologist, barfly, and chaplain. Paul is shaken by Lasher's criticisms but returns home.

By contrast, Finnerty remains with Lasher and forms the Ghost Shirt Society, an underground organization named after a nineteenth-century American Indian movement which resisted white settlement and in the process performed the Ghost Dance. Just as the Indians sought to restore their autonomy in the remaining parts of the American frontier, so the Society seeks to restore Americans' control over technology. Moreover, it looks to the Indian civilization as an example of a healthier and happier social order. Finnerty and Lasher secretly recruit like-minded members of the ruling elite—several of them Paul's associates—and plan a nationwide uprising. Soon, however, the Society's existence becomes known to the authorities, and its members are forced to go into hiding to escape capture. That the original Ghost Shirt Society failed in its task seems not to daunt its successor; if anything, it strengthens the members' resolve.

Paul does not betray his fellow dissidents but refuses to join the Society. Rather, he seeks temporary escape from his problems through acquisition of an old, dilapidated, and, most important, virtually un-mechanized farm. There he plans to live with Anita, who is unaware of Paul's ulterior motives and approves of the purchase under the assump-tion that the farm will be thoroughly mechanized and modernized. Yet eventually Paul finds himself too far removed from nature to become a traditional farmer and abandons this scheme.

The turning point of the story comes during the ruling elite's annual summer retreat on the Meadows, an island in the St. Lawrence River. The retreat is designed to bring together the members of the elite in order for them to celebrate the society they lead. The retreat is re-stricted to men—in this as in so many other utopias women, as epito-mized by Anita, remain subordinates.

From about 1910 to 1955 General Electric operated an annual summer retreat similar to that described in *Player Piano*. The company used its own island (Association Island), as does the ruling elite of the novel, and had its junior and senior executives indulge in the same juvenile games and other activities depicted in the book. Vonnegut himself states that the GE retreat closed in embarrassment after *Player Piano* appeared.[7] However, a larger and more important summer re-treat, the Bohemian Grove, has persisted since the early twentieth century and continues to flourish. North of San Francisco, the Bohe-mian Grove welcomes corporate and political leaders from across Amer-ica for the same purposes as the Meadows: to get better acquainted and to celebrate the "system," here corporate capitalism more than, as in *Player Piano*, technological progress. Two 1974 studies of the Bohemian Grove emphasized its significance for "real world" America's ruling elite.[8] In addition, the Bohemian Grove, like the Meadows, seeks to restore close relationships with nature, but along with its fictional counterpart never achieves more than a superficial return to nature. Like the Meadows as well, the Bohemian Grove is an all-male enclave.

In *Player Piano* the Meadows' participants are divided into four teams. Paul is designated a team leader but accepts the honor reluc-tantly, given his decreasing enthusiasm for the "system." He is much more reluctant to accept an assignment as a double agent, a supposed convert to the Ghost Shirt Society but actually a spy and so subverter of it. The assignment, which he finally accepts, is made a test of his loyalty to that system and a precondition for his promotion.

Ironically, this act of loyalty to the system ends Paul's already shaky marriage. Anita, like most other members of the elite, is deliberately kept ignorant of her husband's "true" intentions and instead sees him publicly branded a "saboteur," the most loathsome designation in society. She then leaves him in disgust for Shepherd. Paul still loves Anita, loves no one else, and is deeply saddened but not altogether surprised by her actions.

The conformity that characterizes both the work and the play of the ruling elite in *Player Piano* was a concern in the "real world" at the time the book appeared. Throughout the late 1940s and 1950s there were studies of the willingness of Americans to conform in order to achieve status and success in a variety of areas. In the area of business the most famous and influential such study, and probably the most critical, was William H. Whyte's *The Organization Man* (1956). Whyte denounced unthinking, uncritical worship of corporate organizations and railed against any organization's use of the concepts of belonging and togetherness to manipulate members and objectives. By the time the book appeared, Vonnegut was presumably already quite familiar with the "organization man" mentality. Yet the book provides useful historical references for understanding the corporate ethos of *Player Piano.*[9]

Ironically, Paul refuses to spy on the Ghost Shirt Society, much less turn its members over to the authorities. Instead, he becomes their nominal leader and is arrested for treason. As his trial proceeds the predicted rebellion begins, the courtroom is invaded, and Paul is liberated. As a result of these developments Paul finally becomes conscious of his hitherto only semiconscious dissatisfactions with his life: namely, its increasing monotony and shallowness. Gradually, too, he becomes aware of the outright desperation of the less fortunate masses, whose lives are far duller and less fulfilling than his.

On the eve of the uprising Paul agrees to sign a letter composed for him by one of the other rebel leaders, Professor von Neumann. The letter is then widely distributed as Paul's own. In it the Ghost Shirt Society declares its intention to make structures and machines subordinate to mankind; to put the well-being and desires of mankind above the ideal of efficiency; to recognize mankind as an imperfect species created by God to improve but never to perfect itself; and to accept mankind's imperfection as a virtue, not a vice.

The Ghost Shirt Society thus questions the basic premises and promises of the Second Industrial Revolution. The term was popularized by Norbert Wiener, professor of mathematics at MIT, in his *The Human Use of Human Beings: Cybernetics and Society* (1950). Wiener was the pioneer in the development of computers who originated the concept of "cybernetics." *The Human Use of Human Beings* was a revised, layman's version of his landmark monograph, *Cybernetics* (1948). Vonnegut certainly used the later book, if not the earlier one, for *Player Piano* not only incorporates the Second Industrial Revolution—to be brought about by cybernetics—but also cites Wiener himself as the source. Far from advocating the wholesale adoption of computers, however, Wiener raised questions about their possible misuse. He warned against allowing computers to make decisions that might eventually lead to their domination over human beings—precisely what occurs in *Player Piano*.

The Ghost Shirt Society uprising nevertheless fails. Although successful in Ilium and a handful of other communities, it never becomes a nationwide upheaval. Ilium and the other rebellious sites are soon surrounded by armed government troops and are informed via messages from robot helicopters that they face fatal besiegement if the Society leaders do not promptly surrender. Paul is already disillusioned not only with the outcome of the uprising but also with the now apparent selfish motivations of his fellow leaders, their manipulation of him and of other participants, the indiscriminate destruction of structures and machines those leaders have allowed, and the paradoxical obsession of many rebels with repairing the most useless structures and machines they have just smashed. Paul therefore joins the other leaders in surrender. Like the nineteenth-century Indians who thought their ghost shirts could stop the white men's bullets, the rebels must pay the supreme price for their act of folly: their rebellion against technological progress.

The rebels' indiscriminate destruction of hardware brings to mind the legendary Luddite "machine breakers" of early nineteenth-century England, the epitome of opposition to the first industrial revolution. Yet later studies of the Luddites have shown them to have been opposed not to technology per se but only to those forms which put them out of work. In this respect they are likewise akin to the rebels of the novel, who hardly oppose technology itself. Unlike those fictional rebels, however, the Luddites never repaired the hardware they destroyed.[10]

Similarly, the rebels' obsession with repairing the most useless hardware they have just smashed recalls the caricatures of unnecessarily complex and invariably inefficient machinery drawn by cartoonist Rube Goldberg early in the twentieth century. Evidence that Goldberg's work influenced Vonnegut is the author's mention of Goldberg's name in connection with Bud Calhoun, Paul's subordinate, who earlier in the novel invents a device to take over his own job.

With the Ghost Shirt Society's elimination, the conclusion of *Player Piano*, like the opening, recalls and reflects the sense of American hegemony in the late 1940s and the early 1950s, the beginning of *Time* editor Henry Luce's envisioned "American Century." Yet the growing fear in those same years of communist subversion of that hegemony both at home and abroad is mirrored in the obsession with the Ghost Shirt Society on the part of the power elite and with the latter's McCarthyite crusades to root out all heretics.

Player Piano has a secondary plot only indirectly related to the central plot. This other plot—or series of subplots—revolves around the official visit to the United States of the Shah of Bratpuhr, the spiritual leader of six million members of the Kolhouri sect. The shah comes to the United States in order to compare his admittedly "primitive" society to this avowedly "advanced" one. His American hosts hope that he will find the United States so progressive, so utopian—in the manner of the post–World War II modernization theorists—that he will readily seek the American technology to transform his own kingdom. Almost from the outset of his visit, however, he raises embarrassing questions—sometimes innocently, sometimes deliberately—about the actual differences between the two societies. In particular, he wonders openly both about the degree to which Americans are slaves to technology in the manner in which many of his subjects are slaves to him or others, and about the fact that Americans, despite their material bounty, are no happier than most of his infinitely poorer subjects.

In the course of his visit the shah meets a soldier who dreams of retirement in twenty-three years and of the opportunity only then of telling off his superiors for making army duty so monotonous; a barber who yearns for his retirement in two years before machines replace all barbers; a housewife who alleviates her boredom by doing the family laundry by hand in the bathtub instead of in the ultrasonic washer, and whose husband, a member of the Reeks and Wrecks, alleviates his by having an affair with a neighbor; and the wife of an aspiring writer who offers herself as a prostitute to earn money for her husband, who stubbornly refuses to write works of officially approved length, depth, and outlook, the only works ever published. The shah also comes into contact with the EPICAC computer, which cannot answer an ancient riddle he puts to it, thereby revealing, at least to him, that it is a false god (incapable of anything heroic, as in an "EPIC").

Ironically, EPICAC is surely a play on the name of one of the first "real" computers, ENIAC (Electronic Numerical Integrator and Computer). Completed in 1946, the huge machine took up the entire fifteen thousand square feet of the basement of the Moore School of Electrical Engineering at the University of Pennsylvania. Its principal inventors were Dr. John W. Mauchly and Dr. J. Presper Eckert, Jr., who went on to invent far smaller and more powerful computers. Significantly, however, Mauchly, Eckert, and the other computer pioneers through the mid-1950s assumed that a mere half-dozen giant computers would suffice for the entire world and would perform complicated calculations for only the largest governmental, business, and academic institutions under the direction of an elite of extensively trained professional programmers. None of these pioneers apparently anticipated the advent of personal computers for everyday use by nonexperts using relatively nontechnical skills.[11] *Player Piano*'s reliance on a single computer for the entire United States thus reflected its times here too.

Throughout his visit the shah is accompanied by a State Department official, Ewing J. Halyard, who later loses all three of his Cornell University degrees—B.A., M.A., and Ph.D.—and so his position and identity because a computer discovers he never completed an undergraduate physical education requirement. Having steadily defended the United States against the shah's criticisms, this official nevertheless becomes a nonperson, one of the masses. Vonnegut himself attended Cornell, majoring in chemistry and biology at his father's insistence rather than the literary studies he preferred; it is interesting that he never graduated.

Through these and other experiences the shah soon reaches conclusions about the nature of American society remarkably similar to those reached more slowly by Paul. Where Paul is too much a part of the "system" to recognize its problems until forced to confront them, the shah is the acute outside observer so characteristic of both science fiction and utopian fiction. He also represents the Oriental observer common in Western literature.

Primarily because of these two plots and the alternation between them throughout the book, *Player Piano* is fragmented. Ironically, a meeting between Paul and the shah not only would have lessened this disjointedness but also might have clarified Paul's anxieties regarding his life and his society. But such a meeting never occurs.

The considerable number of major and minor characters who appear, disappear, and reappear as a result of these alternating plots adds to this incohesiveness. Moreover, none of the characters, including Paul, is as fully developed as one might wish, and most are two-dimensional characters if not outright stereotypes. Paul's surname "Proteus" is ironic, for unlike the classical sea god after whom he is presumably named, Paul fails to change either rapidly or completely. Rather, as indicated, he changes gradually, and then falteringly, and only after being provoked from several quarters.

Paul's surname is equally ironic in another respect. Charles Proteus Steinmetz (1865–1923) was a misshapen German immigrant of socialist views who was nevertheless hired by General Electric in 1892 when that then-new company sought promising scientists and engineers. Steinmetz perfected electric motors and was eventually rewarded with his own laboratory in Schenectady. In turn he gradually altered his socialist views and instead looked to the modern corporation as both the means and the model of social reform in twentieth-century America. He remained at GE until his death. Paul Proteus is hardly the inventive genius Steinmetz was, but like Steinmetz he is the talented industrial manager who can at once fit into the organization and stand out as one of its leaders. Where, however, Steinmetz accommodated himself to large-scale industrialism, Paul obviously does not.[12]

None of the other major characters, save perhaps Finnerty and Lasher, changes as much as Paul, and Finnerty and Lasher themselves seem rebellious by nature, where Paul seems complacent. Moreover, *their* names, like those of other major characters, are more literally true to their stereotyped personalities: Finnerty the irreverent, hard-drinking, emotional Irishman, and Lasher the cynical critic "lashing out" at society. Similarly, Kroner, the supreme manager, and Baer, the Eastern Division's chief engineer, are both cold, efficient, unemotional Germans.

Whether Vonnegut intended his characters to be as limited in personal development, as machinelike in nature, as the avowedly technological society in which they live cannot be determined. Certainly he meant to picture Anita as a machinelike wife and social climber, Shepherd as a machinelike organization man, Kroner as a machinelike man-

ager, and many of the technocrats and rebels alike as machinelike
worshipers of technology. Yet all his characters, including Paul, are
sufficiently complex as to be neither altogether good nor altogether evil.
Just as none of the rebels, including Paul, is without some vices, so none
of the ruling elite, including Kroner, is without some virtues. None of
the elite is as machinelike as the supermen and superwomen (the
Alphas) of Aldous Huxley's *Brave New World* (1932), a book to which, as
will be seen, *Player Piano* is closely akin.

If anything, Vonnegut appears to be sympathetic to virtually everyone in the novel insofar as everyone is ultimately a victim of technological domination. Like Charles Dickens's *Hard Times* (1854) and Emile
Zola's *Germinal* (1885), two pioneering novels of the social consequences of industrialization, *Player Piano* portrays the "winners" of the
Second Industrial Revolution as no happier than the "losers." The
material comforts of the ruling elite do not compensate for their emotional and spiritual deprivations—the same deprivations, admittedly,
affecting the masses as well.

In this regard it is worth noting—and conceding—the limited
serious treatment of workers throughout American fiction. Two notable
exceptions are Rebecca Harding Davis's *Life in the Iron Mills, or the
Korl Woman* (1861), a novella dealing with the early stages of America's
first industrial revolution, and Harvey Swados's *On the Line* (1957), a
novel treating the mature phase of that initial industrial revolution.
Like *Player Piano*, each work reflects both a deep concern for the social
and psychological consequences of technological advance and a first-
hand familiarity with the developments each discusses: iron (and cotton)
mills and automobile assembly lines respectively. Like *Player Piano* as
well, neither blames technology alone for the exploitation and degradation of the workers each graphically portrays, but once again, faults
human nature more.

Like Vonnegut, Davis and Swados portray workers as at least two-
dimensional figures with varied mixtures of virtues and vices. In so
doing these authors, along with Vonnegut, consciously rebelled against
not just that general ignorance of the workplace common to American
writers and critics but, no less important, their tendency to romanticize
and so further distort workers' nature, either lumping workers into a
faceless proletariat or else elevating one or two among them into flaw-
less heroic figures. What, however, distinguishes Davis's and Swados's
workers from Vonnegut's is their need for continued employment to

support themselves and their families in the absence of the utopian welfare state scheme *Player Piano* describes. Significantly, though, where the tragedy portrayed in *Life in the Iron Mills* is nineteenth-century workers' potential aesthetic creativity, as symbolized by a sculpture that survives a worker's death, that portrayed in *On the Line* is twentieth-century workers' actual futility. The latter's labor is meaning-less insofar as it results in unaesthetic if not ugly products—1950s automobiles—that do not and are not meant to last. By the time of *Player Piano*, of course, there is little labor and still less to show for it.

Like most of its characters, *Player Piano*'s style is mechanical, characterized by short sentences, paragraphs, and chapters; a fast pace; and a language that is sometimes journalistic and contrived and rarely eloquent. Perhaps Vonnegut intended the style to mesh with or symbol-ize the book's principal theme of mechanization in society. Given the relative primitivism of television in the early 1950s, when *Player Piano* was written, and contrary to the assertions of some literary critics, it is unlikely that he consciously modeled its style upon stories on televi-sion. The similarity in mechanical style between the book and television is almost certainly coincidental.

In terms of its tone and content, *Player Piano* is not as deadly serious as George Orwell's *1984* (1949), a work with which it is fre-quently compared. Rather, it more closely resembles Huxley's *Brave New World*. Both books mix humor and satire with solemn social crit-icism. They also share a fear of technological domination in the form of rule over the masses by a relative handful of technocrats and myriad of sophisticated structures and machines—in the very name of universal happiness and progress. This thematic overlap is hardly surprising; Vonnegut has confessed that he "cheerfully ripped off the plot of *Brave New World*, whose plot had been cheerfully ripped off from Eugene Zamiatin's *We*"[13] (1920). Each of these four works, however, is suffi-ciently distinctive as to be more than a mere imitation of another.

Indeed, one of the flaws in literary criticism of *Player Piano* is the assumption that the book is nothing more than an imitation of earlier and perhaps subtler works. Thus Mark Hillegas, in a generally fine study of H. G. Wells and the tradition of antiutopian or dystopian writings he largely inspired, claims that *Player Piano* not only is within that tradition but also is as nightmarish as *1984* and the other works within it.[14] I cannot entirely agree. I suggest that the humor of *Player Piano* and the mixture of good and evil in all its characters make it a less *overtly* nightmarish book than *1984* and the other works Hillegas examines, save perhaps *Brave New World.* So too does *Player Piano's* distinctive Americanness, which I will discuss shortly.

Certainly *Player Piano* is an avowedly dystopian work which, like most of those Hillegas studies, views technology as the principal problem. Hillegas is on stronger ground in stating, if much too casually, that "The only difference between Vonnegut's nightmare and its ancestors is that Vonnegut's seems closer to coming reality as we may come to know it." It is precisely here that, as Hillegas himself continues, "*Player Piano* makes its most profound comment."[15] And it is precisely in this respect that *Player Piano* is a subtly nightmarish work and a still more terrifying work than its more overtly terrifying predecessors.

The uniqueness of *Player Piano* can nevertheless best be appreciated through further consideration of the traditions of which it is paradoxically a part. The first of these traditions, the one Hillegas treats, is that of technological dystopianism. This tradition dates back at least as far as Mary Shelley's *Frankenstein* (1818) but does not mature until the appearance of Wells's *The First Men in the Moon* (1901), E. M. Forster's "The Machine Stops" (1912), Karel Čapek's *R.U.R.* (1921), and *We, Brave New World,* and *1984.*

If technology—more precisely, unadulterated technological advance—is the immediate problem in all of these works, human nature, it must be emphasized, is the underlying problem. All recognize that technology's eventual omnipotence reflects mankind's initial desire to dominate the entire world through technology and to have technology solve all problems. If technology somehow comes to dominate mankind, it is, like Victor Frankenstein's unnamed and abandoned creature in Shelley's novel, still a human creation, and ultimate responsibility for technology's domination and possible destructiveness rests with its creators. This fundamental point has frequently been missed by Vonnegut scholars interpreting the novel as primarily an attack on excessive mechanization.[16]

Player Piano treats technology and human nature similarly. Much of the ambivalence toward mankind's future at the novel's conclusion stems exactly from Vonnegut's view of human nature as permanently, inherently flawed. This belief is propounded by the Ghost Shirt Society in its widely circulated letter bearing Paul's signature. The Society's failed uprising itself reflects imperfections in the character of its members—most notably, a degree of authoritarianism remarkably akin to that of the society they would overthrow and that obsession of many of the rebels with repairing the most useless structures and machines they have just destroyed. Consequently, even if the uprising had been successful, there would have been no guarantee either that its replacement society would be qualitatively better or that another technological dystopia would not arise someday. Hence the basis for Vonnegut's ambivalence about the future.

Player Piano must also be seen as part of a reaction against a second and older tradition: that of technological utopianism. Like technological dystopianism, technological utopianism originated in Europe. It can be traced back as far as Johann Andreae's *Christianopolis* (1619), Tommaso Campanella's *The City of the Sun* (1623), and Francis Bacon's *The New Atlantis* (1627). It includes as well Marquis de Condorcet's *Sketch for a Historical Picture of the Progress of the Human Mind* (1795) and the nineteenth-century writings of Henri de Saint-Simon and Auguste Comte. A number of late nineteenth- and early twentieth-century Americans also wrote technological utopias, but Edward Bellamy's *Looking Backward* (1888) is the only prominent work among them.[17] Despite the growing questioning of unadulterated technological advance, technological utopianism persists today in many quarters. Buckminster Fuller (1895–1983) was probably the most popular post–World War II technological visionary.

Without technological utopias, it can be safely assumed, technological dystopias like *Player Piano* either would not exist at all or else would lack power and influence. This is because the same technological developments in the "real world" which in the nineteenth and twentieth centuries spurred the composition of the one set of works gradually spurred the composition of the other. In both cases the issue is not simply the actual or potential impact of technological change upon society. It is also the unprecedented ability to bring about revolutionary social changes hitherto deemed "utopian" exactly because hitherto deemed "impossible." As Frank Manuel and other scholars of utopianism have observed, the conception of utopia moves from the "impossible" to the "possible" to the "probable."[18] But as political theorist George Kateb has aptly put it about dystopian critiques of technological change, "There is not, for the most part, skepticism about the capacity of modern technology and natural science to execute the most vaulting ambitions of utopianism; on the contrary, there is a dread it will."[19]

In addition to being part of these general Western traditions of technological utopianism and dystopianism, *Player Piano* exhibits distinct American strains within both. What makes these American strains distinct is not just the greater prospect for realizing utopias or dystopias in the United States as compared with Europe. (According to this notion, the United States is a potential paradise—or hell—to be brought about through technological change.) Rather, the distinction is also due to what I would characterize as the lesser creativity of American as compared with European writings. American utopias and dystopias alike are generally less imaginative—less enticing and less chilling—than their European counterparts, and not least in regard to technology. Most American technological utopias and dystopias are banal and outright dull, exemplifying, in Hannah Arendt's phrase, the banality of evil—or of good.

To be sure, Americans have usually been enthusiastic about technology, and more enthusiastic than Europeans. Although the absence of accurate polls of public opinion until the mid-twentieth century makes dogmatic pronouncements about earlier periods questionable, it is evident that the anxiety about technological advance that Leo Marx ascribes to America's foremost writers has generally failed to pervade other segments of the American population. Not surprisingly, there have been far fewer American technological dystopias than utopias. The most prominent of these include Mark Twain's *A Connecticut Yankee in King Arthur's Court* (1889), Ignatius Donnelly's *Caesar's Column* (1890), Jack London's *The Iron Heel* (1906), Bernard Wolfe's *Limbo* (1952), Ira Levin's *This Perfect Day* (1970), and portions of Henry Adams's *The Education of Henry Adams* (1907) and *The Degradation of the Democratic Dogma* (1919); plus, of course, *Player Piano* itself. These dystopias have, to repeat, been less frightening than their European counterparts (though certainly disturbing in themselves).

Although more numerous than the technological dystopias, the American technological utopias have likewise suffered by comparison with their European counterparts. The principal criticism invariably leveled against even so well written and well planned a work as *Looking Backward* is that life in that technological utopia would probably be less nightmarish than plain boring. And painfully few American utopian works of any stripe measure up to the style and content of that classic.

The banality of these American technological utopias and dystopias is nevertheless significant, and is not necessarily a liability. Their very banality makes many of them, including *Player Piano*, more believable and so more realistic than their more imaginative European counterparts. If, like *Player Piano*, they suffer from inadequate character and plot development, they do make the prospect of utopia or dystopia more probable than in those European works by providing a narrower gap between preutopia and utopia or dystopia. Moreover, the road to utopia or dystopia is often smoother in the American works than in the European ones. As Vonnegut puts it in the Foreword, "This book is not a book about what is, but a book about what could be"[20]—much as *Looking Backward* is a vision of a quite possible utopia from Bellamy's perspective.

These distinct American strains of technological utopianism and dystopianism clarify Hillegas's too casual comment about the greater realism of *Player Piano* as compared with the other dystopian writings he studied. Nearly all of the latter were written by Europeans and were more creative but less realistic than *Player Piano*. Being more realistic in these respects, *Player Piano* might, despite its humor, actually be a more nightmarish work than its European predecessors.

Player Piano has not had substantial influence as a work of social criticism. Vonnegut did not become a popular novelist until roughly fifteen years after this first novel appeared. Although writing the book prompted Vonnegut to quit his public relations job at GE, it sold only 3,500 copies initially, and he supported himself by writing short stories and popular pieces. Naturally the extraordinary popularity of his later works has generated unprecedented interest in his earlier ones. Still, *Player Piano* has more reflected than shaped attitudes about the early 1950s.

Insofar, however, as Americans' faith in unadulterated technological advance has finally declined, *Player Piano* may be praised for being prophetic if not influential. Equally important, to the degree that concerns for the fate of "technological society" have broadened—or narrowed—from totalitarianism and warfare to everyday life, the book may again be praised for being prophetic. The more sophisticated later critiques of the role of technological domination in everyday life by Jacques Ellul (*The Technological Society;* French, 1954; English, 1964), Herbert Marcuse (*One-Dimensional Man,* 1964), and Langdon Winner (*Autonomous Technology,* 1977), among others, confirm the foresight of Vonnegut in the early 1950s.

Vonnegut's refusal to propose escapism from technology and its problems is also commendable. Vonnegut scholars have often misunderstood the crucial point that the considerable nostalgia in *Player Piano* is for a *less* technological society rather than for a *non*technological society. Not the barely mechanized farm Paul abandons, but a building once used by Edison within the Works complex, the Building 58 he lovingly restores and periodically visits, represents Paul's—and presumably Vonnegut's—degree of nostalgia. Here was a pride in technological progress and in workmanship that was justified, unlike in the present. And here is where Paul and his then young fellow engineers themselves dreamed of perfecting the society they later rebelled against. Every society has had some forms of technology, and American society, Vonnegut understands, has historically been highly receptive to new forms. For Vonnegut it is as much an illusion that utopia—or, for that matter, any good society—can develop without technology as it is that technology is a panacea and the means to utopia. The problem remains more human nature than technology. Hence the reduction of technology and technological domination would not itself bring about utopia—any utopia.

The principal symbol of the book, the player piano in the Homestead bar, reflects Vonnegut's grasp of these issues. The player piano is a comparatively old and amusing mechanical device, dating back to the nineteenth century, and so a symbol of a supposedly happier and more innocent time. Yet it *is* a mechanical device and it *did* replace human finger and foot movements with holes punched on rolls of paper. Similarly, Rudy Hertz, the retired master machinist whose unexpected encounter in the bar with Paul stirs fond memories for both men, is himself a symbol of meaningful labor in a technological society. He epitomizes the kind of work carried out in traditional machine shops. Yet he recalls the past by putting a nickel in the piano and letting it play by itself. Moreover, young Hertz's wonderful—and to Paul, quite musical—hand movements on the lathe were themselves taped by Paul on another mechanical device, in Building 58, no less. Finally, Hertz himself was replaced by still another device, one operated by computer tape. He has become an idle worker and, as Hertz and Paul themselves admit, a living ghost. The question the player piano incident raises is not whether to live in a technological society but rather in what kind of technological society to live. That is an exceedingly difficult question to answer, but it is the proper question to raise if *Player Piano* is not to become a real-life dystopia.

Like the prophecies of numerous other technological utopias and dystopias, those of *Player Piano* have in many respects been borne out in subsequent events—and, as with those other works, frequently earlier than the author expected. For example, the breakup of the Soviet Union, which in many respects embodied the technological culture envisioned by Vonnegut, has brought about a degree of the American hegemony described in the novel and envisioned after World War II by Henry Luce and others. True, Vonnegut, unlike most other such visionaries, provides no specific date for the achievement of, in his case, technological dystopia. Moreover, he might not have had a date in mind but might instead have hoped that the publication of *Player Piano* would prevent at least some of the problems he describes. Yet rooting much of the story as he clearly does in his own time, the early 1950s, suggests a genuine concern on Vonnegut's part for the likelihood of *Player Piano* eventually becoming a real-life dystopia. Despite the collapse of the Soviet empire, the evolution of American society itself since *Player Piano* appeared amply justifies this concern. In this regard the comments of Huxley upon the republication of *Brave New World* in 1946 offer an interesting comparison: "All things considered it looks as though Utopia were far closer to us than anyone, only fifteen years ago, could have imagined. Then, I projected it six hundred years into the future. Today it seems quite possible that the horror may be upon us within a single century. That is, if we refrain from blowing ourselves to smithereens in the interval."[21]

Indeed, Vonnegut may have felt technological dystopia approaching. As historian David Noble has made abundantly clear in his 1984 study of the development of automatically controlled metal cutting machine tools after World War II, GE's record playback (R/P) system, which Vonnegut witnessed in its infancy, gave way to its principal alternative, numerical control (N/C), developed mostly by MIT engineers under contract to the U.S. Air Force, precisely because N/C gave skilled machinists none of the limited power and autonomy that R/P did. For R/P enabled machinists to determine the pace of their work and to modify it if necessary; N/C did not. Where R/P used prepunched paper tapes to run mechanical devices in ways similar to the player piano—capturing on tape the motions of machine tools run initially under manual control—N/C required computers programmed by mathematicians to punch tapes to run those devices. N/C was far more complex, expensive, and prone to breakdown than R/P; and it was suited, if at all, only to large firms (larger than most machine tool firms everywhere). But its appeal was that it shifted the locus of control from the shop floor to programmers and managers obedient to corporate commands. GE, for example, eventually adopted N/C despite its seven-year successful experiment with R/P. Ironically, N/C ultimately proved to be unpopular with corporate management for a variety of reasons, including its negligible effect on labor costs, and was rarely used until recently, when new computer technology made it more practical. Yet Vonnegut's concern with R/P was legitimate even if, as Noble details, R/P was not radical enough for the real-life managers and engineers who inspired him to write *Player Piano*. As Noble puts it, "Although Vonnegut's novel sounded an alarm about the dangers of automation in general, he blurred the distinction between R/P and more total forms of automation"[22] leading to the wholly automatic factory.

Not surprisingly, like Huxley and certain other prophets of technological dystopia, Vonnegut feels sad as well as anxious about the future. The sadness arises from their recognition that, contrary to the beliefs of prophets of technological utopia, technological progress has not meant and probably will never mean equivalent social progress. Rather, the relationship between the two may be partially antithetical. That technological achievements merely dreamed about for so many generations have not, when finally realized, brought about the expected widespread happiness and fulfillment is an irony richly appreciated by both Vonnegut and Huxley, among others. As the well-publicized letter bearing Paul Proteus's signature puts it, " 'Man has survived Armageddon in order to enter the Eden of eternal peace, only to discover that everything he had looked forward to enjoying there, pride, dignity, self-respect, work worth doing, has been condemned as unfit for human consumption.' "[23]

Significantly, as Vonnegut wrote Noble in 1977, some of the older managers and engineers on GE's R/P project were genuinely concerned about "the unhappiness that would be caused by automation. Their unease, in fact, inspired me to write *Player Piano*." But Vonnegut recalled no "negative talk" or "refusal to take part." For there persisted the then "universal belief that all technological advances were by definition good" and "that automation would get rid of dehumanizing work."[24] In this respect Vonnegut wrote *Player Piano* to begin to alter those naive assumptions about modern technology.

For Vonnegut and Huxley alike, technology itself is not, to repeat, the principal problem, which is instead human nature. Yet technology for both is nevertheless a very real and very complex problem, one that can hardly be wished away in the manner of some of technology's most avowedly "humanistic" critics. Apart from altering human nature, as with *Brave New World*'s test-tube babies, the solution for Vonnegut is somehow to live happily and humanely in our pervasively technological society. *Player Piano* provides no blueprint for achieving this kind of good society. But in formulating the issue as such it contributes notably to the possible design of that society.

11

LEWIS MUMFORD'S

ALTERNATIVES TO

THE MEGAMACHINE:

CRITICAL UTOPIANISM,

REGIONALISM, AND

DECENTRALIZATION

. . . .

In a collection of autobiographical reflections published in 1975, Lewis Mumford (1895–1990) confessed to a belated but still fundamental insight about the evolution not merely of technology but of civilization overall:

> Very late in my own development, I discovered what any number of more gifted minds should have discovered long before; namely, that the basic ideology which pervaded the Western mind at the beginning of the [twentieth] century was only a scientifically dressed-up justification for the immemorial practices of the ruling classes—historically attested in Egypt, Babylonia, Assyria, Peru, and indeed, wherever the archetypal megamachine was in control. The dominant institutions of our time, far from being new, were all in the thrall of a myth that was at least five thousand years old. Only one value was acknowledged, and that one was taken for granted: the reality of power in all its forms, from sun power to military power, from manpower to steam power, from cannon power to money power, from machine power and computer power to sex power. . . . The meaning of life was reduced to accelerating movement and change, and nothing else remained. Behold the ultimate religion of our seemingly rational age—the myth of the machine! Bigger and bigger, more and more, farther and farther. . . .[1]

Although the megamachine, as Mumford termed it, embraced more than technology, it reached its culmination in twentieth-century technology and its extraordinary social, economic, cultural, and psychological dimensions.

This chapter will explore the alternatives to the megamachine that Lewis Mumford offered in *Technics and Civilization* (1934), *The Culture of Cities* (1938), *The Myth of the Machine* (1967, 1970; both volumes), and other writings. The chapter will not detail Mumford's familiar descriptions and criticisms of the increasingly powerful and deterministic megamachine as it has evolved over time.[2] Instead, after briefly examining Mumford's ambivalence about technology and mankind's future, I will focus upon his three principal alternatives to it: utopian thought used as social criticism; regional communities and economies; and decentralized living and working arrangements. I will argue that far from being separate alternatives, the three are closely related, and that far from being alternatives suggested at varying stages of Mumford's work, they appear throughout. In addition, I will seek to demonstrate that Mumford is a key bridge figure between the Western utopian tradition and the other philosophical and practical proponents of decentralization and regionalism, ranging from Edward Bellamy and Henry Ford to Patrick Geddes and Howard Odum[3] to E. F. Schumacher and Alvin Toffler.

Mumford is generally ambivalent about technology and mankind's future. Despite his readily acknowledged growing pessimism about the future from *Technics and Civilization* to *The Myth of the Machine*, he retains a degree of optimism. Unlike such critics as Jacques Ellul, whose *The Technological Society* (1964) epitomizes pessimism, Mumford continues to believe that mankind can reexert control over technology. Where Ellul's writings logically have no purpose beyond provoking despair about the future, Mumford's, even at their most pessimistic, ask readers to try to change contemporary "technological society" (a term ironically popularized by the English mistranslation of Ellul's 1954 original French work, *La Technique*).[4] Mumford never sees technology as wholly autonomous, omnipotent, and so enslaving in the way Ellul does, despite the growth of the megamachine. To Mumford, technology is not a Frankensteinian monster come to life, as it is for Ellul (and many other contemporary social critics). Rather, it remains a human invention that mankind can yet reclaim and redirect. As Mumford says as late as *The Pentagon of Power* (*The Myth of the Machine: II*), technology has been changed by human beings as much as it has changed them, and, in any event, our principal purpose is not to master technology (or nature) but to improve ourselves. As he insists in that otherwise bleak work, individuals can still refuse to accept the "Power System." They do have a choice.

Consequently, Mumford disavows the title of "prophet of doom" increasingly ascribed to him following publication of *The Myth of the Machine*. In a letter to historian of technology Melvin Kranzberg following the latter's mixed review of *Technics and Human Development* (*The Myth of the Machine: I*), Mumford insists that he has never considered himself "a prophet, still less . . . a prophet of doom. On the contrary, the whole effort of my work is to diagnose, at an early stage, the conditions that may, if they are uncorrected, undermine our civilization."[5] This disavowal of prophecy is surely less than convincing. Yet Mumford's implicit endorsement here of the jeremiad as a means of spurring change and so saving mankind from an otherwise inevitable fall relates to his general notion of utopianism, about which more shortly.

Given his overall ambivalence, Mumford understandably likewise resents being characterized as an outright opponent of modern technology akin to Ellul. He defends himself against such charges, arguing that his works try to demonstrate that modern society must accept technology as an integral element "capable of serving beauty as well as productivity."[6] Although this defense may be true in many respects, Mumford certainly writes about transcending technology and about creating a healthier biological and social environment, as in *The Culture of Cities*: "The cycle of the machine is now coming to an end. . . . [W]e can no more continue to live in the world of the machine than we could live successfully on the barren surface of the moon."[7]

Regarding utopianism, Mumford is both less ambivalent and more consistent than he is about technology: he believes not in the possibility of genuine utopias, in the sense of literally perfect societies, but rather in the utility of utopias. He allows that, whether as written blueprints or as actual communities, utopias can change existing societies. I call this alternative "critical utopianism." Mumford deems true believers in utopianism of any variety as either naive regarding human nature or overt/covert authoritarians wishing to force conformity to one ideal. (He cites William Morris's *News from Nowhere* [1890]—itself an avowed reaction to and attempted refutation of Bellamy's *Looking Backward*—as an exception to the latter generalization.) Mumford also appreciates the danger of stagnation in proposing an unchanging utopian ideal, however attractive it may be in a particular time and place. New and unanticipated social and material conditions require variety. This is a lesson appreciated by Vonnegut, for example, but lost on Bellamy. As Mumford aptly puts it and then proves, "Fashions Change in Utopia."[8]

Consequently, and to his credit, Mumford refuses to suggest that the garden city scheme of Ebenezer Howard and others, his own preference, be the sole model for cities, towns, and regions in America, Britain, or elsewhere. He is also enthusiastic about small organic communities of the past, like medieval Oxford and Siena, which can still provide models. Moreover, Mumford's zeal for garden cities was qualified by his visits in the 1950s to the British garden cities or New Towns, so far removed were they from his and Howard's ideals—further evidence of the imperfectibility of societies.[9]

In his autobiographical writings, Mumford confesses to having shared, in his youth, the common optimism of pre–World War I America and Europe: "That the March of Progress would in fact lead to worldwide calamity and catastrophe was something the Age of Confidence never saw as the most remote eventuality."[10] Having long ago abandoned that innocence, he has only scorn for those who persist in such ungrounded beliefs and in turn expect us to join them in their self-destructive folly, that is, their various utopian schemes.

Despite these reservations about genuine utopias, Mumford appreciates the fact that by definition they treat most if not all aspects of life, from economics to education to leisure. To this extent, they reflect the organic wholeness (if not the balance) he advocates for "real world" living. Mumford nevertheless properly reads past utopian efforts as telling us less about the future than about the time and place in which they were written or devised. In a manner akin to German philosopher Ernst Bloch, he sees the unrealized and perhaps unrecognized "potentialities"[11] in societies—and in their past—as constituting their legitimate utopian aspirations. Utopian schemes thereby illuminate these potentials and, ideally, help effect positive changes or at least suggest alternatives to existing plans and directions. For Mumford, then, utopian visions are not ends in themselves but means to improving existing society—just like his own jeremiads. He prefers utopias of reconstruction to utopias of escape. If, as he proclaims repeatedly in his writings, life is invariably more interesting and "better than utopia,"[12] its improvement can nonetheless be spurred through such serious utopian schemes. As he puts it in his first book, *The Story of Utopias* (1922), "I have . . . no private utopia . . . for life has still too many potentialities to be encompassed by the projects of a single generation, by the hopes and beliefs of a single thinker." Hence "my utopia is actual life, here or anywhere, pushed to the limits of its ideal possibilities."[13]

Mumford recognizes that the gap between prophecy and fulfillment in so many earlier utopian schemes is now closed and that, as others have argued, the danger is that utopias are all too real, all too capable of realization.[14] For example, Mumford, in 1931, considers that *Looking Backward* "has worn better than perhaps any other nineteenth-century utopia." Bellamy's "picture of utopia is very much like that of the United States in the last months of the [First] World War."[15] Far from heralding this fact, though, Mumford laments it, just as he later does more contemporary technological utopian visions such as those of limited nuclear war and unlimited space colonies. The real gap in *Looking Backward,* he suggests, is the "breach between Bellamy's conception of the good life and the structure he erected to shelter it,"[16] which Mumford deems overly mechanical. The same criticism holds for at least some of those more recent visions of the good life.

Equally important, and probably more original, is Mumford's discussion in *The Pentagon of Power* of the role of utopian writings from Bacon's *New Atlantis* on in providing "ideological preparation"[17] and support for the emerging megamachine to ease its path to dominance. To be sure, Mumford recognizes that few utopian works have had direct concrete influence on any mass movements. Even *Looking Backward,* as I have argued elsewhere, was, despite its enormous sales and popularity, less a major factor in American reform than a reflection of contemporary problems that were addressed more directly by various political and social movements.[18] Mumford contends that indirectly and collectively, these and other utopian writings have had considerable influence. Despite the extreme difficulty of documenting this kind of intellectual power, I would agree. "Utopia," claims Mumford, "is the secret destination of the invisible, all-embracing megamachine. . . . Anyone who had read the literature of utopias during the past two centuries would have had a far better idea of the 'shape of things to come' than a newspaper reader who sedulously followed the random reports of events from day to day."[19]

Mumford further argues that, thanks to the domination of the megamachine, it has become increasingly more difficult to conceive of alternatives to the very world anticipated by Bellamy and other nineteenth- and twentieth-century utopians. Simultaneously, it has become ever more necessary to do so, using utopian (and science fiction) writings to anticipate and try to halt "the future." This is imperative because scientists, inventors, and administrators now have advanced facilities that "have inflated their most sinister technological fantasies and given their projectors a freedom from sensible inhibitions hitherto enjoyed only in the form of nocturnal dreams."[20] Once again, Mumford is hardly alone in his insights, and his analyses here lack the intellectual depth of those of, say, social critic Herbert Marcuse in *One-Dimensional Man* (1964) and other works.[21] But his understanding of the complex and ongoing relationship between utopianism and the megamachine is well founded.

In this light, Mumford has justified contempt for contemporary self-proclaimed utopians like Buckminster Fuller ("that interminable tape recorder of 'salvation by technology' ")[22] and Arthur C. Clarke who ignore history and human nature alike and whose technocratic solutions to fundamentally nontechnocratic problems are shallow, inadequate, and, ironically, unscientific (if not also authoritarian). In addition to criticizing Fuller's plans for cities under gigantic geodesic domes or on huge floating megastructures as excessively large, impersonal, and dehumanizing, he rejects proposed space rockets and colonies on similar grounds—but also as unjustified escapes from terrestrial problems. As early as *Technics and Civilization* he draws parallels between the Egyptian pyramids and early space rockets as expensive megamachines carrying a selected few to seeming paradise, thanks to the labor of untold thousands. In *The Myth of the Machine* he extends the analogy by deeming both huge tombs. Reacting to Clarke's published criticisms of this position, Mumford writes in 1975: "What you [Clarke] call 'life-enhancing' I would characterize as life-cheating or life-defeating—though [yours is] not quite so absurd as Buckminster Fuller's characterization of a space capsule as an ideal environment."[23]

Consequently, Mumford refuses to join the ranks of contemporary futurists. His correspondence with Edward Cornish, president of the World Future Society, is revealing: He refuses to be included in a proposed directory of "individuals active in the futures field" because his concept of the future is allegedly so different from theirs. He claims that where they "conceive of the future as a separate realm from the past and the present," in his scheme "past, present, and future form a continuum that is constantly in process of change." In truth many serious futurists do not make these artificial distinctions, though such prominent futurists as Toffler and John Naisbitt certainly do, as detailed in the final chapter. Moreover, Mumford claims to be less concerned with predicting the future, in questionable contrast again with all contemporary futurists, than with "the continuing process of reacting to the future, in order to take measures to control or arrest forces that threaten the ecological balance of living organisms, and the mental balance of those who equate scientific intelligence with godlike power over all terrestrial phenomena."[24] Hence the significance once again of his half-prophetic jeremiads.

Although Mumford's ideal environment remains the garden city, he is always equally concerned about improving existing communities of all kinds. As early as *The Story of Utopias*, he argues that any future utopias—or, more realistically, any merely good societies—can and should use various modern transportation and communications systems to improve their local communities and to reduce their isolation and parochialism. He contends that if the inhabitants of our would-be utopias will "conduct their daily affairs in a possibly more limited environment than that of the great metropolitan centers, their mental environment will not be localized or nationalized."[25] For unprecedented advances in science and technology have made possible this balance between isolation and engagement. Yet he displays no less concern for keeping local cultures intact amidst internal and external changes alike. Even at this point Mumford recognizes and decries the growing homogeneity of cultures, thanks to the same technological advances that make different cultures accessible in the first place. Technology, he realizes, can be as much a problem as a solution to problems.

Equally important, Mumford is a lifetime advocate of regionalism. As early as *The Story of Utopias*, he embraces regionalism, not as an intellectual abstraction or social imposition but as a welcome fact of life that deserves both recognition and expansion.[26] As in his later, longer writings on regionalism, so here he refuses to specify strict boundaries of size or population (lest regional identity be determined arbitrarily) but instead emphasizes those organic qualities that, more than com-

munications and transportation networks, allegedly hold regions together. Yet in this initial work as in subsequent publications he endorses
comprehensive and "scientific" regional surveys as practical means of
achieving such genuine regionalism. "This common tissue of definite,
verifiable, localized knowledge," he claims, "is what all our partisan
utopias and reconstruction programs have lacked; and lacking it, have
been one-sided and ignorant and abstract—devising paper programs
for the reconstruction of a paper world."[27] Although Mumford does not
deal explicitly with decentralization until later works, the connection
between it and regionalism is already implicit here: regionalism presumes a degree of geographical dispersion from a centralized nation, as
does his emphasis on "localized knowledge."

The volumes on American culture that followed *The Story of Utopias* in the 1920s provide examples from the nineteenth century of the
kind of integrated and balanced culture that Mumford sought in his own
day through regional planning and other deliberate means. His (romanticized) portraits in those books of New England and New York as once
flourishing regions offer interesting comparisons with his later visions of
regionalism in twentieth-century America. He argues that the first two
hundred years of American coastal development saw economic resources being used "with thrift and intelligence" while "industries and
communities were in a state of balance." This produced the "integrated
regional life"[28] of New England and New York his earlier books describe. To his credit, however, Mumford engages in limited nostalgia
and in his writings of the 1930s and 1940s on regionalism generally looks
ahead, not backward. Ironically, though, several reviews of *Technics
and Civilization* chided Mumford for his supposedly "utopian" belief in
the efficacy of economic and social planning.[29]

Whether that criticism is accurate or not, Mumford *has* veered
toward the utopianism he otherwise disavows in his implicit equation of
regionalism with organicism and in turn of organicism with the good
society. Much of his writing depicts regional networks of organic communities as so superior to any others as to constitute de facto utopias.
And this applies not only to similarly envisioned future communities
but also to actual past ones, especially those of the Middle Ages, when
life was supposedly in balance. Although Mumford once again is not
overly nostalgic, he does fall into the common trap of the organic/me-
chanic dichotomy: he separates whole eras and societies into one or the

other of these simplistic, biased, ahistorical sociological categories and describes history as a repeated shifting between them.

Moreover, so given is Mumford to these categories that his overall optimism regarding the world's future, as in *The Culture of Cities* (1938), or pessimism, as in *The Pentagon of Power*, is heavily shaped by his prior assessment of whether modern society is becoming more organic (good) or mechanical (bad). As he puts it in the former work, as long as the mechanical order "was uppermost, people thought quantitatively in terms of expansion, extension, progress, mechanical multiplication, power. With the organism uppermost we begin to think qualitatively in terms of growth, norms, shapes, inter-relationships, implications, associations, and societies. . . . Once established, the vital and social [organic] order must subsume the mechanical one, and dominate it: in practice as well as in thought."[30] In reality, societies of whatever kind usually represent some mixture of the two categories, and organic qualities are not necessarily superior to mechanical qualities, and vice versa. But those kinds of complexities do not engage readers or attract followers as readily as the dichotomy Mumford provides.[31]

Mumford's notion of desirable regionalism thus depends on modern technology but is not, of course, itself technocratic in nature. As he concedes in *The Culture of Cities*, regionalism, like utopianism, is a relative term devoid of meaning until filled in with specific contents—which, for Mumford, include not just geographical and population size and economic base but also environmental quality, cultural opportunities, and other nonquantifiable conditions. Although he advocates no particular scheme, Mumford does favor a balance between agriculture and industry and between open and developed spaces. He rejects the concept of satellite cities, even when composed of garden cities, if it entails a hierarchy rather than an equality of such communities.

Mumford's correspondence in the late 1930s with agrarian renewal proponent George Weller illuminates his belief in a variety of work and leisure settings. He criticizes Weller for "making the notion of domestic production and partial industrial and agricultural self-sufficiency the only possible pattern for future economic change or for urban planning. . . . [F]ar from denying it," Mumford continues, "I have followed it for three years, at least to the extent of running a garden that keeps us provided with vegetables the better part of the year. . . . But it does not seem to me that this pattern of life is necessarily the only valid one;

indeed, my own needs and those of my family are now sending me back to New York again for the winter months. . . . [I]t seems to me that the sort of integration that has been achieved in Radburn and Greenbelt is also worth working for." As Mumford concludes, "you have a far greater bias against collective undertakings than I have against your individualist program. . . . I don't think the apartment is or can be the only type of urban home; but I would not rule it out altogether, as you appear to do—forgetting the existence of bachelors, of childless people, of people who have entered old age, and again of those whose work may temporarily sequester them from active participation in rural industry and rural life."[32]

Mumford's notion of desirable regionalism, whatever its particular manifestations, invariably includes some degree of decentralization. By decentralization he means physically smaller as well as geographically dispersed entities connected to one another in some form of regional network. In *Technics and Civilization* Mumford cites Henry Ford's then ongoing "village industry" experiments as representing the kind of decentralization on a regional scale that he favors. These nineteen modest-sized but quite modern automobile plants in impoverished rural communities were generally (and unfairly) dismissed as either expensive public-relations ventures or subtle union-busting efforts or both.[33] By contrast, and without ever apologizing for Ford's overall labor policies—or politics—Mumford grasps the importance to technology's future direction of transferring the production and assembly processes of certain automobile parts out of the huge Highland Park and River Rouge facilities, the epitome of industrial centralization, to a growing regional network of such avowedly decentralized plants, none of them more than sixty miles from Ford headquarters in Dearborn.

In fact, in *The Culture of Cities* Mumford concedes that prior industrial decentralization schemes, usually in the form of conventional branch plants far away from major ones, have invariably been motivated by either the quest for higher profits or the desire to destroy unions or both. And in that same work he laments the general absence of small-scale, decentralized industries—and, for that matter, of garden cities promoting and sustaining them—from the then-emerging Tennessee Valley Authority (TVA), the epitome of planned regionalism that drew unqualified praise from so many in its early years. Mumford argues that industrial decentralization can be as efficient and as profitable as traditional centralization. Thus "bigger no longer automatically means better," he writes in *Technics and Civilization;* "flexibility of the power unit, closer adaptation of means to ends, nicer timing of operation, are the new marks of efficient industry."[34] Ironically, in a generally favorable review of *Technics and Civilization,* the *New York Times* gently criticized Mumford for not pursuing this further: "There are signs that neotechnic industry will decentralize itself—a possibility that Mr. Mumford does not seem to have considered. With decentralization will go the slums, the diseases of the city, the evils of overcrowding, all that he righteously attacks. . . . And with the possibility of decentralization and a return to the small community comes also the possibility of rational city planning, a subject on which he has written in the past."[35]

Equally important, in both *The Culture of Cities* and *The Pentagon of Power* Mumford sees decentralization in its very diversity and organic qualities as a practical alternative to the uniformity and conformity of "machine civilization." That the former book waxes lyrical about the liberating qualities of electric power lines, aluminum, radios, automobiles, superhighways, and airplanes—as did so many others in the 1930s—does not quite constitute inconsistency; for Mumford, after all, writes in that same work of transcending technology and creating a healthier biological and social environment. Consequently, in both works he sees decentralization as a movement looking to the future, not to the past. And in the latter book, published soon after dozens of Third World countries had gained their independence from European powers, he views decentralized revolts before independence as possible rejections of Western technological—not merely political and cultural—domination, though this has rarely been the case.

Mumford is more accurate and more insightful in refusing to equate the spatial decentralization of such (international, not merely regional) schemes as Marshall McLuhan's "global village" and Toffler's "electronic cottages" with decentralized decision-making and so democracy. (Toffler's vision is explored in the final chapter.) He recognizes the likelihood of decisions continuing to be made from the top and in turn of forced compliance with them. In addition, Mumford demonstrates that he anticipated McLuhan by thirty years—only to have voiced skepticism back in 1934 about the alleged virtues of instantaneous communications insofar as distance of both time and space may be necessary for good judgments and decisions. Moreover, genuine communications may require a common language, if not a common culture.[36] In *The Pentagon of Power* Mumford applies these qualifications about modern communications and transportation systems to computers, whose potential for misuse and abuse he readily recognizes. He therefore calls for decentralized decision-making rather than "remote control."[37]

Curiously, Mumford himself has not always practiced decentralized decision-making or democratic planning. Instead, he has often been as guilty of elitism in this respect as those he repeatedly condemns, albeit with more humane and less technocratic motivations than most of them. In a patrician manner he has often decided what is in the best interest of ordinary citizens, whose views are largely missing from his writings. Moreover, Mumford himself has also relied upon an elite of architects, planners, social critics, and even engineers to effect his vision, at least on paper. In this regard, Mumford's 1933 essay "If I Were Dictator" is revealing. In it he calls for greater regionalism, economic and geographical decentralization, environmental concern, and cultural uplift. He declares: "we must recover the human scale." But he also calls for greater planning, "discipline," and "rehabilitation" from the top down in a manner akin to Bellamy's *Looking Backward* and other schemes he elsewhere rejects on those very grounds.[38] Hence one must be cautious about taking too literally his 1937 pronouncement that "planning demands for its success not an authoritarian society but a society in which free thought and voluntary action and experimental effort still play a major part in its existence."[39] Like former TVA director David Lilienthal, whose popular *TVA: Democracy on the March* (1944) created an image of decentralized "grass-roots democracy" contradicted by the organization's actual practices, including Lilienthal's own, Mumford, had he his way, would not necessarily have practiced what he preached.[40]

In conclusion, for Mumford, decentralization and regionalism are not panaceas and do not provide the royal road to utopia.[41] Nor does Mumford believe in the prospect of any utopia anywhere. Instead, he values utopias as means of criticizing, and so trying to change, existing societies. Nevertheless, decentralization, regionalism, and even critical utopianism can offer supposedly practical alternatives to the megamachine, the antiutopian or dystopian "technological society" that drives Ellul to despair but that Mumford still somehow hopes to eliminate. Mumford's jeremiads, from *The Story of Utopias* on, have obviously failed to accomplish this, as he is painfully aware in later writings. As he laments in 1975, "It seems to me that, on the basis of rational calculations, derived from what must admittedly be incomplete evidence, if the forces that now dominate us continue on their present path they must lead to collapse of the whole historical fabric, not just this or that great nation or empire."[42] Yet his major works have surely made readers—and sometimes policymakers—much more sensitive to the need for "human scale"[43] in individual buildings, whole cities, towns, regions, and entire nations. His desire for human scale carries over to all of his areas of social concern and integrates them. To this extent his lifelong efforts were hardly in vain. He is indeed a key bridge figure between the Western utopian tradition and the twentieth century's other philosophical and practical proponents of decentralization and regionalism.

IV

HIGH-TECH

CULTURE

RECONSIDERED

12

HIGH TECH AND THE

BURDEN OF HISTORY;

OR, THE MANY IRONIES

OF CONTEMPORARY

TECHNOLOGICAL

OPTIMISM

. . . .

If the 1991 Persian Gulf War quickly rekindled the long-dormant spirit of technological utopianism throughout America, that spirit has certainly faded amid lingering postwar questions over the actual efficiency of America's computerized weapons systems (as well as, of course, over the long-term political, economic, social, and environmental costs of the conflict). It would be simplistic, however, to assume that technological utopianism is once again dormant, much less dead. Just the opposite is the case, as elaborated here. "High tech" has for many years now waged an elaborate campaign on several fronts to revitalize the spirit—and, no less important, the values—of technological utopianism, not only in the United States but also abroad. Among these values is a peculiar, sometimes contradictory stance toward the past. The apparent failure of the Gulf War's high-tech weapons systems to prove as decisive or as reliable as initially believed has undermined but hardly ended this campaign.[1]

Before analyzing that campaign, it is necessary to define "high tech," a term used occasionally earlier in the book. In general, high tech can be broadly defined as computers, satellite communications, robotics, space travel, genetic engineering, and other post–World War II technologies. True, other, less glitzy technologies have emerged since 1945—in the chemical industry, for example. I exclude them not because they are less significant but because commonly accepted notions of high tech exclude them. More precisely, high tech is usually contrasted with traditional dirty, large-scale manufacturing and power facilities through its greater cleanliness and efficiency and its smaller size as well as through its allegedly "paperless" communications systems. High tech fits neatly within the framework of a contemporary postindustrial society, given high-tech industries' foundation on information collection, analysis, and distribution.

Admittedly, "high tech" itself is a relative term applicable to earlier periods, not least the prior industrial revolution of large-scale factories. Just as technology has been present to some degree in every society, so numerous prior eras have had their own "cutting edge" technologies. A 1935 article by David Cushman Coyle, a consulting engineer, contains the earliest reference I have found to high tech. Significantly, Coyle pleads for the decentralization of large-scale factories.[2] Still, contemporary high tech has its own particular identity and self-image and can be used without apology.

So defined, contemporary high tech has been and remains a notable exception to the perception of technology in much of the modern world as having gradually shifted from a social solution to a social question. High tech, by contrast, embodies and promotes otherwise largely discarded beliefs in progress per se and in the causal connection between technological progress and social progress. "Star Wars" is perhaps the foremost example of this persistent strain of technological utopianism associated with high tech, but it is hardly the only one, as the Persian Gulf War weapons systems example makes clear. High tech, in fact, appears not only as optimistic about the future as, but also more indifferent toward and, in other respects, more manipulative of the past than earlier technologies have been. Indeed, high tech is eager to proclaim itself the supreme technological revolution while enjoying an unprecedented ability to articulate and spread its message, thanks to the very communications and transportation systems it exalts.

But this unqualified faith in the future, unlike that of earlier technological utopians, is only a facade. Behind it is a largely unacknowledged ambivalence about the future and, equally important, a sometimes desperate desire to connect to the past for intellectual legitimacy—even when this means, paradoxically, manipulation of the past or seeming contempt for it. In this context, I will examine four leading ways in which high tech, misusing and abusing as well as ignoring history, promotes high tech's products and its ideology: prophecies, advertising, world's fairs/theme parks, and the technological literacy crusade. However diverse these phenomena, they are linked by a common vision of technological utopia or at least of high tech's notion of the "good society."

I

High tech has spawned a new generation of technological utopians whose principal allegiance is not to the public sector, unlike earlier such visionaries, but to the private; whose favored institution is not big government but the big corporation; and whose principal motivation is not serious social change but personal gain—or prophecy for profits' sake. Once the province of generally well-intentioned if often fumbling amateurs, technological forecasting has become an increasingly big business, populated by "professionals." Their clients are generally major corporations plus those government agencies and educational institutions that can afford their enormous consulting fees. These forecasters' success is a tribute to the spirit of free enterprise they espouse, and it is hardly surprising that their overall message is resolutely optimistic, no matter if things seem to be going in wrong directions. These high-tech prophets insist that to the extent to which they are considered, most national and international problems will be solved through ever more and better technology and through the sheer determination to use it decisively.

The most popular high-tech prophets, though hardly the only ones, are Alvin Toffler and John Naisbitt. It is a measure of high tech's underlying ambivalence about the future that their respective messages, however different, are so passionately embraced as gospel by business and professional people above all. They need the reassurance these best-selling prophecies amply provide. High tech dearly wants to be told that its products and services are bringing the world closer to some kind of utopia.

Like most earlier technological utopians, Toffler and Naisbitt largely extrapolate from today to tomorrow while showing painfully limited interest in yesterday. Yet, as with their predecessors, it is the unacknowledged past that invariably provides the actual basis of these contemporary prophecies, whether as the extrapolation source or as the supposed contrast with the great age ahead. Try as they may, they can never escape history's grasp.

Toffler has written and edited several books about the future, the most popular of which are *Future Shock* (1970), *The Third Wave* (1980), and *Powershift* (1990), each neatly appearing at the start of a new decade. *Future Shock* was published five years after Toffler coined the term while writing an article. It was the first futurist best-seller.[3] In those five years he visited people and places concerned with change and coping behavior. The term "future shock" is variously defined in his book, but in general it means the cumulative effects of the acceleration of change on individuals and societies and the limitations to the amount of change that ordinary persons can absorb in a short time. It is a form of culture shock applied more to time than to space. According to Toffler, an unending number of changes in everyday life—enormous technological advances, information overload, immense diversity of choices and decisions, instability of human relationships, intensive urbanization, instant communications—have created an unprecedented "collision with the future." Future shock is the dizziness brought on by "the premature arrival of the future."[4] How the future can arrive ahead of schedule is beyond me. The more interesting point, however, is the consequent separation of the future from the past and in turn the irrelevance of history to present and future alike.

At first glance, Toffler's description of the contemporary world, written in the breathless prose of *Time* magazine in its heyday (he once worked at *Fortune*), is rather depressing to contemplate. Toffler has taken the concept of "cultural lag" identified with sociologist William Ogburn (whom he characteristically simplifies and distorts) to an absurd degree. Ogburn suggested that disequilibrium results from the slow speed with which nonmaterial culture adapts itself to technological advances. Neither personally nor organizationally, Toffler contends, can existing means of adaptability to change save us. Rather, we need new ways of looking at and responding to the future at hand and, not surprisingly, new visionaries to guide us to the better world ahead. Toffler, of course, is happily available to save the world from "massive adaptational breakdown."[5] (Jargon like this runs throughout all of Toffler's works and, even for his many admirers, invariably becomes a barrier to the readability he otherwise seeks and achieves.)

Among other things, Toffler recommends that individuals turn off sensory stimuli and maintain personal stability zones, or patterns of relative constancy. In specific terms, this means, for example, turning on air conditioners to lower street noise, seeking silence on deserted beaches, traveling less, keeping clothes and cars for additional years, and reorganizing companies, churches, and community groups less often. For societies he suggests the reform of education and the control of technology. Schools must cease preparing their students for the past, for the world of the nineteenth-century industrial revolution, and must instead literally teach the future. Information that will be useless for the future should simply be forgotten, and that presumably includes the information gleaned from history, or history altogether. Significantly, Toffler rarely mentions and barely criticizes advertising as a major cause of future shock, with its endless creation of artificial wants.

Lest I misrepresent his position on technology, Toffler here as in later writings is no technological pessimist. Far from it! He despises the so-called antitechnologists allegedly epitomized by Jacques Ellul, Erich Fromm, Herbert Marcuse, and Lewis Mumford. Modern technology, he argues, is the great "engine of change" in societies and the foremost guarantor of much of our freedom, particularly our freedom of choice and of diversity. "It is only primitive technology," he claims, "that imposes standardization." No technological plateau for him. Similarly, Toffler rejects as "myth" the vision of future "man as a helpless cog in some vast organizational machine." Instead, bureaucracy will vanish, replaced by "ad-hocracy"—short-term, professional, problem-solving task forces.[6]

The fact that untold individuals and societies throughout history have, despite enormous challenges and costs, adapted to changes as profound and as accelerated in their own day as those Toffler details for the 1970s naturally is of no interest to him; for then he would have precious little originality save perhaps regarding specific recommended adaptations to high tech. And the equally important fact that all technological developments, whether beneficial or harmful, are the products of human actions and decisions and not autonomous forces, is likewise something Toffler needs to ignore in order to sell his argument. Moreover, his predicted "death of permanence" hardly means the end of history and might be turned around to justify accelerated historical study just to keep track of so many changes and to contribute to the "soft landing" on the future he seeks.[7]

At the outset of *Future Shock* Toffler makes a brief, carefully low-key disclaimer that can be applied to his later writings as well:

. . . I have taken the liberty of speaking firmly, without hesitation, trusting that the intelligent reader will understand the stylistic problem. The word "will" should always be read as though it were preceded by "probably" or "in my opinion." Similarly, all dates applied to future events need to be taken with a grain of judgment.[8]

This is hardly a mere "stylistic" issue, but it is certainly a problem. Like so many other "scientific" futurists, Toffler thereby qualifies his predictions, not only to avoid being wrong but also to concede his apparent ambivalence about the future. However plentiful his statistics, examples, and jargon, his prophecies are anything but guaranteed. Yet he wants his readers and other audiences to go along with the traditional American positive thinking that helps account for his works' popularity (and that places them in proper historical context). Positive thinking has the wonderful advantage, especially to the business and professional people in a position to alter the world, to substitute willpower and self-improvement for the fundamental economic, social, political, and other changes that one might innocently assume essential to avert lasting future shock.

True, Toffler advocates continuing popular plebiscites on the future ("social future assemblies") and the elimination of traditional technological planning—not that technological planning, much less the social planning that should accompany it, has a long or popular history in the United States. Like Naisbitt, Toffler places unlimited faith in the capacity of mass communications, including television and computers, to liberate individuals and to invigorate democracy. Such faith was as clearly misplaced in 1970 as it is today. Toffler's failure to discuss political power in America and its future distribution is as revealing as anything else of his ironic actual commitment in *Future Shock* to at least the political status quo. The "anticipatory democracy" he forecasts may thus remain a pipe dream.[9]

Like all good futurists, Toffler actually deals with the present and the past as much as the future, his denials notwithstanding. "Future shock," to the extent it exists, is really "present shock." Paradoxically, so much contemporary upheaval should logically restrain, not prompt, serious speculation about tomorrow, lest further change undermine the prescriptions offered at the present moment. This is or should be the price to be paid for the unprecedented acceleration Toffler insists we accept as reality. But he chooses not to pay it.

In *Future Shock* Toffler does allow for one small use of history: as respite from the present and the future. He argues on behalf of "living museums" where people could, in effect, take a holiday from change.

For example, "children from the outside world might spend a few months in a simulated feudal village, living and actually working as children did centuries ago."[10] That "living history museums" already exist in the United States and elsewhere is something Toffler apparently is unaware of. The more telling point is his indifference to anything such museums might teach us, including just how fast or slow life really was in earlier times; Toffler obviously assumes it was profoundly slow. Ironically, though, he again cannot escape the past despite manipulating it for his own purposes.

At first glance, *The Third Wave* is more historically grounded, treating as it does the whole of history. The First Wave began about 8000 B.C., when roving bands of hunters, having learned to till the soil, settled in villages. It lasted until the Industrial Revolution of about A.D. 1650–1750. The Second Wave, which gave us the industrialized, standardized society that most of us grew up in, is itself giving way to the postindustrial Third Wave, which could last forever if only people listened to sages like Toffler. Among the Third Wave's characteristics are an increased emphasis on leisure, the decline of the nuclear family, the replacement of outdated political institutions and processes, and the growing use of genetic engineering. As in *Future Shock*, Toffler happily views technology as deterministic. Computers, word processors, and microprocessors are the 1980s' "engines of change." In fact, the Third Wave, still more than future shock, is beyond human control. "In a great historical confluence," Toffler contends, "many raging rivers of change are running together to form an oceanic Third Wave of change that is gaining momentum with every passing hour."[11] Where *Future Shock* emphasized the cost of rapid change, *The Third Wave* emphasizes the cost of not changing rapidly enough.

True, the Third Wave will utilize technology to create a new society combining some aspects of both of its predecessors. This includes the ability to work at home or nearby in high-tech "electronic cottages" reminiscent of the First Wave; decentralized and "demassified" customized production derived from Second Wave centralized mass production, and the restoration of producers and consumers, divorced in the Second Wave, into "prosumers" recalling the First Wave.[12] But the Third Wave will not celebrate any legacies of its predecessors; it will instead wash them out into oblivion. The real possibility that new technologies will reinforce rather than subvert the status quo never occurs to Toffler. Meanwhile the transitions to the Third Wave will generate tensions and, if we are foolish, conflict and perhaps self-destruction. Those with vested interests in the Second Wave will fight fiercely against the inevitable. Yet the eventual outcome is, of course, positive, if mankind changes its ways.

To his credit, Toffler here deals with anticipated changes in political power and process more seriously than in *Future Shock.* In the concluding chapter of *The Third Wave* he outlines a new form of decentralized participatory democracy appropriate for a "demassified" age. Majority rule by mass political parties is to give way to temporary "modular parties" reflecting shifting pluralities of various interest groups. Going further, elected representatives may be replaced or complemented by ordinary citizens using high-tech communications systems to learn about and then vote on issues. Toffler seems genuinely concerned about the breakup of Second Wave governments and institutions possibly leading to authoritarianism. Hence the need for "anticipatory democracy" to save the day is more urgent than he thought it was in 1970.[13] Once again, however, his vision lacks the critique of the fundamental obstacles (like multinational corporations) to genuine participatory democracy in the future.

"As Third Wave civilization matures," Toffler predicts, "we shall create not a utopian man or woman who towers over the people of the past, not a superhuman race of Goethes and Aristotles (or Genghis Khans or Hitlers) but merely, and proudly, one hopes, a race—and a civilization—that deserves to be called human." Yet Toffler believes that the Third Wave will evolve into a "practopia," or practical utopia.[14] Significantly, *The Third Wave* hedges its predictions much more than *Future Shock,* and Toffler is sometimes at pains to let his optimism overcome the pessimistic portrait he paints of an industrial civilization otherwise heading for chaos and collapse. Even Edward Cornish, president of the World Future Society and a Toffler admirer, wondered "just where Al spells out exactly what the Third Wave is," so deliberately qualified and vague is the content.[15] Once more Toffler's ambivalence about the future comes through.

For this reason Toffler needs to have the otherwise neatly separated Second and Third Waves overlap until the latter someday triumphs. This temporary overlap creates uncertainty and confusion. Any serious student of history would recognize the simultaneity today of agriculture and industrialization amid postindustrialization and the likelihood of continuities among them for the foreseeable future. For Toffler, however, the Second Wave must finally give way entirely to the Third, just as the First allegedly gave way to the Second. Historical discontinuity is crucial for his argument, lest the future not roll in as he repeatedly insists it will.

At the beginning of *The Third Wave* Toffler writes that "beneath the clatter and jangle of seemingly senseless events there lies a startling and potentially hopeful pattern. . . . the human story, far from ending, has only just begun."[16] Notice the further forced separation of, in effect, all of history from the future, as if "the human story" had no past but only a (new) beginning; or, going further, as if no one had ever transformed the "seemingly senseless events" of earlier times into a coherent pattern. Revealingly, in *Previews and Premises: An Interview with the Author of "Future Shock" and "The Third Wave"* (1983), Toffler brands persons who are not interested in the future—dare I say not obsessed with the future?—as "nostalgiacs" and "reversionists" who naively imagine a return to a mythical past.[17] Responding here to provocative questions posed by a Boston leftist publishing collective, he denounces as romantic antitechnologists the German Greens, the "anti-nukes," and the other alleged reactionaries who align themselves with First Wave forces to try to prevent Toffler's future from emerging intact. And it is definitely Toffler's future as he conceives and conveys it.

To be sure, in *Previews and Premises* Toffler rejects the related notions that he is a technological determinist and that the future is predetermined: "I don't believe any single force drives the system. . . . Different causal forces emerge as salient at different moments, and . . . the attempt to find a single dominating causal force is a misguided search for a unique 'link that pulls the chain.'" Consequently, "the future is not entirely deterministic" as there is always the role of chance. "I certainly don't believe that the Third Wave is an inevitability. . . . The system can go in any number of directions. . . . All changes . . . are made by people, including ordinary people, making decisions, choices."[18] This is considerably different from both *Future Shock* and *The Third Wave*, whether conceded by Toffler or not. The earlier supreme optimism has been shaken.

By 1990, with *Powershift: Knowledge, Wealth, and Violence at the Edge of the 21st Century*, Toffler has become still less optimistic. The ongoing, generally positive powershift throughout the world toward knowledge economies, decentralized governments, and participatory democracies is increasingly threatened by the possible rise of one or more racist, tribal (read nationalist), eco-fascist, or fundamentalist states all too ready to suppress human rights, freedom of religion, and, not least, private property. The broader context for this grave prospect is the continuing reapportionment of traditional authority throughout the world and the varying reactions to it. In tones reminiscent of *The Third Wave* he declares that "We live at a moment when the entire structure of power that held the world together is now disintegrating. . . . we stand at the edge of the deepest powershift in human history," as if history really mattered to him. The proletariat is finished, replaced by the "cognitariat."[19]

Power, Toffler argues, comes in threes (like so much else)—violence, wealth, and knowledge—but has been steadily moving from the first two to the last. For example, the contemporary maldistribution of telecommunications facilities is allegedly more serious than our unequal food distributions. Violence and wealth alike, Toffler claims, are ever more dependent upon knowledge in order to be efficiently used or amassed. Traditional nations are steadily losing power to extranational forces ranging from multinational corporations to ethnic groups to organized religions to criminal networks. The same technology that could achieve and sustain the glories of the Third Wave could instead be used to bring about a new Dark Age filled with violence as well as knowledge. Here Toffler is clearly correct if hardly original, as the 1989 and 1990 upheavals in China and Eastern Europe made abundantly clear. In any case, Toffler remains a virtual technological determinist notwithstanding his 1983 disavowal.

Still, like all good jeremiads, *Powershift* holds out hope for silver linings if not outright redemption. Not only is the United States, along with Japan and reunited Germany, likely to dominate the coming international economy, but the United States is best positioned to remain the world's most powerful country, economy, and democracy—provided, of course, that the decision-makers read and accept Toffler's latest gospel. (Again, his 1983 disavowal aside, Toffler ultimately writes for elites, not ordinary folks.) The obvious fact that the very global telecommunications and computer networks that Toffler here as before routinely exalts may be making books, above all big books, obsolete is an irony he nicely ignores.

Despite his regular and well-publicized hobnobbing with the world's corporate and governmental elite, Toffler in *Powershift* as in *The Third Wave* wants to come across as a democrat, a friend of common citizens, someone who wants technology to promote democracy. He may genuinely believe that the sheer accumulation and generation of information through computers to unprecedented numbers of persons inevitably translates into a powershift from the centralized few decision-makers to the decentralized many. Ironically, he thereby reveals a principal failing of his book: its inability to prove that increased information necessarily means increased knowledge and so increased power. Toffler simply assumes this, when the compelling evidence is over-whelmingly negative. It is indicative of Toffler's "methodology" that he tries to distinguish among "data," "information," and "knowledge," only to give up and use them interchangeably, "even at the expense of rigor."[20] As before, he carefully avoids a serious critique of his de facto patrons, multinational corporations, as obstacles to true participatory democracy, focusing instead on easier targets like drug cartels, radical ecologists, and fundamentalists.

According to Toffler himself, *Powershift* is the final volume in his trilogy. *Future Shock* "looks at the *process* of change—how change affects people and organizations." *The Third Wave* "focuses on the *directions* of change—where today's changes are taking us." Meanwhile *Powershift* "deals with the *control* of changes still to come—who will shape them and how."[21] This is a useful if oversimplified compartmen-talization of his major works. One naturally wonders if he anticipated a trilogy when he began or if his works just conveniently became one. It will be interesting to see if, by the year 2000, Toffler nevertheless feels compelled to publish yet another tome and if such a work is as ambiva-lent and as anxious about the future as *Powershift* is, Toffler's surface optimism to the contrary.

Naisbitt's *Megatrends: Ten New Directions Transforming Our Lives* appeared in 1982, two years after Toffler's *The Third Wave*. Like his later works, it is written in flat, colorless prose, broken up repeat-edly by topic sentences with bold letters. A self-styled "book of synthe-sis in an age of analysis,"[22] *Megatrends* professed to distill the insights about the near future gleaned from twelve years' worth of six thousand newspapers a month for a total of two million articles. Ironically, Nais-bitt and his associates in the Naisbitt Group use the very traditional methodology of content analysis. Notwithstanding the limitations of print in an age of broadcast media otherwise ironically celebrated by Naisbitt, analyzing minor local newspapers' daily content supposedly reveals current trends. Naisbitt's dubious assumption is that newspapers publish only those stories of most interest to their readers. What about their editors or their owners? And which comes first, public awareness or media coverage? In any case, the methodology transcends these questions insofar as more space in newspapers translates into more public concern, regardless of who saw the light first and who prompted its publication. In addition, the book's footnotes more often cite major newspapers and magazines than minor local ones, thereby relegating Naisbitt's data base to second place.

Like Toffler, Naisbitt uses many diverse events and developments that may seem random at first glance but that, not surprisingly, coalesce into identifiable megatrends. Naisbitt's acknowledged historical indebtedness is limited and dates back only to 1956–57. By 1956, the United States had become a white-collar work force of technical, managerial, and clerical personnel who outnumbered blue-collar workers, the traditional majority. And in 1957, with the successful Soviet launching of Sputnik, global telecommunications became a reality. The dual shift in the work force and in communications ushered in the glorious information revolution.

Naisbitt's megatrends combine the obvious with the questionable. They include American movements (1) from an industrial to an information society; (2) from an internal to a global economy and marketplace, no longer producing and consuming most of what we need; (3) from northern to western and southern cities; (4) from short-term to long-term considerations and rewards; (5) from a representational to a participatory democracy; (6) from a hierarchical "top-down" to a "bottom-up" society; (7) from formal chain-of-command communications to informal communications networks in business, politics, and the home; and (8) from institutional to self-help in areas ranging from exercise and nutrition to job counseling. The other, no less important megatrends are (9) the matching of every successful high-tech advance with "high touch," or a positive human response; and (10) the expansion of choices in everyday life from few if any to a multiplicity. That several of these megatrends are clearly applicable elsewhere in the world is, of course, a confirmation of their validity. It remains to be seen, however, if especially megatrends (4), (5), (6), (7), (9), and (10) apply as universally as Naisbitt contends, or just within the United States. High tech certainly has the capacity to reinforce or impose both hierarchy and traditional communications and to reduce choices. And high tech hardly guarantees "high touch" in any given situation.[23]

As more than one reverential reviewer observed at the time, Naisbitt was not a traditional futurist, offering "grand theories, imaginative projections, or reviews of past history."[24] (Toffler, for all his pretensions of uniqueness, *is* to that extent a traditionalist.) Rather, Naisbitt was describing, in his own words, "a new American society that is not yet fully evolved," but is "already changing our inner and outer lives"[25]—as if traditional futurists were not also invariably treating the present along with the future. But Naisbitt is again special, in the eyes of some worshipers, for simply telling like it is, "neither trying to predict the future nor convince the reader of a pet theory."[26] This focus on the present and near future, this dissociation among the past, the present, and the future, is thus a badge of honor for those concerned only with the short-term. Is that not ironically contrary to one of Naisbitt's own megatrends? Ironically, too, Naisbitt actually has a pet theory beyond his true belief in free market capitalism as panacea: that once a megatrend develops, it will continue to develop, only more so. Here Naisbitt is anything but unique, as the historical study of forecasting's successes and failures makes painfully clear. Toffler himself takes a similar stance. Still, the American tradition of positive thinking, of which *Megatrends*, along with Toffler's works, is only the high-tech installment, prevails. Problems become challenges; challenges become opportunities. Millions of readers presumably share Naisbitt's conclusion: "My God, what a fantastic time to be alive!"[27]

But that was in 1982. By 1990, when Naisbitt and Patricia Aburdene published *Megatrends 2000*, things were looking still better. "We stand at the dawn of a new era," they claim at the outset. "Before us is the most important decade in the history of civilization, a period of stunning technological innovation, unprecedented economic opportunity, surprising political reform, and great cultural rebirth. It will be a decade like none that has come before because it will culminate in the millennium, the year 2000."[28] Once again the past supposedly has no hold on the present, much less the future.

Naturally there are ten new megatrends to ponder and then act upon: (1) a global boom free from past limits on growth and without any future limits; (2) the emergence of "free market socialism" (an oxymoron) in Eastern Europe; (3) the privatization of the welfare state as in Britain under Margaret Thatcher; (4) the rise of the "Pacific Rim" extending from California to every other country, including those in South America, fronting on the Pacific; (5) global lifestyles and cultural nationalism, including the attempted preservation of national or regional cultures amid global homogenization; (6) a renaissance in the arts so popular as to replace sports as some societies' dominant leisure activity; (7) unprecedented leadership of women in business and the professions; (8) worldwide religious revivalism from fundamentalism to New Age; (9) an age of biology and biotechnology (the only megatrend that at all troubles them ethically and otherwise); and (10) the triumph of the individual over the collective through high-tech computers, cellular phones, and fax machines. *Megatrends 2000* is more international in scope than its predecessor. As *Megatrends 2000* happily concludes, "On the threshold of the millennium, long the symbol of humanity's golden age, we possess the tools and the capacity to build utopia here and now."[29]

Paradoxically, Naisbitt and Aburdene here claim to be truly forecasting, if only for a decade, whereas their forecasts are, if anything, more obvious, less imaginative and insightful, and less based on compelling hard data than those in *Megatrends*, which avowedly steered away from forecasting. Virtually all of their major points have already been detailed in such periodicals as *Time, Newsweek, Business Week,* and the *Economist,* while megatrends (6) renaissance of the arts and (10) the triumph of the individual surely remain to be confirmed. Global environmental crises, hunger, crime, drugs, AIDS, and other genuine crises are either ignored or minimized. Where *Megatrends* at least appeared when most of the developments it described were not yet part of the conventional wisdom, *Megatrends 2000* is behind the times, so to speak, in its revelations. Ironically, Naisbitt and Aburdene defend both books by arguing in the sequel that *Megatrends'* trends are on schedule but that the latest shift is the quickened pace of information growth, thereby requiring *Megatrends 2000.*

Significantly, Naisbitt and Aburdene's conclusion also includes the following statement: "By identifying the forces pushing the future, rather than those that have contained the past, you possess the power to engage with your reality."[30] Once again history is irrelevant save as the supposed contrast with the golden age ahead and, more than with Toffler, is simply ignored. It is as if high tech arrived and flourished in a historical vacuum of no more than a few decades and as if everything before it can forever be forgotten. Such conscious historical amnesia (combined with Naisbitt and Aburdene's dismissal of caution on the road to utopia and their contempt for "naysayers") reveals their unacknowledged anxiety that history in some fashion may indeed repeat itself; that technological progress may once more be a mixed blessing; and that unanticipated trends or events may wreck or detour their smooth scenarios. It is precisely when American business and professional people, among others, are so unsure of the country's or the world's future, so desperate to be handed the sugar-coated soma pills of Aldous Huxley's *Brave New World* in book form, that *Megatrends 2000*, like *Megatrends*, can be so successfully packaged, purchased, and consumed.

What, however, is most troubling about Toffler, Naisbitt, and like-minded high-tech prophets is the virtual absence of any moral critique of the present, any deep-seated concern driving them to their speculations about tomorrow. Even the late Buckminster Fuller or the late Gerard O'Neill, with their naive beliefs in the prospect for achieving versions of technological utopia either on spaceship earth or in space colonies, had a fundamentally nonpecuniary interest in the future. Both wrote and spoke out of the conviction, however misplaced, that they had panaceas worth putting into effect. In this respect they continued the tradition of utopian—and, equally important, antiutopian—writing and organization dating back at least to Thomas More if not to Plato. By contrast, with Toffler and Naisbitt, one senses little more than crass opportunism, including a willingness to revise radically their predictions to meet the marketplace, and absolutely no sense of their analyses being part of any historical movement. It is no accident that Toffler and Naisbitt alike praise what Toffler calls "wealth creation" as mankind's greatest achievement. It is something they do know about.

II

By contrast, high-tech print and television advertising boldly uses historical structures and figures to promote its products but in so doing at once misappropriates and trivializes the past and bespeaks an anxiety about the present and the future akin to that of Naisbitt and Toffler. The modeling of Dallas's Infomart, housing information processing systems and services, after London's 1851 Crystal Palace, site of the first world's fair, is the most provocative recreation of an historical structure. The most provocative recastings of historical figures are Xerox's use of Leonardo da Vinci; Apple Computer's use of Isaac Newton; Bell South's use of Ralph Bunche, Winston Churchill, and Albert Schweitzer; and IBM's use of Charlie Chaplin's Little Tramp.

As a student of American culture, I am hardly surprised by the use of major historical figures or structures to increase sales and profits. Every February, for instance, I anticipate ever cruder commercials proudly showing George Washington and Abraham Lincoln—our apostles of truth—as happy salesmen for items ranging from cars to televisions to dishwashers. I do wonder whether their association convinces a single potential consumer to make a purchase. Likewise, I am no longer shocked by the association of, say, the Statue of Liberty or the Liberty Bell with commercial wares having absolutely nothing to do with either's history and significance. Yet these associations, however crass, are not a recent development and at least stir a bit of genuine nostalgia for "the good old days," variously defined, when America's leaders and symbols were more uplifting and respected than in recent years.

As a student of technology, however, I am disturbed by the false nostalgia created when high-tech companies and institutions—or their advertising agencies—adopt wholly inappropriate persons and buildings to push their products. Take the case of Infomart, which opened in 1985 at a cost of $100 million.[31] Just as London's Crystal Palace showcased the products of the British industrial revolution, Infomart is supposedly doing the same for those of high tech. Its designers, we are told in an early promotion brochure, "have meticulously adapted [Joseph] Paxton's original plans for the Crystal Palace. . . . Great care has been taken to maintain the historical integrity of the original structure while designing a state-of-the-art facility. . . ."[32] A 1992 promotion publication goes still further. Infomart has somehow "been recognized by Great Britain's Parliament as the official successor to the Crystal Palace. It reflects not only the Crystal Palace's architecture, but its spirit and forward-thinking purpose."[33] Moreover, the same Italian company that designed the Crystal Palace's fountain, Barovier-Toso, designed Infomart's crystal fountain, while one company that exhibited at the Crystal Palace—Siemens and Halske Telegraph, then manufacturing railway telegraph and signal devices—has a showroom at Infomart as Siemens Information Systems, now manufacturing automation devices. But not only is the 1.6-million-square-foot, eight-story Infomart almost one and a half times the size of the Crystal Palace, both its exterior and interior are hardly identical with the latter, as befits an ultramodern convention and exhibition facility; inside it more closely resembles the kind of multistory atrium found in architect John Portman's hotels. A similar contemporary structure that is more successful is New York City's Jacob

Javits Convention Center, a public facility that also has ties—albeit less explicit and less pretentious—to the Crystal Palace.[34]

More important, Infomart's purpose is not to generate world peace or serious cultural exchange, or even wholesome amusement, as were the additional purposes of the Crystal Palace, but only to promote commerce. The presence of a high-tech electronic library and resource center and of endless seminars, demonstrations, and showcases, and the absence of salespeople, may provide a more relaxed, more "user friendly" atmosphere conducive to comparison shopping; but selling the products and services displayed, not satisfying intellectual curiosity, remains Infomart's sole objective. Boldly describing Infomart as "the education center for the Information Age"[35] hardly alters that fact. And in a world of instantaneous communications and "electronic cottages," as elaborated in section III below, it is no longer necessary, as was the case with the Crystal Palace and other pre-1980 world's fairs, for business and professional people to come to one central location to examine the hardware and the software; they can remain in their home offices and receive the information through their computer and television screens and fax machines. Ironically, the same high-tech firms leasing space in Infomart are those who make just such claims in other contexts, such as print and media advertisements. Infomart's own quarterly magazine has an article praising videoconferencing for doing precisely this and so eliminating unnecessary business and professional travel to distant sites![36] Ironically, too, the Dallas Infomart was intended as just the first in a series of Infomarts yet to be constructed in New York City, Atlanta, Chicago, Los Angeles, Frankfurt, and elsewhere; one in Paris is now open. So much for literal adherence to the one-place-at-one-time centralization of exhibits in traditional world's fairs like the Crystal Palace. In addition, rival computer marts are in the works.

If Infomart is a cultural symbol at all, it surely represents high tech's lack of self-confidence, its ambivalence about the present and the future, and its consequent need to establish close ties to the past. Infomart's intriguing facade thus remains merely a facade. Only insofar as it houses an equally new Information Processing Hall of Fame, including John Cullinane, Grace Hopper, H. Ross Perot, and An Wang, has Infomart any historical or cultural bent. And the idea of a hall of fame in technology perpetuates the simplistic, romantic notion of a "heroic theory of invention" generally rejected by serious students of technology's past.

Despite all this, Infomart at least has its commercial connection with the Crystal Palace, which indeed had business high on its agenda. By contrast, Leonardo (1452–1519) has no ties whatsoever with high tech save as a pioneer designer and inventor.[37] Somehow we are supposed to see this individual genius as a loyal corporate employee, happily embracing photocopiers, fax machines, laser printers, and entire workstations. Presumably such high-tech equipment would have enabled Leonardo to design, invent, sketch, and perhaps paint better. Yet the Xerox ads sometimes show Leonardo as a befuddled time-traveler unable to cope with the modern office. The tag line that "Xerox brings out the genius in you" may, then, be an implicit criticism of eccentric souls who couldn't last a day in the modern high-tech corporation—not on "Team Xerox" anyway—as much as an obvious paean to the hardware and software themselves. The tag line is certainly an implicit relegation of Leonardo's intellect to second place behind the high-tech equipment he now hawks. Once again, though, high tech feels it necessary to look backward for reassurance as it otherwise looks only ahead.

By coincidence, in the early 1980s IBM (and Bechtel) sponsored a traveling exhibit, "Leonardo's Return to Vinci," which toured several of America's university art museums. Most viewers were dazzled by the actual art and models of inventions (tank, parachute, helicopter, car, paddlewheel ship, etc.) of this archetypal Renaissance man. They probably missed the exhibit's ulterior purpose: to demonstrate that high culture and high tech mesh as readily in our time as in Leonardo's.[38] Another newspaper article of the time suggested that if Leonardo were alive today he would contentedly be working (if not at Xerox then) as an artist in the electronic media, with the TV screen as his canvas and with knobs and computer keyboards as his brushes and paints.

Ironically, and unintentionally, the exhibit demonstrated the very opposite, and in ways that were as revealing as the displays themselves. The truth about Leonardo is that his age—unlike ours—tolerated and actually encouraged the diverse activities that made him a Renaissance man beyond chronology alone. Moreover, notwithstanding his individual talents, he was hardly unique in his time. Attributing Leonardo's manifold achievement in painting, sculpture, design, architecture, and engineering solely to his singular genius is to miss the point: he was multifaceted in part because there did not then exist both the tremen-

dous gaps between technology and culture and the occupational specialization we today accept as almost inevitable. Technology in its present
meaning also did not then exist, and the engineer and architect (if not
artist) were invariably the same person.

Leonardo would not, of course, have fit the conservative corporate
molds of IBM or Bechtel any better than that of Xerox. Nor would any of
these three corporate cultures have granted him the relative independence he enjoyed in his own day. Still, among these corporate sponsors
there likely lurks a hope that similar inventive geniuses will reappear to
rescue the United States from its present technological and economic
malaise and that corporate America will somehow find a way to accommodate them. The traditional American admiration for alleged lone-
wolf inventors like Eli Whitney, Henry Ford, and Thomas Edison
persists. Like them, Leonardo actually invented considerably less than
he is credited with; and, like them, what he did "invent"—at least in his
sketches—was frequently the result of collaborative efforts.

Persons of Leonardo's nevertheless impressive intellectual stature
do, of course, occasionally appear, but they no longer resemble our
Renaissance man. And that is the subtext of this exhibit and of the Xerox
advertisements: that the past is not recoverable by the present. Or, to
quote, of all persons, the operations manager of Xerox's facility at
Dallas's Infomart, praising Infomart's integration of goods and services,
"I imagine it's very annoying to see technology out of context."[39] I'll say
it is! High tech will have to look elsewhere for its cultural heroes.

Ironically, this Renaissance pseudoheritage came to haunt high
tech when, on March 6, 1992, a new computer virus named Michelangelo struck at least five large and one thousand small businesses in
the United States and an untold number of individuals. Given high
tech's self-proclaimed universality, the virus also struck around the
world, infecting an estimated five million personal computers. The
occasion was the Renaissance painter and sculptor's 517th birthday, and
among the American high-tech firms affected was, most ironically, the
Da Vinci Systems Corporation, a maker of electronic-mail software. It
had recently mailed out some nine hundred infected demonstration
disks. Other software and hardware manufacturers were also victim-
ized. True, well-publicized warnings and the availability of software
that detects and removes viruses greatly reduced the damage. And
antivirus software manufacturers and their advertisers benefited tre-

mendously. Yet every March 6 for the foreseeable future Michelangelo the Renaissance artist and humanist will have to compete with Michelangelo the destroyer of knowledge.[40]

On a more positive note, perhaps, we can anticipate any number of charming advertisements when Apple Computer begins selling its recently unveiled Newton, a pocket-size, pen-based computer named after scientist Isaac Newton. The first in a projected line of "personal digital assistants," the Newton combines an electronic calendar, a phone directory, a card index, a note taker, and other personal organizing functions. Although the front of Newton's plastic case houses a flat liquid crystal screen like those found in portable computers, Newton has no keyboard. Instead, its users print on the screen with a high-tech pen. In turn Newton recognizes their words and acts accordingly, as in making appointments or in saving and filing quick notes. Whether this device will prove commercially popular, especially with nonusers of conventional computers, remains to be seen, as does—more pertinent here—the role of that preeminent scientist in promoting it. Newton is widely associated with apples in his experiments on gravity, particularly gravity's extending to the moon, but its association with his discoveries about gravity may have been his own clever invention, intended to backdate those discoveries to establish priorities over rival claims. In any case, there is no logical connection between those seminal discoveries about gravity and Apple Computer's Newton. The latter's incorporation of "smart agents" or "intelligent assistance," software terms referring to organizing information without telling computers what to do, is the only conceivable tie—that is, both Newtons' being terribly bright. (Whether, like Leonardo in the Xerox advertisements, the original Newton's intelligence will be deemed inferior to that of his high-tech namesake will be interesting to observe.) In Isaac Newton's day science and technology were separate realms with different agendas, unlike, as with Leonardo, architecture and engineering.[41]

By contrast, there is no tie whatsoever between Ralph Bunche, Winston Churchill, and Albert Schweitzer and the components of Bell South, one of the "Baby Bells" created by the court-mandated breakup in 1984 of American Telephone and Telegraph. The fact that each of these persons had multiple talents—athlete, college professor, author, statesman, and negotiator (Bunche); war correspondent, author, painter, and world leader (Churchill); theologian, physician, organist, author, and humanitarian (Schweitzer)—is somehow to place Bell

South itself in a new light: "everything you expect from a leader" in telecommunications, information services, mobile communications, and even advertising. This crass association of the allegedly "most admired telecommunications company in the United States" with three individuals hardly revered for anything technological and having precious little in common with one another is historical stretching of the worst kind. It is compounded by the ridiculous notions that the "remarkable talents" found in each man can be molded to fit conservative corporate cultures, much like Leonardo's creativity, and that strong-willed individuals like these can be inspired to work together to solve problems. It is unfortunate that Bell South feels compelled to look back to such irrelevant historical figures to sell its products.[42]

Perhaps the most offensive high-tech advertisements, however, are IBM's caricatures of the Little Tramp.[43] These helped launch IBM's personal computer in 1981 and ran until 1987. They were revived in 1991 to celebrate IBM's tenth anniversary in the personal computer business. Cleverly playing on the pervasive fears of modern technology itself creating chaos—not least on the assembly line, as epitomized by Chaplin's classic 1936 film *Modern Times*—the IBM advertisements instead show a benign view of personal computers, as devices bringing order, profits, and happiness into the Little Tramp's previously disorderly, inefficient, and unhappy life. Whether the setting is a house, an office, a bakery, or a hat shop, the outcome is always the same and is always happy, supposedly in accordance with the film's ending and view of life. Indeed, several IBM advertisements call the personal computer "a tool for modern times," and the film, not just the Little Tramp, was clearly on the minds of the ad campaign's creators. At the same time the advertisements humanize the world's preeminent computer company, the epitome of the impersonal large corporation. In so doing they completely misrepresent Chaplin's critical views of modern technology and its social impact and of the large corporations responsible for so much of both. Contrary to the IBM advertisements, *Modern Times* finally seeks escape from modern technology and industrial society and, if anything, is wholly inadequate in not suggesting any (other) solutions to the dehumanization of work and leisure it depicts. If only the Little Tramp had had a PC at hand! Ironically, the film's subtext is that human beings cannot master modern machines. Like the recent television commercials for luxury cars, financial securities, jogging accessories, and other "upscale" goods that use popular songs—and sometimes singers—from the 1960s with originally antimaterialist messages, the IBM advertisements create a particularly distorted view of the past, an utterly false nostalgia.

Ironically, high tech *has* a history, or is creating one, as with the several "generations" of computers that have come into existence since World War II—the term "generations" itself a telling comment on the rapid pace of change within high tech. Appropriately, the computer now has its first major museum, in Boston, housed in what, a century ago, was a warehouse. Here there is no contradiction between the building and its contents, for the structure, despite the parallels between the earlier industrial revolution and the present information revolution, lacks the architectural and cultural pretensions of Infomart. A nonprofit enterprise, the museum has no commercial aspirations and has recently and significantly modified its initial basic message of computers' evolution as constituting unadulterated technological and social progress alike.[44] Infomart's Information Processing Hall of Fame would be inappropriate in the revamped Computer Museum. Would that Infomart, Xerox, IBM, and other high-tech institutions felt secure enough to present a more balanced picture of modern technology's mixed blessings. Their doing so would be a reflection of high tech's genuine self-confidence.

It is, of course, entirely possible that these and other high-tech companies and their advertising arms care not a wit about historical accuracy and happily misuse historical figures and structures just because they sell their products—or seem to sell their products, given the notorious difficulty of connecting advertisements with sales. Or, for all I know, these companies and advertisers may be blithely unaware of their perversion of history and may believe that they are somehow promoting history in a manner akin to corporate sponsorship of other historical and cultural enterprises. Still worse, these companies and advertisers may, as with the IBM Little Tramp ad campaign, believe that their historical figures would have embraced their high-tech products if only they'd seen them in action; that Chaplin himself would have been genuinely liberated by a personal computer and would have become a contented entrepreneur. The linkages between high tech and high culture are sufficiently unexplored to allow for all these possibilities.

Other high-tech companies utilize historical figures and buildings in more historically responsible advertisements (if advertisements for commercial products can ever be historically responsible). These include Sun Microsystem's adoption of Mozart at the piano to boast that "Only one other ten-year-old has ever performed so well on a keyboard" on the computer company's tenth birthday; Storer Communications' comparison of a nineteenth-century telegraph operator who "could tap out about twenty-five words a minute" with computers that "can deliver a 300-page report in seconds"; Storer's similar comparison of nineteenth-century Pony Express riders through whom "communications traveled about fifteen miles per hour" with contemporary systems through which "communications can travel at the speed of light"; and Lockheed's use of William the Conqueror's mounted cavalry on stirrups against the English Anglo-Saxons in 1066 to proclaim its own "air superiority" in the then-ongoing Cold War against the Warsaw Pact's aircraft.[45] In addition, a 1992 issue of ElAl Airlines' bimonthly magazine carried an advertisement for an Israeli tool manufacturer, Iscar, comparing the artworks of Michelangelo and Leonardo, among others, with its own—its hard metal cutting tools, that is, "which grace no famous museum but are utilized regularly in industrial sites around the world."[46] An audacious comparison, perhaps, but a valid one insofar as art and (what we call) technology historically were inextricably connected and often equated. In 1829, Harvard professor Jacob Bigelow's *Elements of Technology*, which, along with his lectures, largely introduced the term in the United States, defined technology as the "application of the sciences to the useful arts."[47] "State-of-the-art technology," a term invoked so frequently today by high-tech promoters, thus has a deeper meaning than imagined by nearly all who employ it.[48]

Yet the more widely promoted misuse and, equally important, trivialization of avowedly humanistic historical symbols like Leonardo and the Little Tramp by Xerox, IBM, and others cannot be so easily excused as oversight or indifference or good intentions gone wrong. One need not be conspiratorial to recognize other forces at work and to suggest high tech's deep-seated need to connect to the past. If, then, high tech feels compelled to look backward for reassurance or legitimacy—or simply for greater profits—let it be more honest in its historical appropriations. Otherwise, its false nostalgia may someday prove self-defeating.

III

Another form of advertising that high tech increasingly finances is world's fairs. In so doing, however, high tech fails to achieve the intellectual significance of prior fairs and ironically raises fundamental questions about the continuing relevance of world's fairs. This heretical notion first occurred to me, of all places, at a 1980 symposium commemorating the 1939–40 New York World's Fair held on the very site of that fair, Flushing Meadows (also the site of the 1964 New York World's Fair). Although other international expositions from 1851 onward displayed no less impressive exhibitions than New York's did, the 1939–40 fair alone announced the prospect of creating a veritable utopia in the very near future: in 1960, to be exact. Its achievement quite literally awaited the magic touch of the fair's several prominent industrial designers: Norman Bel Geddes, Henry Dreyfuss, Raymond Loewy, and Walter Dorwin Teague.[49] Or so they—and thousands of fair visitors—naively believed.

As with so many other technological utopias—and not only world's fairs but model communities and visionary writings too—the problem has been twofold: the inability to predict the "real" future technologically and nontechnologically, and the inability to translate actual technological advances into equivalent social advances. The same problem, of course, plagues high tech's prophets. By 1960 American society resembled the 1939–40 fair's "world of tomorrow" only in bare outline—in its sleek skyscrapers and superhighways. Much remained to be filled in, and obviously still does.

Planners of recent and coming world's fairs both at home and abroad manifest painfully modest concern for the future of fairs, much less for their past, as significant social and cultural artifacts. Like Toffler and Naisbitt, these high-tech visionaries are ahistorical, so ahistorical that they fail to ask themselves how past world's fairs have affected those who created, visited, and read or heard about them, if only to compare with present and future fairs. Yet this is precisely where world's fairs are—or at least have been—most significant: they have revealed much about the times and places that produced them and far less about the future. As scholars in several disciplines are gradually recognizing, fairs embody the real or ideal self-image of their respective organizers and exhibitors and so provide a wonderful opportunity to probe deeply into any number of societies and cultures on display. This is, if anything, more important today than ever before just because, ironically, the alleged shrinkage in time between the problematic present and the future perfect—as exemplified in Buckminster Fuller's persistent demand that we either create utopia immediately or face oblivion—

likewise lessens the role and excitement of world's fairs as previews of the future. If our high-tech future is virtually at hand, what can fairs actually teach us about the world of, literally, tomorrow?

The historic importance of world's fairs does not, then, guarantee their permanent importance. Apart from the always sensitive question of finances, given their common failure to turn a profit, there is a no less weighty question of the continuing utility of world's fairs as conveyers both of ideals and of technical information. Like postage stamps, peace ships, and peace congresses, world's fairs can no longer be viewed as efficient means of achieving international harmony. Simply bringing together masses of people into one geographical space is hardly a serious route to that admirable goal. Other means to world peace more suitable to the late twentieth century should be sought.

Technology comes readily to mind, whether as a military deterrent or in more positive forms. Yet it is the advance of technology since 1939–40 that, ironically, more than anything else, has rendered fairs obsolete. The revolution in electronics and information processing, not even envisioned in 1939–40, has made possible instantaneous visual and other communication throughout most of the globe. Why travel to distant points if satellites, computers, word processors, and other high-tech advances can at once deliver the needed data and enable one to see the latest technological developments on a screen or a fax rather than in person? Those who still wish, and can afford, to view technological developments in the flesh can of course do so, perhaps at the local, regional, national, and international trade fairs that predated the Crystal Palace Exhibition and that persist today; or at Dallas's Infomart and similar structures elsewhere. But save for Infomart, these enterprises have no serious social and cultural pretensions, including those that call themselves a "World's Fair for Consumer Electronics" or a "World's Fair of Imaging."[50] Hence the other principal purpose of international expositions—bringing technological advances to the attention of the largest number of people in the most effective way—has likewise been severely undermined.

True, world's fairs have traditionally promoted entertainment and good times as well as peace and technology. And many of the medieval precursors of the Crystal Palace mixed trade shows and carnivals. It is hardly accidental that amusement parks are more commonly associated with world's fairs for many persons than anything else. Yet here, too, international expositions are obsolete. They have been replaced by permanent "theme" parks exemplified by Disneyland and Walt Disney World, which are the entertainment counterparts of Infomart. Theme parks are now the rage throughout the world. They increasingly encompass every conceivable popular activity and fantasy, from computerized high-tech roller coasters and other thrilling rides to movie studio recreations to foreign travel to themes like country music, sports, cars, toys, and celebrities. Yet the opening in 1983 of Tokyo Disneyland and in 1992 of Euro Disney near Paris should be construed as the triumph not of true internationalism but of American cultural imperialism. Calling Euro Disney "a cultural Chernobyl," as did at least one widely quoted French intellectual, is, however, going a bit too far.[51] These new Disneylands are more akin to the American fast-food eateries that now dot so much of the "global village." They carefully blend popular features from their California and Florida counterparts with appealing aspects of Japanese and French culture respectively but remain fundamentally American in character and content. That they are so popular with the Japanese and the French themselves doesn't contradict this. Their popularity ironically lessens the motivation for non-Americans to visit Disneyland and Walt Disney World and to this extent undermines the internationalism celebrated by traditional world's fairs and by some theme parks themselves.

In the case of Disney's EPCOT Center, visitors are provided with a still more romanticized vision of both the past and the future than temporary fairs once offered, and as strong a dose of technological determinism as in Toffler's and Naisbitt's writings. Officially named Experimental Prototype Community of Tomorrow, EPCOT was envisioned by Disney as a dome-covered actual city of twenty thousand full-time residents. Before he died in 1966, Disney left few specifics as to how his technological utopia should look and operate. Eventually his successors decided to do without people—perhaps the ultimate high-tech dream—and to create, adjacent to Walt Disney World, exhibitions divided into World Showcase and Future World. World Showcase offers replicas of buildings from nine nations (plus the United States) to allow visitors the opportunity to experience foreign lands without leaving American soil. It is as artificial and as superficial as any traditional world's fair; or perhaps worse, for in EPCOT other countries don't display their latest inventions, only corporations do.[52]

Future World exalts the ability of its giant corporate sponsors to solve problems confronting mankind through more and more technology. The notion of corporate responsibility for any problems is naturally left out. Moreover, problems that ordinary citizens might deem serious, much less fundamental, are conveniently ignored: war and peace, over-population, poverty, unemployment, crime, drugs, etc. Here as else-where in the Disney empire, painful reminders of everyday life are, along with each day's litter, religiously swept away. Ironically, visitors to EPCOT and to Walt Disney World have increased so much since the former's 1982 opening that they are often confronted with real-world problems upon arriving and departing if not during their stay, from poorly planned surrounding areas to inadequate public transporta-tion.[53] More ironically, few of the Future World exhibits treat the future; most celebrate existing and, still more ironically, past tech-nologies. Robots act out everyday scenes from prehistoric times on. The General Motors pavilion includes the model for Leonardo's *Mona Lisa* tapping her feet and scowling while our Renaissance hero works on his flying machine. So here Leonardo sells cars, in effect. One could hardly ask for clearer confirmation of high tech's inability to escape the past in the name of promoting the future.

Significantly, EPCOT does not merely sanitize the past, in the manner of other temporary world's fairs and permanent theme parks, it outright "improves" it. History as presented here is devoid of what Disney employees call "downers," such as famine, plague, or genocide. Like Walt Disney World's Main Street, it is history as it should have been or should be. The American pavilion, sponsored by American Express and Coca-Cola, uses robots dressed as Benjamin Franklin and Mark Twain to romp through American history in twenty-nine minutes. Unlike the rest of EPCOT, it doesn't completely omit wars, depres-sions, and suffering, but the overall thrust is naturally upbeat. Coverage of the 1960s and 1970s, for instance, totally ignores race riots, Water-gate, and Vietnam, among other unpleasantries. The feminist move-ment is also carefully left out. Lest this still prove taxing to visitors, there is, by EPCOT's own admission, World Showcase to relieve infor-mation overload.

As historian Mike Wallace has put it so well, EPCOT overall "pro-motes a sense of history as a pleasantly nostalgic memory, now so completely transcended by the modern, corporate order as to be irrele-vant to contemporary life." Hence the tone of gentle mockery and wry amusement in the Future World reconstructions of past futile efforts of lone inventors and small businessmen to satisfy consumers as naturally only large corporations can successfully manage nowadays. That in turn "dulls historical sensibility and invites acquiescence to what is" or what is soon coming.[54] This distortion and detachment of history applies, of course, to high-tech prophecies and advertisements.

Ironically, EPCOT is praised by Disney executives and (other) public relations professionals as not merely another Disneyland, but a serious educational enterprise, testing ideas and inventions. Contrary to Walt Disney's dream for EPCOT, however, the lessons learned do not begin to apply to solving especially urban problems. Like so much of high tech, EPCOT is an escape from rather than an illumination of reality. As a senior Disney executive confessed in 1982, "We're interested in seeing technology work to accomplish a story point. We wanted to make a point about America, that dreaming and doing things is an ongoing thing." This is very different from showing how things actually work, much less how they came about. As he continued, EPCOT is a necessary "voice of optimism" amid mounting uncertainties. "Industry has lost credibility with the public, the government has lost credibility, but people still have faith in Mickey Mouse and Donald Duck."[55]

Going a step further away from actually addressing urban problems, Hollywood's Universal Studios, already operating a Florida theme park in competition with Walt Disney World, is completing a four-block entertainment and retail area in Los Angeles, called City Walk, that re-creates a Los Angeles that never existed, and then terms that pseudo-past the wave of the future. Combining shops, restaurants, and clubs amid a mixture of such architectural styles as art deco, cyberpunk, and southwestern, City Walk provides a "safe, thematically correct" locale for pleasurable activities free from reminders of Los Angeles's more mixed and less appealing actual development. City Walk's features include a replica of a giant surfboard as one building's roof, a section of pavement embedded with fake litter, and street performers. The absence of a sustained sense of history often attributed to Los Angeles— along with the scant number of actual places like City Walk to gather and to walk—allegedly justifies this historical "reconstruction." According to a project architect, City Walk is the "architectural equivalent of artificial insemination." Its ultimate objective is to "jump-start" the local culture "by infusing it synthetically and letting it evolve from there."[56] This might become the goal of other theme parks as well.

Missing from these theme parks and recent world's fairs, as from Toffler's and Naisbitt's writings, is any genuine moral critique of the present, any serious effort to alter society in the manner of the 1939–40 New York and other major pre-1950 fairs. As socially and culturally conservative as those earlier fairs admittedly were in their common embrace of corporate capitalism, not to mention their at least implicit sexism and racism, they did offer a view of the future intended to inspire change, not simply to entertain. And it is increasingly difficult, perhaps impossible, for world's fairs' organizers to match the expertise and imagination of theme parks' professional entertainment specialists and designers; or to avoid hiring them in order to compete for a season or two with the Disneylands and EPCOTS.

These contemporary professionals, moreover, generally lack the cosmopolitanism of a Bel Geddes or a Loewy, for whom fairs were but one of many diverse projects rather than preoccupations. They did not spend their time attending meetings of the International Association of Fairs and Expositions, now a quarter-century old.[57] It is revealing of such groups' ahistorical perspective that their very invocations of history, like those of Toffler and Naisbitt, are at best embarrassingly shallow and at worst plain wrong. At the 1980 symposium commemorating the 1939–40 New York fair, for example, the only participant who appeared fully confident that the future really could still be fashioned and improved in the manner of the "world of tomorrow" was such a professional world's fair organizer. His talk "From Out of History Comes Energy Expo '82—the Knoxville World's Fair" demonstrated absolutely no grasp of the historical discontinuities that had already made the Knoxville fair obsolete before its opening day. For him, as for Toffler and Naisbitt, the past was a convenient if barely acknowledged launching pad for the future, and whatever trend or wave currently existed— in this case, ever more world's fairs celebrating one technological achievement after another—presumably would continue indefinitely. Similarly, the head of marketing and communications for Vancouver's Expo '86, a much more successful world's fair than Knoxville in strictly quantitative and financial terms, boasted in a subsequent trade publication interview of "How PR Packed 'Em In at Expo '86" by promoting it as "a world exposition in the grand tradition." His historical knowledge, alas, was limited, as per his muddled assertion of "trying to reference to the people and the media that we were going back to what it was like in London, and what it was like in 1861, when the very first world exposition took place." That he presumably meant 1851 was only the more obvious of his errors, the more serious of which was the assumption that what life was like at the 1851 Crystal Palace could readily be duplicated, and, of course, surpassed in 1986.[58]

Finally, the principal sponsorship of world's fairs has, like so much else, gradually shifted from the public to the private realm. As fewer and fewer cities and states and even nations have been able to afford to spend enormous sums on world's fairs, and as Chicago, Oklahoma City, St. Louis, Paris, and Venice have consequently canceled long-anticipated fairs, giant high-tech multinational corporations have taken their place.[59] Where, to take the two most recent American fairs, the federal government contributed two hundred million dollars to Knoxville's 1982 extravaganza, it gave only ten million to New Orleans's 1984 effort. Meanwhile the American pavilion at Seville's 1992 world's fair was nearly left unfinished because of allegedly inadequate government funding. Seville, in fact, marks the first time that the federal government, under intense congressional pressure, has sought private sector funding for its world's fair pavilion.[60] This is considerably different from earlier times, when major corporations either displayed their products in government-sponsored exhibition halls or, when constructing their own halls, did not dwarf those built by the many cities, states, and nations also in attendance. It is no accident that Dallas's Infomart bills itself as the "largest privately owned exhibit hall in the world" and deems that a mark of prestige.[61]

Moreover, and more so than in the past, these contemporary corporations treat world's fairs, like theme parks, as little more than huge advertisements for their products, and if world's fairs are to survive, they will assuredly have to contribute substantially to the "bottom line." The legacy of the Knoxville and New Orleans fairs not only in losing tens of millions of dollars but also in leaving unoccupied, unusable buildings would hardly be tolerated by profit-minded corporations. The example of the futuristic United States Knoxville exhibition hall standing vacant and deteriorating would tarnish the image of any self-respecting corporation with a similar white elephant, while the preclosing declaration of bankruptcy by the New Orleans fair organization would obviously be the height of embarrassment for any corporation in a comparable situation.[62] For these reasons it is increasingly common for corporations to promote their products as official fair suppliers (clothing, for example) or representatives (airlines, for instance) rather than, in traditional fashion, as outright exhibitors. This in turn gives new meaning to the phrase "selling the future" associated with world's fairs, theme parks, and related enterprises.[63] Not surprisingly, the author of a disappointing study comparing the "participant outcome perspective" of visitors to the Knoxville and New Orleans fairs concludes with a plea to increase "advertising and marketing events to tell the individuals what to expect from the experience" and to provide assistance "to interpret and understand their experience on-site."[64] Apparently, left to their own devices, visitors might get the wrong message about the future and, more important, about its corporate sponsors.

Pleading, in November 1991, for the six million dollars then needed to complete the underfunded United States pavilion for the Seville world's fair opening the following April, one Henry Raymont wrote in the *Boston Globe* that most Americans failed to grasp the enormous symbolic significance of an appropriate American presence there. The problem, he contended, was not "partisan politics or genuine budgetary concerns" so much as "a lack of historical imagination."[65] As the chair of the Culture Committee of the Christopher Columbus Quincentenary Jubilee Commission, Raymont naturally had a vested interest in having the pavilion completed on time; it had already been criticized as consisting of little more than two recycled geodesic domes used in European trade fairs over the last twenty years. Yet the irony of his historical reference cannot go overlooked, not least because, for political reasons above all, what began as a celebration of the five-hundredth anniversary of Columbus's first voyage to the New World ended, by the host country's own doing, as a celebration instead of Spanish democracy, culture, and technology. Spain's king didn't even mention Columbus's now controversial name when he officially opened what has been billed as the biggest world's fair ever, in terms of the number of countries represented and of exhibits constructed and costs incurred.

If, for once, the United States was not the biggest exhibitor, that could be the healthy start of rethinking the continuing significance of world's fairs in the age of high tech. Contrary to Raymont and other defenders, the same technological progress that formerly inspired so many fair designers and patrons has ultimately and ironically rendered the object of their affections irrelevant to the future. At best, fairs are historical artifacts, beloved by nostalgia buffs. Nowhere among recent fairs has this point been demonstrated better than at Vancouver's Expo '86, whose very theme was "World in Motion, World in Touch." The communications and transportation technology most prominently displayed unintentionally but repeatedly confirmed the technological obsolescence of world's fairs. The fact that the Vancouver fair's overall message was that technology cannot solve all world problems only compounds the irony, as does the fact that visitors dazzled by the high-tech displays rarely got this message. No other recent fair has shown such courage in suggesting modern technology's mixed blessings, and Vancouver itself lacked the "historical imagination" to illuminate historical developments leading to the end of technological optimism.[66] Far more common is the message at a major pavilion at the 1985 Tsukuba, Japan, world's fair, whose overall theme was unadulterated technological progress: "What mankind can dream, technology can achieve."[67] As with high-tech prophecies and advertisements, the surface glow of technological optimism expressed in Tsukuba, in Seville, in Knoxville, in New Orleans, and elsewhere only partly conceals the underlying anxiety about the future and the ultimate inability to restore the more understandable hopefulness of earlier world's fairs.

Henry Adams, the great American historian and man of letters, was profoundly moved by his visit to the Paris exposition of 1900. At a time when so many other Americans, among others, predicted ever greater technological and in turn social progress, Adams expressed grave doubts about the future based in part precisely upon his experience at that world's fair. As he wrote in *The Education of Henry Adams* (1907),

> Until the Great Exposition of 1900 closed its doors in November, Adams haunted it, aching to absorb knowledge, and helpless to find it. He would have liked to know how much of it could be grasped by the best informed man in the world. . . . Historians undertake to arrange sequence,—called stories, or histories—assuming in silence a relation of cause and effect. These assumptions, hidden in the depths of dusty libraries, have been astounding, but commonly unconscious and childlike; so much so, that if any captious critic were to drag them to light, historians would probably reply, with one voice, that they had never supposed themselves required to know what they were talking about. Adams, for one, had toiled in vain to find out what he meant. . . . Where he saw sequence, other men saw something quite different, and no one saw the same unit of measure. . . . Satisfied that the sequence of men led to nothing and that the sequence of their society could lead no further, while the mere sequence of time was artificial, and the sequence of thought was chaos, he turned at last to the sequence of force; and thus it

happened, that after ten years' pursuit, he found himself lying in the Gallery of Machines at the Great Exposition of 1900, his historical neck broken by the sudden eruption of forces totally new.[68]

Would that any future world's fairs, building on the message of Vancouver's Expo '86, have a similarly profound impact on at least a few of their visitors.[69]

IV

Finally, high tech promotes "technological literacy" but in so doing at once displays a narrow, ahistorical conception of literacy and suggests a defensiveness about what genuine technological literacy reveals about technology's past, present, and future. The indifference to technology's past here is no worse—but no better—than the obsession with technology's past regarding high-tech advertising. Like the high-tech prophets and world's fairs' sponsors, though, the promoters of technological literacy ultimately cannot escape the historical burden of technology's mixed blessings.

More than three decades after C. P. Snow at once identified and lamented the growing gap between the "two cultures"—the sciences and the humanities—technological literacy is being widely hailed as the long-sought bridge between them.[70] Curricular reforms at several leading liberal arts colleges, supported by the private Alfred Sloan Foundation, have been introduced to institutionalize technological literacy. They include courses and research projects ranging from computer-generated art and music to bridge, cathedral, and skyscraper design to game theory and national security to the social and psychological effects of noise pollution. And these so-called New Liberal Arts programs are merely the forerunners of anticipated nationwide educational reforms intended to restore America's economic as well as technological supremacy. Not since the upheavals in American education after the 1957 Sputnik satellite launching has so much concern been expressed about technical (and scientific) education.[71] In the representative words of two technological literacy advocates, "technological development" is accelerating so much that "fewer and fewer people will understand these changes." This could create a "technologically illiterate nation." Shades of Toffler's *Future Shock!* Thus everyone must "understand technology if we are to function as citizens in such roles as voters, workers, employers, consumers, and . . . family members."[72]

Yet the concept—and practice—of technological literacy, as evidenced by these initial efforts, may be more problematic than its advocates realize. Technological literacy is riddled with several ironies that call into question its ultimate utility for its intended beneficiaries: those outside the ranks of engineers and other technical experts who wish to know more about and participate more fully in our avowedly technological society, particularly future decision-makers, not simply ordinary citizens.

The first irony of technological literacy is that, contrary to what one might expect, the term does not mean simply becoming acquainted with technology as hardware, that is, as computers, word processors, faxes, and the other devices of the contemporary revolution in electronics and information processing. Technological literacy is only partly a vocational enterprise, only partly a matter of learning the new alphabet of that revolution. But insofar as it is such, the most diehard humanists alone could reject this reform. Consequently, many self-proclaimed humanists have openly embraced the hardware.

In truth, however, as represented by the New Liberal Arts agenda, technological literacy also means becoming familiar with the nature of technology itself, or what I like to call technology as software: its principles, functions, and values. Here the hardware is quite secondary, and technology is appropriately deemed as much an intellectual as a material phenomenon. Hence the emphasis within the New Liberal Arts on basic engineering principles, applied mathematics, computer models, and other aspects of "quantitative reasoning"—to use one of its favorite terms. Not surprisingly, the persons most often requiring such enlightenment are those in the humanities, some of whom still pride themselves on their ignorance of—if not hostility toward—technology. That such persons have usually been the most fervent advocates of forcing engineering (and science) students to acquire a liberal arts education as well is the second irony of technological literacy; for they themselves refuse to become well rounded.

Yet those humanists' traditional assumptions about technology being separate(d) from its human creators and potentially harmful to their interests retain a certain validity today, as Americans' long-standing faith in technical experts and in their allegedly "fail-safe" systems declines (even in the face of the temporary resurgence of technological utopianism during the Persian Gulf War). Certainly technology has always been and continues to be very much a human creation, as the

New Liberal Arts programs properly try to demonstrate. However, the fundamental fear on the part of such humanists that contemporary forms of technology—whether robots or computers or nuclear weapons—will get out of control is not without basis. For that matter, the more nonexperts learn about modern technology the more they may become concerned as much as converted. Their much-vaunted new ability to "do" technology rather than, as with many older Science, Technology, and Society programs, merely talk about it, may thus prove harmful to technology's own advance.[73] This is the third irony of technological literacy.

The fourth irony is that many scientists are also in need of enlightenment about the nature of technology. As Snow himself recognized, scientists can be as patronizing toward engineers and other technologists as any self-proclaimed humanists. He thus deemed technology a separate or third culture—a point widely ignored by commentators on his work.[74] Appropriately, the New Liberal Arts have illuminated the profound differences between science and technology and have suggested that technology is not merely the application of scientific principles but rather a highly intellectual, design-oriented enterprise in itself. As Princeton civil engineer David Billington, perhaps the leading practitioner of the New Liberal Arts, has argued, "Science is discovery, engineering is design. Scientists study the natural, engineers create the artificial. Scientists create general theories out of observed data; engineers make things, often using only very approximate theories." Engineers' "primary motive for design is the creation of an object that works."[75] Such differences between science and technology surely bolster the case for including technology in the liberal arts curriculum as an independent intellectual construct, along with science. Not all scientists, though, would be comfortable with so broadening the liberal arts.

The fifth irony of technological literacy, however, is that some of its advocates appear to desire not just the discussion but the outright acceptance by humanists of technological thinking and values, above all, that pervasive assumption among engineers and technologists generally that the fundamental problems of the world are technical in nature and that those problems both have been and are being routinely solved by technology. True, as Billington observes, engineers often see more than one solution to a problem; and problem solving in itself can certainly be a creative endeavor. But the idea that there may *not* be a solution to every given problem, technical or not, is alien to engineers, just as it is to the high-tech prophets, advertisers, world's fair/theme park designers, and their collective corporate employers and patrons. Writings that suggest this, such as Franz Kafka's *The Trial* and *The Castle*, are deeply disturbing to engineering students (and their mentors), as I have learned from my own teaching experience. Not surprisingly, one still finds genuine technological utopians among the advocates of robotics, genetic engineering, space colonies, nuclear power, and, of course, "Star Wars." Nor is it accidental that engineering students assigned Huxley's *Brave New World* often misinterpret the work as a genuine utopia, a technocrat's dream world, with themselves as the Alphas, or leaders of society. The skeptical, often critical, view of the world and of its imperfect inhabitants that one commonly associates with the humanities—from Greek tragedies to Shakespearean plays to antiutopian novels—is thereby threatened by this extension of technological literacy. By contrast, civil engineer and popular writer Samuel Florman, a prominent advocate of integrating engineering with the "old" liberal arts, repeatedly emphasizes the "tragic view of life" gleaned from a more traditional humanities curriculum and its value to engineers and nonengineers alike. Hardly an opponent of technological progress, Florman nevertheless tempers his optimism with an appreciation of mankind's limitations which his own exposure to the humanities has taught him. Florman thus would not, I believe, favor transforming the liberal arts curriculum in the new directions outlined here.[76]

Significantly, as reported in the educational press, certain of the initial Sloan-supported efforts to advance the New Liberal Arts have been criticized by the foundation for insufficient attention to quantitative reasoning and other "technological modes of thought" in their teaching and research.[77] The assumption that the most fundamental issues and values can be quantified in one way or another—and that those not quantifiable aren't truly important—equally distinguishes technology from the traditional liberal arts, where such assumptions are invariably rejected as naive and shallow. Furthermore, the kind of precise, analytical thinking found in technology may not apply as readily to the liberal arts as some of its advocates suggest. Consequently, no matter how warmly humanists embrace technology, this profoundly different worldview remains.

The sixth irony is that technological literacy may not be as essential to the daily functioning of our high-tech society as its advocates would have us believe. For all the hype about the acknowledged need for ordinary citizens, but especially non-technically trained decision-makers, to understand better the world in which they live, it has yet to be demonstrated, as one curriculum development expert concedes, "exactly how much knowledge and skill in scientific and technical fields an individual needs to work as an accountant, a construction worker, a clerk, a secretary, or a teacher"—or, for that matter, as a corporate executive or a government official.[78] If, as in the exemplary case of computers, high tech has become so "user friendly" that one hardly requires extensive technical expertise to operate them successfully, what is the compelling case for technological literacy in the broader sense espoused by its advocates? Is it really true that, as a leading New Liberal Arts advocate assumes, "If people understand what's going on inside a computer or TV, they will enjoy it more"?[79] Could one not argue that high tech's very advances in cases like computers (and televisions) have ironically undermined rather than advanced technological literacy's utility?

The seventh irony is that an appreciation of technology's own past might well make one cautious about technological literacy's future. Where, however, the humanities provide a sense of history, most advocates of technological literacy seem to have little interest in history, including the history of technology. (The teaching and scholarship of Billington on machines and structures, two very different sides of technology, is a notable exception.) For them, as for other high-tech visionaries, technology is only future oriented, and what is past is literally "bunk."[80] In fact, technology has a rich history, as its scholars have made abundantly clear in recent decades, and technological literacy ought to be broadened to encompass that history. For that matter, the very idea of spreading technological literacy in America can be traced back at least as far as the nineteenth-century mechanics institutes that provided basic technical instruction to working-class citizens. Are the proponents of technological literacy aware of these antecedents? Or do they see themselves as the originators of this crusade?

Equally troublesome, the majority of those few technological literacy crusaders who do incorporate history in their teaching and research appears to believe that history shows technology to have always been a positive and progressive force, only solving problems, never creating them; this naturally leads to technological utopianism. Yet the history of technology, far from being an exemplar of the overly optimistic Whig

Theory of history, invariably reflects technology's mixed impact on and reception by virtually every society, from the most technologically primitive to the most advanced. Hence the real lesson to be learned from the serious study of technology's past is that technological progress and social progress do not necessarily go hand-in-hand but often conflict. The same lesson, of course, can be derived from the serious study of such contemporary technological advances as pesticides, organ transplants, nuclear weapons, and space shuttles. A course or program in technological literacy that suggested this might nevertheless risk loss of foundation, corporate, governmental, or, for that matter, college and university support. So might a course or program that led newly enlightened citizens to control (their) technology by, say, opposing the nuclear power plants or nuclear weapons they now truly understood. Has the technological literacy crusade sufficient "self-confidence"—to use another of its favorite terms—to accept serious questioning of its worldview? Or, in the words announcing a recent national conference on technological literacy, to consider seriously the "ethical and value implications" of technology, much less the political implications?[81]

The eighth irony of technological literacy is that its advocates' democratic rhetoric does not quite mesh with the elitism inherent in both the major engineering schools and the prestigious liberal arts colleges that have nearly monopolized public and private funds for the New Liberal Arts. This situation does show signs of changing—as with the excellent Sloan-supported program at the State University of New York at Stony Brook, a large public and to this extent nonelitist institution—but the persistent emphasis on (re)educating present and future decision-makers loses some of its appeal outside those charmed circles.[82] Subsequent Sloan funding at twelve historically black colleges is another step in the more democratic direction. Can technological literacy be as effectively applied to mass higher education as it has been to date to those elite institutions? For that matter, can technological literacy "trickle down" to mass secondary and elementary education as readily as its advocates suggest it can? No less important, can the managerial ethos endemic to the training of future engineers be tempered in the direction of sharing responsibility for technology's future with ordinary citizens? And can characteristically indifferent engineering and other technical students be stirred politically or socially?

The ninth and final irony is that the very push for technological literacy ultimately reflects ambivalence, or at least anxiety, on its proponents' part about technology's future. This is not to deny their surface optimistic views and values but rather to suggest their underlying concern as to why such optimism is not widely shared among other educated persons. In varying ways the same concern accounts for the overcompensatory zeal of high-tech prophets, advertisers, world's fair/ theme park designers, and their corporate sponsors. Admittedly, technological literacy efforts *are* winning converts away from the hostility toward technology (and science) found in some of the Science, Technology, and Society (STS) programs of the late 1960s and early 1970s. These efforts might actually sway certain programs in the opposite direction, toward what Langdon Winner has called HSTS—"Hooray for Science, Technology, and Society."[83] Nevertheless, if technological literacy is truly to bridge the three separate cultures Snow described without simultaneously threatening the humanities and alienating the sciences, it must somehow incorporate a critical, historical perspective. Just as being literate in a conventional sense today entails more than being able to read and write—it now also means being able to function in society and to develop one's knowledge and potential[84]—so being technologically literate should properly entail more than being comfortable with the hardware or even the software.

V

With technological literacy, then, as with prophecies, advertising, and world's fairs/theme parks, contemporary high tech cannot let go of the past as it otherwise passionately embraces the present and the future. It is as if, deep down, high tech's promoters fear that the world of tomorrow may prove considerably less than utopian, their public stances notwithstanding. In this regard let me add a concluding point. The eminent philosopher of science Nicholas Rescher has examined the findings of leading pollsters and concluded that Americans and, by extension, citizens of comparably industrialized societies generally find technological advances insufficient in themselves to constitute perceived increases in personal happiness. By and large people do not oppose advances that enhance domestic comforts or contribute to the national welfare. But they simultaneously yearn for the "good old days," when, despite these advances, life was supposedly happier; they also simultaneously desire ever more such advances to meet the ever rising expectations created by the most recent advances. Hence a terribly complicated, sometimes contradictory, set of assumptions colors conventional Western attitudes toward technological progress and social progress.[85] What most concerns Rescher, however, is the growing tendency to blame technology—and science—rather than ourselves, for not producing the satisfying increase in personal happiness that they were supposed to produce. This concern is surely legitimate if, I suggest, exaggerated by him and others. The deeper problem is determining what to do next, once it is agreed that, in Rescher's words, "Science and technology cannot deliver on the $64,000 question of human satisfaction . . . because, in the final analysis, they simply do not furnish the stuff of which real happiness is made."[86] This is what led me to that prospect of a technological plateau discussed in chapter 3, the prospect partially undermined by the resurgence of technological utopianism during and after the Persian Gulf War.

Contemporary high tech is thus replete with many ironies of the unanticipated consequences of technological progress along the route to technological utopia. That such consequences are painfully familiar to those truly knowledgeable about technology's past is yet another irony. So long as its various promotional enterprises turn a profit and generate positive public relations, high tech may not care what ordinary citizens, much less cultural critics, feel about these dilemmas. Yet ordinary citizens, not simply intellectuals, may care a good deal more than high tech and its promoters believe (or allow themselves to believe). The ideological and other ends being served by unjustified technological optimism may turn out to be every bit as questionable as those being served by technological pessimism in other quarters. However successful its individual technologies, then, high tech is lacking in the very historical consciousness that would in turn temper its optimism and thereby, most ironically of all, perhaps strengthen its appeal.

NOTES

· ·

1. INTRODUCTION

1. The two principal collections of primary historical sources on public attitudes toward American technology reflect a fundamentally hopeful outlook, an outlook only periodically tempered by negative developments akin to those listed above. See *Readings in Technology and American Life*, ed. Carroll W. Pursell, Jr. (New York: Oxford University Press, 1969), and *Changing Attitudes Toward American Technology*, ed. Thomas P. Hughes (New York: Harper and Row, 1975). Hughes's Introduction and Conclusion are especially illuminating in this regard. By contrast, the now infamous nationally televised speech of President Jimmy Carter on July 15, 1979, about the nation's malaise, reprinted in the *New York Times* of July 17, 1979, is notably simplistic in its assumption of an unchanging American faith in technological progress until quite recent times. See also Henry Allen, "Give Us This Day Our Daily Dread: Doom, Defeat, and Despair Have America Dragging Its Tailfeathers," *Washington Post National Weekly Edition*, December 17–23, 1990, 11–12.

2. See Howard P. Segal, "Let's Abandon the Whig Theory of the History of Technology," *The Chronicle of Higher Education* 18 (July 9, 1979): 64. See also John M. Staudenmaier, *Technology's Storytellers: Reweaving the Human Fabric* (Cambridge: MIT Press, 1985), chap. 5; Staudenmaier, "Comment: Recent Trends in the History of Technology," *American Historical Review* 95 (June 1990): 715–25; and Melvin Kranzberg, "The Uses of History in Studies of Science, Technology, and Society," *Bulletin of Science, Technology, and Society* 10 (1990): 6–11.

3. Definitions of "technology" abound. For perhaps the most sensible, see David P. Billington, "Structures and Machines: The Two Sides of Technology," *Soundings* 57 (Fall 1974): 275–88.

4. Jacques Ellul, *The Technological Society*, tr. John Wilkinson (New York: Vintage Books, 1964). The book was originally published in French in 1954 as *La Technique ou l'Enjeu du Siècle*. My chapter 11 on Lewis Mumford elaborates on the significance of the book's English title.

5. On the development of the history of American technology as an area of scholarship, see Staudenmaier, *Technology's Storytellers;* Staudenmaier, "Comment: Recent Trends"; Kranzberg and William H. Davenport, "Introduction: At the Start," in *Technology and Culture: An Anthology,* ed. Kranzberg and Davenport (New York: Meridian Books, 1975), 9–20; and *In Context: History and the History of Technology: Essays in Honor of Melvin Kranzberg,* ed. Stephen H. Cutcliffe and Robert C. Post (Bethlehem, Pa.: Lehigh University Press, 1989).

6. On the writing of American history, especially for secondary schools, see Frances Fitzgerald, *America Revised: History Schoolbooks in the Twentieth Century* (Boston: Atlantic–Little, Brown, 1979), and Paul A. Gagnon, *Democracy's Half-Told Story: What American History Textbooks Should Add* (Washington, D.C.: American Federation of Teachers, 1989).

7. See Daniel J. Boorstin, *The Republic of Technology: Reflections on Our Future Community* (New York: Harper and Row, 1978). Despite the title, chapters 5 and 6 have nothing to do with technology. Significantly, Boorstin nowhere mentions America's use of advanced military technology in Vietnam, Cambodia, and other foreign lands in the 1960s and 1970s.

8. On the development of American Studies as an area of scholarship, see Karen J. Winkler, "For Scholars in American Studies, the Intellectual Landscape Is Changing," *The Chronicle of Higher Education* 20 (March 10, 1980): 3–4, and an interview by Bruce Tucker with Gary Kulik, editor of *American Quarterly,* the field's leading journal, "Assessing the Field: An Oral History Interview," *Canadian Review of American Studies* 23 (Fall 1992): 1–14.

9. The most recent of these studies, and one of the most penetrating, is C. Vann Woodward, *The Old World's New World* (New York: New York Public Library/Oxford University Press, 1991).

10. See Boorstin, *The Genius of American Politics* (Chicago: Phoenix Books, 1959), esp. chap. 1, and David M. Potter, *People of Plenty: Economic Abundance and the American Character* (Chicago: Phoenix Books, 1954), chap. 7.

11. See Frank E. Manuel, "Toward a Psychological History of Utopias," in *Utopias and Utopian Thought,* ed. Manuel (Boston: Beacon Press, 1967), 69–98.

12. As historian Francis Jennings puts it so well, "American society is the product not only of interaction between colonists and natives but of contributions from both." Yet "Civilization was not brought from Europe to triumph over the Indians; rather the Indians paid a staggering price in lives, labor, goods, and lands as their part in creation of modern American society and culture. . . ." For, finally, "The American land was more like a widow than a virgin" (*The Invasion of America: Indians, Colonialism, and the Cant of Conquest* [New York: Norton, 1975], vi–vii, 41, 30).

13. On the revisionist interpretations of American abundance summarized in this and succeeding paragraphs, see Daniel M. Fox, *The Discovery of Abundance: Simon N. Patten and the Transformation of Social Theory* (Ithaca, N.Y.: Cornell University Press, 1967); Zane L. Miller, "Scarcity, Abundance, and American Urban History," *Journal of Urban History* 4 (February 1978): 131–55; and Kenneth E. Boulding, Michael Kammen, and Seymour Martin Lipset, *From Abundance to Scarcity: Implications for the American Tradition* (Columbus: Ohio State University Press, 1978). Potter's *People of Plenty* is a landmark pioneering study of American abundance but suffers from a false assumption of persistent abundance throughout American history. As Jennings observes, "Europeans explorers and invaders discovered an inhabited land. Had it been pristine wilderness then, it would possibly be so still today, for neither the technology nor the social organization of Europe in the sixteenth and seventeenth centuries had the capacity to maintain, of its own resources, outpost colonies thousands of miles from home" (Jennings, *Invasion of America*, 15). See also ibid., 33–34.

14. It is ironic that one of the earliest, most penetrating, and most publicized reports on industrialization in America made the very connections among natural resources, technological advance, and abundance overlooked by American historians who wrote after its publication. It is further ironic that this work, *The Report of the Committee on the Machinery of the United States* (1854–1855), was written by a group of prominent British citizens sent by their government to examine the nature and uses of American structures and machines in what was beginning to be called "The American System of Manufacturing." And it is yet more ironic that delays in the opening of the New York Industrial Exhibition of 1853, the American counterpart to the British Crystal Palace Exhibition of 1851 and the particular occasion of their journey, gave the visitors an unexpected opportunity to investigate American industry outside of the Exhibition itself. See *The American System of Manufactures: The Report of the Committee on the Machinery of the United States, 1855, and the Special Reports of George Wallis and Joseph Whitworth, 1854*, ed. Nathan Rosenberg (Edinburgh: Edinburgh University Press, 1969), 387–88. Despite its deficiencies, Potter's *People of Plenty*, it should be noted, correctly recognizes the transformations needed to convert natural resources into finished products. See Potter, 161–62. On this point, see also Cecelia Tichi, *New World, New Earth: Environmental Reform in American Literature from the Puritans through Whitman* (New Haven, Conn.: Yale University Press, 1979), 70, 90, 153.

15. On the biographical background and visionary writings of these antebellum technological utopians, see Segal, *Technological Utopianism in American Culture* (Chicago: University of Chicago Press, 1985), 3, 77, 78, 88, 89–91, 173–74.

16. Tichi, *New World, New Earth*, viii, and Sacvan Bercovitch, *The American Jeremiad* (Madison: University of Wisconsin Press, 1979), 179. On the nature and persistence of this "ideology," see the whole of both books but esp. Tichi, ix, 49–50, 66, 72–73, 148–49, 215, and Bercovitch, 9, 178.

17. See Tichi, *New World, New Earth,* 55, 64, 85–86, 89–90, 103–105, 134, 165, 168, 190, 216, and Bercovitch, *American Jeremiad,* 111, 142, 162–63.

18. Tichi, *New World, New Earth,* x, 114, 69.

19. On the fate of industrial design in general and of streamlining in particular in the years after 1939, see Jeffrey L. Meikle, *Twentieth-Century Limited: Industrial Design in America, 1925–1939* (Philadelphia: Temple University Press, 1979), 209–10. See also Donald J. Bush, *The Streamlined Decade* (New York: Braziller, 1975), and Bush, "Futurama: World's Fair as Utopia," *Alternative Futures* 2 (Fall 1979): 3–20.

2. THE "MIDDLE LANDSCAPE"

1. Leo Marx, *The Machine in the Garden: Technology and the Pastoral Ideal in America* (New York: Oxford University Press, 1964), 3, 4.

2. Ibid., 4.

3. Ibid., 30, 28.

4. Marx emphasizes the years 1840–60 as, in economist Walt Rostow's phrase, the period of "take-off"—a concept that was more respectable at the time Marx wrote. Marx even singles out a specific year as his starting point: 1844, the date of Nathaniel Hawthorne's first encounter with the machine intruding in the garden.

5. Marx, *Machine in the Garden,* 5, 32.

6. Marx elaborates upon the American aversion to "raw" wilderness in his "Technology and Ecology as a Driving Force in Literature," in *Civil Engineering: History,· Heritage, and the Humanities: Selected Papers from the First National Conference, Princeton University, 1970* (Princeton, N.J.: Princeton University Press, n.d.), n.p. On mankind's ancient and seemingly eternal fear of "raw" wilderness, see Roderick Nash, *Wilderness and the American Mind* (New Haven, Conn.: Yale University Press, 1967), chaps. 1–2.

7. See Alan Marcus and Howard P. Segal, *Technology in America: A Brief History* (San Diego: Harcourt Brace Jovanovich, 1989), chap. 1.

8. Marx, *The Machine in the Garden,* 141–42.

9. Henry Nash Smith, *Virgin Land: The American West as Symbol and Myth* (Cambridge: Harvard University Press, 1950), 259.

10. For Jefferson, writes Bender, "commerce was an element of an advanced agricultural economy and was without urban implications" (*Toward an Urban Vision: Ideas and Institutions in Nineteenth Century America* [Lexington: University Press of Kentucky, 1975], 22).

11. See Marvin Fisher, *Workshops in the Wilderness: The European Response to American Industrialization, 1830–1860* (New York: Oxford University Press, 1967).

12. On the nature of these communities and their significance for republican ideology, see Fisher, esp. chap. 6; John Coolidge, *Mill and Mansion: A Study of Architecture and Society in Lowell, Massachusetts, 1820–1865* (1942; reprint ed., Amherst: University of Massachusetts Press, 1993); Christopher

Tunnard, *The City of Man* (New York: Scribner, 1953), 158–64; John W. Reps, *The Making of Urban America: A History of City Planning in the United States* (Princeton, N.J.: Princeton University Press, 1965), 415–20; Bender, *Toward an Urban Vision*, chaps. 4–5; and John Kasson, *Civilizing the Machine: Technology and Republican Values in America, 1776–1900* (New York: Grossman/Viking, 1976), chaps. 1–2.

13. Marx, *The Machine in the Garden*, 353. For criticism of Marx's literary selections and interpretations, see Paul Levine, "The Region of Culture," *American Scholar* 34 (Spring 1965): 298–300; Nicolaus C. Mills, "The Machine in the Anglo-American Garden," *Centennial Review* 14 (Spring 1970): 201–12; and John Lark Bryant, "A Usable Pastoralism: Leo Marx's Method in *The Machine in the Garden*," *American Studies* 16 (Spring 1975): 63–72.

14. Marx, *The Machine in the Garden*, 5, 365. Despite an old-fashioned "humanistic" stance against technology implicit in his book and made explicit in his "American Institutions and Ecological Ideals," *Science*, n.s., 170 (November 27, 1970): 945–52, Marx, in his Princeton Conference paper and later writings, indicates a more sophisticated, more even-handed attitude toward technology in general and criticizes primarily its misuse rather than its nature; its incorporation in contemporary governmental, corporate, and military systems he understandably condemns more than the structures and machines that enable them to function so well. See also his "Technology and the Study of Man," in *The Sciences, the Humanities and the Technological Threat*, ed. W. Roy Niblett (New York: Wiley, 1975), 3–20, an abridged version of which appeared under the same title in Phi Beta Kappa's *The Key Reporter* 39 (Spring 1974): 2–4, 8. Significantly, however, one of Marx's most recent publications, a review in the Society for the History of Technology's official journal of a festschrift honoring the Society's—and the field's—founder, questions the value of the history of technology as a separate scholarly enterprise. Marx regards "its existence as another manifestation of that very tendency of mind it was designed to explain: our increasingly fragmented, technocratic view of life and learning" (Marx, review of *In Context: History and the History of Technology—Essays in Honor of Melvin Kranzberg, Technology and Culture* 32 [April 1991]: 396. See also the follow-up correspondence between Kranzberg and Marx in *Technology and Culture* 33 [April 1992]: 406–407).

15. Bender, *Toward an Urban Vision*, 77. One major problem confronting Lowell and other similar communities was the necessity of replacing departing well-bred farm girls with poor, less-acculturated, and sometimes foreign-born males.

16. Smith, *Virgin Land*, 123, 259. As Alan Trachtenberg argued in an early, and otherwise quite favorable, review of *The Machine in the Garden*, "Marx's treatment of the dialectic [between machine and garden] within history is not as strong nor as convincing as his treatment of the contradictions within consciousness" ("The American Way of Life," *The Nation* 201 [July 19, 1965]: 45).

17. First, in regard to the "middle state ethic," the source of the concept of

the middle landscape: "this is a scheme that admits of no absolute solutions, and looks to an endless series of *ad hoc* decisions, compromises, and adjustments in resolving problems" (Marx, *Machine in the Garden*, 100); and second, in regard to Jefferson: "the controlling principle" of his politics is his "dialectical" image of society, "his recognition of the constant need to redefine the 'middle landscape' ideal, pushing it ahead, so to speak, into an unknown future to adjust it to ever-changing circumstances" (ibid., 139). Nash contends that the conditions of wilderness as well underwent continual change. See Nash, *Wilderness and the American Mind*, 6–7.

18. Bender, *Toward an Urban Vision*, 92. On cemeteries, walkways, and parks, see Bender, chap. 4, and Reps, *Making of Urban America*, 325–30.

19. See Albert Fein, *Frederick Law Olmsted and the American Environmental Tradition* (New York: Braziller, 1972). Of contemporary "landscape architects," and Olmsted was more than a landscape architect in any case, only Horace William Shaler Cleveland, Robert Morris Copeland, and Charles Eliot approached his achievement. Although his work influenced Olmsted's, Andrew Jackson Downing was not urban enough in his orientation to warrant further attention here. On Olmsted's accomplishments, see, besides Fein, Bender, *Toward an Urban Vision*, chap. 7 and epilogue; Reps, *Making of Urban America*, 331–39, 342–45, 348, 498; and Norman T. Newton, *Design on the Land: The Development of Landscape Architecture* (Cambridge: Harvard University Press, 1971), chaps. 19–26, 32, 40–41. The definitive biography is Laura Wood Roper, *FLO: A Biography of Frederick Law Olmsted* (Baltimore: The Johns Hopkins University Press, 1973).

20. On Olmsted's suburban designs, see Fein, *Frederick Law Olmsted*, 32–35; Bender, *Toward an Urban Vision*, 171–72, 181–84; Newton, *Design on the Land*, 464–71; Reps, *Making of Urban America*, 342–45, 348; Roper, *FLO*, 305, 308, 318–19, 321–26; and Tunnard, *City of Man*, 192–95.

21. The pioneering, if rather brief, accounts of these early suburbs are in Carl Bridenbaugh's *Cities in the Wilderness: Urban Life in America, 1625–1742* (New York: Capricorn Books, 1964), 306, and his *Cities in Revolt: Urban Life in America, 1743–1776* (New York: Capricorn Books, 1964), 24–25.

22. On the electrified street railways, see Glen E. Holt, "The Changing Perception of Urban Pathology: An Essay on the Development of Mass Transit in the United States," in *Cities in American History*, ed. Kenneth T. Jackson and Stanley K. Schultz (New York: Knopf, 1972), 324–43, and Joel A. Tarr, "From City to Suburb: The 'Moral' Influence of Transportation Technology," in *American Urban History: An Interpretive Reader with Commentaries*, ed. Alexander B. Callow, Jr., rev. ed. (New York: Oxford University Press, 1973), 202–12. For their impact upon the growth of Boston, see Sam Bass Warner, Jr., *Streetcar Suburbs: The Process of Growth in Boston, 1870–1900* (Cambridge: Harvard University Press, 1962); upon Milwaukee, Clay McShane, *Technology and Reform: Street Railways and the Growth of Milwaukee, 1887–1900* (Madison: State Historical Society of Wisconsin, 1974); and upon Norfolk and else-

where, Charles N. Glaab and A. Theodore Brown, *A History of Urban America* (New York: Macmillan, 1967), 157–58, 281–83.

23. On Shaker Heights, see Glaab and Brown, *History of Urban America,* 283–84. On the Country Club District, see ibid., 292–95, and Newton, *Design on the Land,* 471–74.

24. On Pullman, see Reps, *Making of Urban America,* 421–24, and esp. Stanley Buder, *Pullman: An Experiment in Industrial Order and Community Planning, 1880–1930* (New York: Oxford University Press, 1967). On Gary, see Raymond A. Mohl and Neil Betten, "The Failure of Industrial City Planning: Gary, Indiana, 1906–1910," *Journal of the American Institute of Planners* 38 (July 1972): 203–14.

25. On Howard, see Walter L. Creese, *The Search for Environment: The Garden City: Before and After* (New Haven, Conn.: Yale University Press, 1966), and Peter Batchelor, "The Origin of the Garden City Concept of Urban Form," *Journal of the Society of Architectural Historians* 28 (October 1969): 184–200. On Forest Hills Gardens, see Newton, *Design on the Land,* 474–78. On Sunnyside Gardens and Radburn, see ibid., 489–95. On the New Deal communities, see ibid., 502–507; Paul K. Conkin, *Tomorrow a New World: The New Deal Community Program* (Ithaca, N.Y.: Cornell University Press, 1959), chap. 14; and Joseph L. Arnold, *The New Deal in the Suburbs: A History of the Greenbelt Town Program, 1935–1954* (Columbus: Ohio State University Press, 1971).

26. According to Donald Worster, the German scientist and philosopher Ernst Haeckel coined the term "ecology" in 1866. (Introduction, *American Environmentalism: The Formative Period, 1860–1915,* ed. Worster [New York: Wiley, 1973], 3). Worster properly includes an 1871 Olmsted report in his excellent collection of primary materials and in his penetrating introduction to them persuasively justifies his doing so.

27. See Samuel P. Hays, *Conservation and the Gospel of Efficiency: The Progressive Conservation Movement, 1890–1920* (New York: Atheneum, 1969).

28. See Roy Lubove, *Community Planning in the 1920's: The Contribution of the Regional Planning Association of America* (Pittsburgh: University of Pittsburgh Press, 1963).

29. On the TVA, see Thomas K. McCraw, *Morgan vs. Lilienthal: The Feud Within the TVA* (Chicago: Loyola University Press, 1970); McCraw, *TVA and the Power Fight, 1933–1939* (Philadelphia: Lippincott, 1971); Robert E. Barde, "Arthur E. Morgan, First Chairman of TVA," *Tennessee Historical Quarterly* 30 (Fall 1971): 299–314; and Roy Talbert, Jr., *FDR's Utopian: Arthur Morgan of the TVA* (Jackson: University Press of Mississippi, 1987).

30. See Jean Gottman, *Megalopolis: The Urbanized Northeastern Seaboard of the United States* (Cambridge: MIT Press, 1961).

31. See Warner, *The Urban Wilderness: A History of the American City* (New York: Harper and Row, 1972), 63 and chap. 5. Robert M. Fogelson, in contrast, is highly critical of Los Angeles's development. See his *The Frag-*

mented Metropolis: Los Angeles, 1850–1930 (Cambridge: Harvard University Press, 1967).

32. John L. Thomas, *Alternative America: Henry George, Edward Bellamy, Henry Demarest Lloyd and the Adversary Tradition* (Cambridge: Harvard University Press, 1983), 359.

33. See Henry Olerich, *A Cityless and Countryless World; An Outline of Practical Co-operative Individualism* (Holstein, Ia.: Gilmore and Olerich, 1893).

34. Albert Waldo Howard, *The Milltillionaire* (Boston: n.p., 1895), 9.

35. Marx, *The Machine in the Garden*, 141.

36. On the European origins and manifestations of the middle landscape, see Mark B. Lapping, "The Middle Landscape and American Urban Theory" (Ph.D. diss., Emory University, 1972), chap. 2, and esp. Raymond Williams, *The Country and the City* (New York: Oxford University Press, 1973).

37. Paul Lukacs, "The Critic in the Garden," review of *The Pilot and the Passenger, American Scholar* 58 (Autumn 1989), 601. This lengthy review (pp. 600–604) is notable for recognizing in Marx's essays the general problem I raise here and raised in the 1977 earlier version of this essay.

38. See William L. Bowers, *The Country Life Movement in America, 1900–1920* (Port Washington, N.Y.: Kennikat, 1974); Don S. Kirschner, *City and Country: Rural Responses to Urbanization in the 1920's* (Westport, Conn.: Greenwood, 1970), chaps. 2, 7; James L. Machor, *Pastoral Cities: Urban Ideals and the Symbolic Landscape of America* (Madison: University of Wisconsin Press, 1987); Peter J. Schmitt, *Back to Nature: The Arcadian Myth in Urban America* (New York: Oxford University Press, 1969); Reynold M. Wik, *Henry Ford and Grass-roots America* (Ann Arbor: University of Michigan Press, 1972); and Peter G. Rowe, *Making a Middle Landscape* (Cambridge: MIT Press, 1991).

39. Marx, "American Literary Culture and the Fatalistic View of Technology," in his *The Pilot and the Passenger: Essays on Literature, Technology, and Culture in the United States* (New York: Oxford University Press, 1988), 197–98.

40. Marx, *Machine in the Garden*, 365. In addition to the 1978 essay cited in n. 39, see also his essays in *The Pilot and the Passenger* on "The Neo-Romantic Critique of Science," "Susan Sontag's 'New Left Pastoral,'" and "The American Revolution and the American Landscape." All have considerable political content.

41. See, for example, his two essays on F. O. Matthiessen in *The Pilot and the Passenger* published in 1950 and 1983 respectively.

42. Marx, "Pastoralism in America," in *Ideology and Classic American Literature*, ed. Sacvan Bercovitch and Myra Jehlen (New York: Cambridge University Press, 1986), 40, 49. In his 1978 essay cited in n. 39 Marx had written that "The pastoral world-view is particularly appealing to disaffected members of the professional middle class and intelligentsia who, for several reasons, are

better able to identify with residual than emergent elements of the culture. If the experience of the Vietnam era is any indication, their political protest against the dominant culture is likely to be eruptive, unstable, and transient in character. The much sought after alliance with the civil rights or labor movements proved to be unattainable, and without such an alliance the politics of pastoralism might well become reactionary or, as in the late 1960s, simply evaporate" (206–207).

43. See Marx's later extension of the basic argument of *The Machine in the Garden* to artistic treatments of railroads in his "The Railroad-in-the-Landscape: An Iconological Reading of a Theme in American Art," in *The Railroad in American Art: Representations of Technological Change*, ed. Susan Danly and Marx (Cambridge: MIT Press, 1988), 183–208. As with his book, as noted above, so with this article, Marx concludes with a provocative statement crying out for elaboration: "How foolish it is . . . to hold any machines or implements of power responsible for the damage people have done, or may yet do, with their help" (206). See also Marx, "The American Ideology of Space," in *Denatured Visions: Landscape and Culture in the Twentieth Century*, ed. Stuart Wrede and William Howard Adams (New York: Museum of Modern Art, 1991), 62–78.

3. THE AUTOMOBILE AND THE PROSPECT OF AN AMERICAN TECHNOLOGICAL PLATEAU

1. For partial—but only partial—confirmation of this proposition, see James J. Flink, "Three Stages of American Automobile Consciousness," *American Quarterly* 24 (October 1972): 451–73; Blaine A. Brownell, "A Symbol of Modernity: Attitudes Toward the Automobile in Southern Cities in the 1920's," ibid. 24 (March 1972): 20–44; Mark S. Foster, "City Planners and Urban Transportation: The American Response, 1900–1940," *Journal of Urban History* 5 (May 1979): 365–96; Foster, "The Western Response to Urban Transportation: A Tale of Three Cities, 1900–1945," *Journal of the West* 18 (July 1979): 31–39; and Foster, *From Streetcar to Superhighway: American City Planners and Urban Transportation, 1900–1940* (Philadelphia: Temple University Press, 1981).

2. Nearly all of the arguments in this paragraph in favor of the auto can be found in the 1895 editorial "The Horseless Age" quoted at the outset. *The Horseless Age* itself was merely one of several national auto journals established in the 1890s and early 1900s. Similar editorials and arguments can be found in virtually every one of them. On the contribution of auto advertising to this appeal, see Park Dixon Goist, *From Main Street to State Street: Town, City, and Community in America* (Port Washington, N.Y.: Kennikat Press, 1977), 40–44.

3. See Foster, "Western Response to Urban Transportation"; Foster, "The Model-T, the Hard Sell, and Los Angeles' Urban Growth: The Decentralization of Los Angeles during the 1920's," *Pacific Historical Review* 44 (November 1975): 459–84; Robert M. Fogelson, *The Fragmented Metropolis: Los Angeles,*

1850–1930 (Cambridge: Harvard University Press, 1967); Brownell, "Symbol of Modernity"; Brownell, *The Urban Ethos in the South, 1920–1930* (Baton Rouge: Louisiana State University Press, 1975), chaps, 3, 4; and Howard L. Preston, *Automobile Age Atlanta: The Making of a Southern Metropolis, 1900–1935* (Athens: University of Georgia Press, 1979).

4. See Reynold M. Wik, *Henry Ford and Grass-roots America* (Ann Arbor: University of Michigan Press, 1972).

5. In addition to Goist, *Main Street to State Street,* chap. 3, see Warren J. Belasco, *Americans on the Road: From Autocamp to Motel, 1910–1945* (Cambridge: MIT Press, 1979); Richard J. S. Gutman and Elliott Kaufman, *American Diner* (New York: Harper and Row, 1979); Paul Hirshorn and Steven Izenour, *White Towers* (Cambridge: MIT Press, 1979); and Daniel I. Vieyra, *Fill'er Up: An Architectural History of America's Gas Stations* (New York: Macmillan, 1979).

6. On this approach to American technology, see Alan Marcus and Howard P. Segal, *Technology in America: A Brief History* (San Diego: Harcourt Brace Jovanovich, 1989).

7. See Kenneth M. Roemer, *The Obsolete Necessity: America in Utopian Writings, 1888–1900* (Kent, Ohio: Kent State University Press, 1976); Sacvan Bercovitch, *The American Jeremiad* (Madison: University of Wisconsin Press, 1979); and esp. Cecelia Tichi, *New World, New Earth: Environmental Reform in American Literature from the Puritans through Whitman* (New Haven, Conn.: Yale University Press, 1979).

8. It is worth repeating that Leo Marx calls the (initial) middle landscape an "imaginative and complex" version of the pastoral ideal (*The Machine in the Garden: Technology and the Pastoral Ideal in America* [New York: Oxford University Press, 1964], 5).

9. On the dangers of dogmatic prophecies of whatever kind about the auto, see Foster, "City Planners and Urban Transportation," and Foster, *From Streetcar to Superhighway.* As Foster also shows, city planners, traffic engineers, public transit officials, and other experts intimately involved in the first decades of the auto's existence disagreed sharply among themselves about its immediate, much less its long-range, potential. Not surprisingly, their predictions were often contradictory and incorrect. Wisely, however, Foster refrains from using the advantage of hindsight to condemn these "experts" for lacking foresight.

10. See Flink, *The Automobile Age* (Cambridge: MIT Press, 1988).

11. See Robert Fishman, *Urban Utopias in the Twentieth Century: Ebenezer Howard, Frank Lloyd Wright, and Le Corbusier* (New York: Basic Books, 1977), and Jeffrey L. Meikle, *Twentieth-Century Limited: Industrial Design in America, 1925–1939* (Philadelphia: Temple University Press, 1979). Wright's plans for a totally decentralized "Broadacres" city, or series of cities, the antithesis of Le Corbusier's "Radiant City" save for their dependence on the auto, have ironically suffered the same fate: neglect.

12. On the history of this concept, see Segal, *Technological Utopianism in American Culture* (Chicago: University of Chicago Press, 1985), chap. 8.

13. Lewis Mumford, "If I Were Dictator," *The Nation* 83 (December 9, 1933): 631.

14. Mumford, *Technics and Civilization* (1934; reprinted New York: Harcourt, Brace and World, 1963), 429.

15. Ibid., 432, 430.

16. Mumford, *The Pentagon of Power: The Myth of the Machine: II* (New York: Harcourt Brace Jovanovich, 1970), 433.

17. On the fate of the auto and its future role within American society and culture, see, for example, Richard M. Ketchum, "Letter from the Country," *Blair and Ketchums Country Journal* 6 (June 1979): 20–21; Michael Barone, "Our Romance with the Auto Is Over," in *The Automobile and American Culture*, ed. David L. Lewis and Laurence Goldstein (Ann Arbor: University of Michigan Press, 1983), 353–55; Andrew Malcolm, "On the Road Again, With a Passion," *New York Times*, October 10, 1988, A10; and Matthew L. Wald, "In Cars, Muscle vs. Mileage: Gas Can Be Saved, But It's Up to Drivers," *New York Times*, August 16, 1990, D1, D7.

4. ALEXIS DE TOCQUEVILLE AND THE DILEMMAS OF MODERNIZATION

1. [No author] "Chronicle," *New York Times*, August 26, 1991, B5.

2. On the distortions of Alexis de Tocqueville's work by his admiring scholarly interpreters beyond those indicated here, see Lynn L. Marshall and Seymour Drescher, "American Historians and Tocqueville's *Democracy*," *Journal of American History* 55 (December 1968): 512–32.

3. Susan M. Matarese, "Foreign Policy and the American Self-Image: Looking Back at *Looking Backward*," *ATQ (The American Transcendental Quarterly)*, special issue on "American Utopias: Texts and Contexts," ed. Jean Pfaelzer, 2d ser., 3 (March 1989): 46.

4. See Seymour Drescher, *Dilemmas of Democracy: Tocqueville and Modernization* (Pittsburgh: University of Pittsburgh Press, 1968). Drescher has convincingly established that Tocqueville had no explicit or even implicit theory of modernization, given his and his contemporaries' approach to social change.

5. Alexis de Tocqueville, *Democracy in America*, ed. Phillips Bradley, tr. Henry Reeve, Francis Bowen, Bradley. 2 vols. (New York: Vintage Books, n.d.), 1:452.

6. Tocqueville, *The Old Regime and the French Revolution*, tr. Stuart Gilbert (Garden City, N.Y.: Doubleday Anchor Books, 1955), vii.

7. Tocqueville, *Democracy*, 1:355.

8. Quoted in Drescher, *Dilemmas of Democracy*, 24 n. 5.

9. Tocqueville, *Democracy*, 1:3; 2:108.

10. Ibid., 1:8.

11. Ibid., 1:334.

12. Ibid., 1:73. On Tocqueville's fundamentally psychological approach to social change, see Drescher, *Dilemmas of Democracy*, 23–25, and Melvin

Richter, "Tocqueville's Contribution to the Theory of Revolution," in *Revolution, Nomos 8: Yearbook of the American Society for Political and Legal Philosophy*, ed. Carl J. Friedrich (New York, Atherton, 1966): 75–121. Only in his last years did Tocqueville begin to perceive the inadequacy of analyses based primarily upon human character rather than at least equally upon geography, institutions, ideology, and so forth.

13. Drescher, *Dilemmas of Democracy*, 25.

14. Tocqueville, *Democracy*, 1:15. C. Vann Woodward argues that here and elsewhere Tocqueville (and other European observers) used America as a metaphor for what was later termed the process of modernization, a process even then making the West unrecognizable, and not necessarily for the better. See his *The Old World's New World* (New York: New York Public Library/ Oxford University Press, 1991), Preface.

15. Tocqueville, *Democracy*, 1:239; 1:261–62.

16. Ibid., 1:199; 1:279. Tocqueville was also aware of the possible tyranny of a minority: "The exercise of the right of association becomes dangerous, then, in proportion as great parties find themselves wholly unable to acquire the majority" (ibid., 1:204).

17. Ibid., 1:279; 2:11. The fullest account of the differences between the two volumes of *Democracy* is Drescher, "Tocqueville's Two *Démocraties*," *Journal of the History of Ideas* 25 (April 1964): 201–16. As historian James T. Schleifer has written, where in the first volume of *Democracy* Tocqueville "distinguished between governmental and administrative centralization, admitting that the first was necessary for a nation to be unified and strong, but insisting that the second was destructive to social energy and dangerous to freedom," in the second volume he portrayed "the new despotism of the bureaucratic state" that had since come about. "By contrast, England and especially America served as his models to illustrate the economic, political, social, and moral advantages of administrative decentralization" ("Tocqueville and Centralization: Four Previously Unpublished Manuscripts," *Yale University Library Gazette* 58 [October 1983]:29).

18. Tocqueville, *Democracy*, 2:263.

19. Ibid., *The Old Regime*, 119, 174.

20. Tocqueville, *Democracy*, 1:9; Sasha Reinhard Weitman, "The Sociological Thesis of Tocqueville's *The Old Regime and the Revolution*," *Social Research* 33 (Autumn 1966): 405. Tocqueville, says Weitman, saw the Revolution as "the dramatic outcome of a long period of psychological and cultural conversion of the French people to the centralizing, equalizing, and standardizing mentality which had guided the monarchy in its relentless expansion throughout the seventeenth and eighteenth centuries" (ibid., 397). On Tocqueville's conception of revolution, see also Richter, "Tocqueville's Contribution to the Theory of Revolution."

21. Tocqueville, *The European Revolution and Correspondence with Gobineau*, ed. and tr. John Lukacs (Garden City, N.Y.: Doubleday Anchor Books, 1959), 126.

22. On Tocqueville's envious comparisons in the 1850s of French democracy with English and American versions, see ibid., 97–98, 113, 164–65, and Drescher, *Tocqueville and England*, Harvard Historical Monographs, 55 (Cambridge: Harvard University Press, 1964), 170–71. His reliance on human habits as his primary explanatory device did not, as indicated here, completely disappear.

23. Tocqueville, *Recollections*, ed. J. P. Mayer and A. P. Kerr, tr. George Lawrence (Garden City, N.Y.: Doubleday Anchor Books, 1971), 15.

24. Samuel P. Huntington, "Conservatism as an Ideology," *American Political Science Review* 51 (June 1957): 458.

25. Ibid., 470.

26. Ibid., 473.

27. See Chong-Do Hah and Jeanne Schneider, "A Critique of Current Studies on Political Development and Modernization," *Social Research* 35 (Spring 1968): 130–58; Dean C. Tipps, "Modernization Theory and the Comparative Study of Societies: A Critical Perspective," *Comparative Studies in Society and History* 15 (March 1973): 199–225; L. E. Shiner, "Tradition/ Modernity: An Ideal Type Gone Astray," *Comparative Studies in Society and History* 17 (April 1975): 245–52; Immanuel Wallerstein, "Modernization: Requiescat in Pace," in *The Uses of Controversy in Sociology*, ed. Lewis A. Coser and Otto N. Larsen (New York: Free Press, 1976), 131–35; and Michael Adas, *Machines as the Measure of Men: Science, Technology, and Ideologies of Western Dominance* (Ithaca, N.Y.: Cornell University Press, 1989), "Epilogue: Modernization Theory and the Revival of the Technological Standard," 402–18.

28. See Huntington, "Political Development and Political Decay," *World Politics* 17 (April 1965): 393–405, and *Political Order in Changing Societies* (New Haven, Conn.: Yale University Press, 1968); and S. N. Eisenstadt, "Breakdowns of Modernization," *Economic Development and Cultural Change* 12 (July 1964): 345–67, and *Modernization: Protest and Change* 12 (Englewood Cliffs, N.J.: Prentice-Hall, 1966). See also Eisenstadt, *Tradition, Change, and Modernity* (New York: Wiley, 1973); *Post-Traditional Societies*, ed. Eisenstadt (New York: Norton, 1974); *Patterns of Modernity*, ed. Eisenstadt, 2 vols. (New York: New York University Press, 1987); and David E. Apter, *Rethinking Development: Modernization, Dependency, and Postmodern Politics* (Newbury Park, Calif.: Sage, 1987).

29. See, for example, the contrasting approaches to the relationship between technological advance and democracy outlined in (no author) Associated Press, "Africa's Old Order in Decline: End of the Cold War Dealt Harsh Blow to Autocratic Rulers," *Boston Sunday Globe*, November 3, 1991, 19, and Colin Nickerson, "As South Korea Celebrates Democracy, 1-Party Rule Goes On," *Boston Sunday Globe*, December 20, 1992, 10–11.

30. Arthur Kaledin, "Tocqueville's Apocalypse: Culture, Politics, and Freedom in *Democracy in America*," *The Tocqueville Review* 7 (Charlottesville: University Press of Virginia, 1985/86): 32 n. 10, and Edgar Leon Newman, "The French Background of Tocqueville's *Democracy in America*," ibid., 44. See also

Edward Pessen, "Tocqueville's Misreading of America, America's Misreading of Tocqueville," ibid., 4 (Spring/Summer 1982): 5–22. *The Tocqueville Review* itself, now an annual volume, formerly a quarterly journal, is the official organ of another Tocqueville Society, this a serious international organization concerned with the kind of large issues that its namesake investigated.

31. Significantly, Michael Adas's monumental study of Western dominance over the centuries, *Machines as the Measure of Men*, does not mention Tocqueville yet convincingly argues that modernization theory was rooted in earlier, imperialistic ideologies based literally on "machines as the measure of men." See his Epilogue. By way of confirmation of Adas's appropriate neglect of Tocqueville, James T. Schleifer's equally monumental work, *The Making of Tocqueville's "Democracy in America"* (Chapel Hill: University of North Carolina Press, 1980), chap. 6, concedes that Tocqueville's published work paid insufficient attention to the technological transformations he witnessed in his travels; his unpublished work, which Schleifer examines in extraordinary detail, reveals greater sensitivity to technological advances.

32. Richard D. Brown, *Modernization: The Transformation of American Life, 1600–1865* (New York: Hill and Wang, 1976), 19. Brown hopes that this is not the case, that modernization in fact is a useful concept to illuminate the evolution of American society. Yet his Epilogue concedes contemporary Americans' disenchantment with so much of what was once deemed perfection. He cites Bellamy's *Looking Backward* as projecting "fulfillment in a future where modernization had solved all problems, answered all questions, resolved all doubts" (189) and contrasts that optimism with today's pervasive American skepticism about the future. Interestingly, Brown never cites Tocqueville in his book.

33. See Richard Bernstein, "Ideas and Trends: Judging 'Post-History,' The Theory to End All Theories," *New York Times*, Sunday Week in Review, August 27, 1989, E5; Bernstein, "Ideas and Trends: The End of History, Explained for the Second Time," *New York Times*, Sunday Week in Review, December 10, 1989, E6; and Francis Fukuyama, *The End of History and the Last Man* (New York: Free Press, 1992).

34. Significantly, Eisenstadt, in his 1974 "revisionist" introduction to *Post-Traditional Societies*, states that "unlike the 'classical paradigms' of modernization," his approach "does not assume that 'development' or 'modernization' constitutes a 'unlinear' demographic, social, economic, or political process, extending, even if haltingly or intermittently, to some plateau whose basic contours will be everywhere the same, despite differences in detail" (7). Like Brown, Eisenstadt, writing at about the same time, tries to modify the concept to avoid the major weaknesses outlined above without giving up on it altogether.

5. THE MACHINE SHOP IN AMERICAN SOCIETY AND CULTURE

1. See John Bowditch, "Armington and Sims: In Providence, Rhode Island, and Greenfield Village, Dearborn, Michigan," *Henry Ford Museum and Greenfield Village Herald* 12 (1984): 110–19.

2. Jacob Abbott, "The Novelty Works," *Harper's New Monthly Magazine* 2 (May 1851): 721–22, 724.

3. Monte A. Calvert, *The Mechanical Engineer in America, 1830–1910: Professional Cultures in Conflict* (Baltimore: Johns Hopkins University Press, 1967).

4. W. J. Rorabaugh, *The Craft Apprentice: From Franklin to the Machine Age in America* (New York: Oxford University Press, 1986).

5. John F. Kasson, *Civilizing the Machine: Technology and Republican Values in America, 1776–1900* (New York: Grossman/Viking, 1976), chap. 2.

6. John F. Kouwenhoven, *The Arts in Modern American Civilization* (New York: Norton, 1967); this is a reprint of his 1948 original work.

7. See Kasson, *Civilizing the Machine,* chap. 4, and Bowditch, personal conversations based on his expertise as curator of machinery at the Henry Ford Museum and Greenfield Village.

8. See Alan Marcus and Howard P. Segal, *Technology in America: A Brief History* (San Diego: Harcourt Brace Jovanovich, 1989), chaps. 3–6.

9. Robert S. Woodbury, *Studies in the History of Machine Tools* (Cambridge: MIT Press, 1972), New Preface, no page number.

10. The report is summarized and analyzed in *American Machinist* 124 (October 1980): 105–28.

11. On machine shops and academia, see Bernard Burke, "The Quiet Shops of Academe," *Science* 204 (June 8, 1979): 1041, and Thomas J. Slattery, "Machine Shop Renaissance," *Automation* 35 (June 1988): 44–45.

12. See, for example, Bert Casper, "Nurture Your People Resources," *Modern Machine Shop* 57 (January 1985): 98, 100; Casper, "What Do Employees Really Think?" ibid. 59 (November 1986): 110, 112; Casper, "Large Contracts— And How Not to Become a Captive Shop," ibid. 61 (February 1989): 104, 106; William Hubbart, "Communicating Workplace Hazards," ibid. 59 (January 1987): 82–88; Woodruff Imberman, "What's New in Management Fads?" ibid. 60 (January 1988): 128, 130; [No author] "Industrial America Can Fight Back," ibid. 57 (May 1985): 128, 130, 132, 134, 136; [No author] "No Square Pegs in Round Holes," ibid. 61 (October 1988): 98, 100; and Seymour Melman, "How the Yankees Lost Their Know-How," *Technology Review* 86 (October 1983): 56–64.

13. See Paul J. Dvorak, "Mechanical Components: Getting Lighter and Smaller," *Machine Design* 59 (April 9, 1987): 120–27.

14. E. Ray McClure et al., *The Competitive Status of the U.S. Machine Tool Industry: A Study of the Influences of Technology in Determining International Industrial Competitive Advantage* (Washington, D.C.: National Academy Press, 1983), 1.

15. See Victor E. Repp and Willard J. McCarthy, *Machine Tool Technology,* 5th ed. (Encino, Calif.: Bennett and McKnight, 1984), 582.

16. [No author] "Blacksmith Shop Family Opened in 1875 Adapts, Hammers Out a Future," *Bangor Daily News* (June 29–30, 1991): 32.

17. In this regard see the notice calling for possible contributions to a Los Angeles machine tool museum in *Production Engineering* 33 (November 1986): 15.

6. ON TECHNOLOGICAL MUSEUMS

1. George Basalla, "Museums and Technological Utopianism," in *Technological Innovation and the Decorative Arts*, ed. Ian M. G. Quimby and Polly Anne Earl (Charlottesville: University Press of Virginia, 1973), 355–73, and Larry Lankton, "Reading History from the Hardware," *Henry Ford Museum and Greenfield Village Herald* 10 (1981): 23–28.

2. Paul E. Rivard, *Made in Maine: An Historical Overview* (Augusta: Maine State Museum, 1985), iii.

3. Rivard and Marilyn Norcini, "Made in Maine," *History News* 40 (November 1985): 12.

7. COMPUTERS AND MUSEUMS

1. Exceptions are contemporary "science centers" where computers are indeed common. But these centers generally lack the intellectual objectives of technological museums.

2. Joseph J. Corn, "Tools, Technologies, and Contexts: Interpreting the History of American Technics," in *History Museums in the United States: A Critical Assessment*, ed. Warren Leon and Roy Rosenzweig (Urbana: University of Illinois Press, 1989), 252.

3. Computer Museum Fact Sheet dated September 17, 1992.

4. See, for example, Michal McMahon, "Exhibit Review: The Romance of Technological Progress: A Critical Review of the National Air and Space Museum," *Technology and Culture* 22 (October 1981): 281–96.

5. *The Computer Museum News*, July–August 1988: 2.

6. John F. Kasson, *Civilizing the Machine: Technology and Republican Values in America, 1776–1900* (New York: Grossman/Viking, 1976), chap. 4.

7. Computer Museum Press Release, "The Smart Machines Gallery: Artificial Intelligence and Robots," undated, 1.

8. I cannot ignore the delightful noninteractive robot in a rear corner of "Beyond the Limits" who calmly folds and launches paper airplanes—a welcome bit of comic relief from the seriousness and complexity of it all (even if the paper airplanes contain a glossary of terms and a reading list for interested visitors).

9. As a label in the manufacturing section revealingly puts it, "Many advantages gained in Computer-Aided Design are lost if drawings cannot be linked directly to computers in the manufacturing process. Before computers, there was agreement on the meaning of symbols and directions in blueprints. Today, the variety of computer languages and programs often produces communication problems between the design workstation and the factory floor."

10. See Paul Ceruzzi, "An Unforeseen Revolution: Computers and Expec-

tations, 1935–1985," in *Imagining Tomorrow: History, Technology, and the American Future*, ed. Joseph J. Corn (Cambridge: MIT Press, 1986), 188–201.

11. See Samuel A. Batzli, "From Heroes to Hiroshima: The National Air and Space Museum Adjusts Its Point of View," *Technology and Culture* 31 (October 1990): 830–37.

12. In May 1990 the National Museum of American History, also part of the Smithsonian Institution, opened a large major permanent exhibition entitled "Information Age: People, Information, and Technology." This exhibition covers a longer period (150 years) and more technologies (including the telegraph, telephone, radio, and TV) than either the Computer Museum or "Beyond the Limits." Here computers, while hardly neglected, are placed in the context I, among others, seek. "Information Age" has its faults, but overall it is a model for all future exhibits on computers and society.

8. EDWARD BELLAMY AND TECHNOLOGY

1. Edward Bellamy, *Talks on Nationalism* (1938; reprinted Freeport, N.Y.: Books for Libraries Press, 1969), 45–46.

2. See E. F. Schumacher, *Small Is Beautiful: Economics as if People Mattered* (New York: Harper and Row, 1973), and George McRobie, *Small Is Possible* (New York: Harper and Row, 1981).

3. See Alvin Toffler, *The Third Wave* (1980; reprinted New York: Bantam Books, 1981), 10.

4. Bellamy, "Progress of Nationalism in the United States," *North American Review* 154 (June 1892): 743.

5. Bellamy, *Looking Backward, 2000–1887* (1888; reprinted New York: Penguin, 1982), 140.

6. John L. Thomas, *Alternative America: Henry George, Edward Bellamy, Henry Demarest Lloyd and the Adversary Tradition* (Cambridge: Harvard University Press, 1983), 359.

7. See Howard P. Segal, *Technological Utopianism in American Culture* (Chicago: University of Chicago Press, 1985).

8. Burton J. Bledstein, "Edward Bellamy, Storyteller to the Middle Class. *Looking Backward, 1888–1988*," *Annals of Scholarship* 5 (1988): 480.

9. See Milton Cantor, "The Backward Look of Bellamy's Socialism," and Franklin Rosemont, "Bellamy's Radicalism Reclaimed," in *Looking Backward, 1988–1888*, ed. Daphne Patai (Amherst: University of Massachusetts Press, 1988), 21–36 and 147–209.

10. Bellamy, *Looking Backward*, 55.

11. Bellamy, *Equality* (New York: Appleton, 1897), 296.

12. Bellamy, *Looking Backward*, 232.

13. Ibid., 137.

14. Ibid., 139.

15. Ibid., 176–77.

16. Arthur Lipow, *Authoritarian Socialism in America: Edward Bellamy*

and the Nationalist Movement (Berkeley and Los Angeles: University of California Press, 1982).

17. Bledstein, "Storyteller to the Middle Class," 481, 499, 501.

18. Thomas, *Alternative America*, 364.

19. William A. Simonds, "Rural Factories along Little Streams," *Stone and Webster Journal* 41 (November 1927), 653. See also Segal, "'Little Plants in the Country': Henry Ford's Village Industries and the Beginning of Decentralized Technology in Modern America," in *Prospects: The Annual of American Culture Studies*, ed. Jack Salzman, 13 (New York: Cambridge University Press, 1988), 181–223.

20. See David E. Lilienthal, *TVA: Democracy on the March* (New York: Harper, 1944).

21. Aldous Huxley, *Brave New World* (1946; reprinted New York: Harper and Row, 1969), vii–viii.

22. Lewis Mumford, *The Story of Utopias* (1922; reprinted New York: Viking Compass, 1962), 306–307.

23. Bledstein, "Storyteller to the Middle Class," 500.

9. THE FIRST FEMINIST TECHNOLOGICAL UTOPIA

1. Krishan Kumar, "Primitivism in Feminist Utopias," *Alternative Futures: The Journal of Utopian Studies* 4 (Spring/Summer 1981): 61–62.

2. See Daphne Patai, "British and American Utopias by Women (1836–1979): An Annotated Bibliography," ibid.: 184–206.

3. Kumar, "Primitivism in Feminist Utopias," 61.

4. Elaine Hoffman Baruch, "'A Natural and Necessary Monster': Women in Utopia," *Alternative Futures* 2 (Winter 1979): 38.

5. Murat Halstead, Preface to Mary E. Bradley Lane, *Mizora: A Prophecy* (New York: Dillingham, 1890), vi. Gregg Press, a division of G. K. Hall, reprinted the book in 1975 in its "Science Fiction" series. A portion of the book was later reprinted in *Daring to Dream: Utopian Stories by United States Women: 1836–1919*, ed. Carol Farley Kessler (Boston: Pandora, 1984), 119–37. My references below are to the original 1890 edition.

6. The Saturday issues of the *Commercial* in which, beginning on November 6, 1880, and ending on February 5, 1881, *Mizora* originally appeared, of course say nothing about the real author of the purportedly autobiographical "Narrative of Vera Zarovitch." Nor do other issues of the newspaper for those months. Other possible sources have proved no more illuminating. Neither the Cincinnati Historical Society nor the Cincinnati Public Library nor the Ohio Historical Society—nor, for that matter, any other known research facility—contains any additional materials, published or unpublished, by or about Mary Lane.

7. Ann D. Wood, "The 'Scribbling Women' and Fanny Fern: Why Women Wrote," *American Quarterly* 23 (Spring 1971): 24.

8. On utopian attitudes toward the role of women in society in the heyday

of American utopian writing, see Kenneth M. Roemer, *The Obsolete Necessity: America in Utopian Writings, 1880–1900* (Kent, Ohio: Kent State University Press, 1976), chap. 6. On the actual roles of women in nineteenth-century American utopian communities, see Raymond Lee Muncy, "Women in Utopia," in *France and North America: Utopias and Utopians*, ed. Mathé Allain (Lafayette: University of Southwestern Louisiana, Center for Louisiana Studies, 1978), 57–69, and Carol A. Kolmerten, *Women in Utopia: The Ideology of Gender in the American Owenite Communities* (Bloomington: Indiana University Press, 1990). On the alleged antifemale bias of prominent male utopian writers and community organizers throughout history, see Lyman Tower Sargent, "Women in Utopia," *Comparative Literature Studies* 10 (December 1973): 302–16, and Sylvia Strauss, "Women in 'Utopia,'" *South Atlantic Quarterly* 75 (Winter 1976): 115–31.

9. Ann J. Lane's introduction to a reprinting of *Herland* (New York: Pantheon, 1979) contains a superficial summary paragraph of *Mizora* which dismisses the latter as an "utterly preposterous story" (xix)—presumably to emphasize the uniqueness of *Herland*. Lane does, however, concede that *Mizora* "is the only self-consciously feminist utopia published before *Herland* I have been able to locate" (xix). Significantly, neither *Mizora* nor its author is even mentioned in Lane's *To Herland and Beyond: The Life and Work of Charlotte Perkins Gilman* (New York: Pantheon, 1990).

10. According to research by a University of Texas zoologist and psychologist, parthenogenesis actually exists in the natural world. The desert grassland whiptail lizard, which lives in the American Southwest and in northern Mexico, is an all-female species that reproduces itself successfully. See Sarah Boxer, "Does Pseudosex Enhance Virgin Birth?" *Discover* 8 (April 1987): 5–6.

11. Mary Lane, *Mizora*, 256.

12. On attitudes toward the role of women in society in American utopian writing oriented toward scientific and technological advance, see Howard P. Segal, *Technological Utopianism in American Culture* (Chicago: University of Chicago Press, 1985), 31 and 191–92 n. 58.

13. To my knowledge, there exists no scholarly analysis of these works. But see, for example, Timothy Savage, *The Amazonian Republic, Recently Discovered in the Interior of Peru* (New York: Colman, 1842); J. L. Collins, *Queen Krinaleen's Plagues; or, How a Simple People Were Destroyed* (New York: American News, 1874); and Frank Cowan, *Revi-Lona: A Romance of Love in a Marvelous Land* (Greensburg, Pa.: Tribune Press, 1890).

14. Peter Steinfels, "Idyllic Theory of Goddesses Creates Storm," *New York Times*, February 13, 1990, C1, C12.

15. Mary Lane, *Mizora*, 312.

16. See Dee Garrison, "Immoral Fiction in the Late Victorian Library," *American Quarterly* 28 (Spring 1976): 71–89.

17. See Helen Waite Papashvily, *All the Happy Endings* (New York: Harper, 1956); Elaine Showalter, *A Literature of Their Own: British Women Novelists*

from Brontë to Lessing (Princeton, N.J.: Princeton University Press, 1977); and Sandra M. Gilbert and Susan Gubar, *The Madwoman in the Attic: The Woman Writer and the Nineteenth-Century Literary Imagination* (New Haven, Conn.: Yale University Press, 1979).

18. Baruch, "'Natural and Necessary Monster,'" 44.

19. Mary Lane, *Mizora*, 21.

20. Kumar, "Primitivism in Feminist Utopias," 66.

21. See Ruth Schwartz Cowan, "The 'Industrial Revolution' in the Home: Household Technology and Social Change in the Twentieth Century," *Technology and Culture* 17 (January 1976): 1–23, and her *More Work for Mother: The Ironies of Household Technology from the Open Hearth to the Microwave* (New York: Basic, 1983).

22. See, for example, the expression of such optimistic belief in some of the responses to questions about "Women and the Future" in *Alternative Futures* 4 (Spring/Summer 1981): 161–67.

23. So, too, do several other respondents in ibid.

24. See *Machina Ex Dea: Feminist Perspectives on Technology*, ed. Joan Rothschild (New York: Penguin Press, 1983).

25. On *The Handmaid's Tale* and related works, see Frances Bartowski, *Feminist Utopias* (Lincoln: University of Nebraska Press, 1989).

26. Mary Lane, *Mizora*, 9.

27. Kessler, *Daring to Dream*, Introduction, 7.

28. Kumar, "Primitivism in Feminist Utopias," 66.

10. KURT VONNEGUT'S *PLAYER PIANO*

1. Kurt Vonnegut, *Player Piano* (1952; reprinted New York: Dell, 1974), 11.

2. As several literary critics have noted, the opening paragraph of *Player Piano* parodies the opening paragraph of Julius Caesar's *Commentary on the Gallic War*.

3. Vonnegut, "Science Fiction," *New York Times Book Review* (September 5, 1965): 2. On Vonnegut's experiences at General Electric, see Robert Scholes, "A Talk with Kurt Vonnegut, Jr.," in *The Vonnegut Statement*, ed. Jerome Klinkowitz and John Somer (New York: Delta, 1973), 91–94.

4. Vonnegut, interview with David Standish in *Playboy* 20 (July 1973): 68. See also David F. Noble, *Forces of Production: A Social History of Industrial Automation* (New York: Knopf, 1984), Appendix II, which quotes Vonnegut further on his experience at GE and on his motivation to write *Player Piano*, as quoted below.

5. Vonnegut, *Player Piano*, 10.

6. On planning in modern America, see Otis L. Grahan, Jr., *Toward a Planned Society: From Roosevelt to Nixon* (New York: Oxford University Press, 1976).

7. See Scholes, "A Talk with Kurt Vonnegut," 93–94.

8. See John Van der Zee, *The Greatest Men's Party on Earth: Inside the Bohemian Grove* (New York: Harcourt Brace Jovanovich, 1974), and G. William Domhoff, *The Bohemian Grove and Other Retreats: A Study in Ruling-Class Cohesiveness* (New York: Harper and Row, 1974).

9. Of historical interest in this regard are Bellamy's *Looking Backward*, with its highly conformist civilian "industrial army," and Sinclair Lewis's *Babbitt* (1922), with its obsessive concern with conformity. On the latter's many parallels with *Player Piano*, see Mary Schniber, "You've Come a Long Way, Babbitt! From Zenith to Ilium," *Twentieth Century Literature* 17 (April 1971): 101–6.

10. For revisionist interpretations of the Luddites, see Eric J. Hobsbawm, "The Machine Breakers," in his *Labouring Men: Studies in the History of Labour* (Garden City, N.Y.: Doubleday, 1967), chap. 2, and Malcolm I. Thomas, *The Luddites: Machine-Breaking in Regency England* (New York: Schocken, 1972).

11. See Paul Ceruzzi, "An Unforeseen Revolution: Computers and Expectations, 1935–1985," in *Imagining Tomorrow: History, Technology, and the American Future*, ed. Joseph J. Corn (Cambridge: MIT Press, 1986), 188–201.

12. On Steinmetz's life and thought, see James Gilbert, *Designing the Industrial State: The Intellectual Pursuit of Collectivism in America, 1880–1940* (Chicago: Quadrangle Books, 1972), chap. 7, and Ronald Kline, *Steinmetz: Engineer and Socialist* (Baltimore: Johns Hopkins University Press, 1992).

13. Vonnegut, *Playboy* interview, 68.

14. Mark Hillegas, *The Future as Nightmare: H. G. Wells and the Anti-Utopians* (1967; reprinted Carbondale and Edwardsville: Southern Illinois University Press, 1974), 159–62.

15. Ibid., 161.

16. See, for example, David Y. Hughes, "The Ghost in the Machine: The Theme of *Player Piano*," in *America as Utopia: Collected Essays*, ed. Kenneth M. Roemer (New York: Burt Franklin, 1981), 108–14; Thomas L. Wymer, "Machines and the Meaning of Human in the Novels of Kurt Vonnegut, Jr.," in *The Mechanical God: Machines in Science Fiction*, ed. Thomas P. Dunn and Richard D. Erlich (Westport, Conn.: Greenwood, 1982), 41–52; Thomas P. Hoffman, "The Theme of Mechanization in *Player Piano*," in *Clockwork Worlds: Mechanized Environments in SF*, ed. Erlich and Dunn (Westport, Conn.: Greenwood, 1983), 125–35; and Lawrence Broer, "Pilgrim's Progress: Is Kurt Vonnegut, Jr., Winning His War with Machines?" in ibid., 137–61.

17. See Howard P. Segal, *Technological Utopianism in American Culture* (Chicago: University of Chicago Press, 1985).

18. See Frank E. Manuel, "Toward a Psychological History of Utopias," in *Utopias and Utopian Thought*, ed. Manuel (Boston: Beacon Press, 1967), 69–98.

19. George Kateb, *Utopia and Its Enemies* (New York: Free Press, 1963), 14–15.

20. Vonnegut, *Player Piano*, 7.

21. Aldous Huxley, *Brave New World* (1932; reprinted New York: Harper and Row, 1969), xiii–xiv.

22. Noble, *Forces of Production*, 166. Noble *has* been criticized for either ignoring or minimizing other, equally legitimate motivations for MIT and Air Force technical experts in favoring N/C over R/P and for not bringing his account up-to-date as of his book's 1984 publication. Additional serious criticisms of his account by MIT insiders are summarized in David Warsh, "An Engineering Revolution By the Numbers," *Boston Sunday Globe*, July 21, 1991, Business, 45, 47. Moreover, Noble has a nostalgia for skilled machinists akin to Vonnegut's; indeed, a greater fondness for R/P than Vonnegut has, given that R/P would also have meant technological unemployment for many of those same skilled machinists.

23. Vonnegut, *Player Piano*, 284.

24. Vonnegut quoted by Noble, *Forces of Production*, Appendix II, 359.

11. LEWIS MUMFORD'S ALTERNATIVES TO THE MEGAMACHINE

1. Lewis Mumford, *Findings and Keepings: Analects for an Autobiography* (New York: Harcourt Brace Jovanovich, 1975), 375.

2. On the nature of the megamachine in Mumford's work, see Donald L. Miller, *Lewis Mumford: A Life* (New York: Weidenfeld and Nicholson, 1989), 509–10 and chap. 27, and Miller, *"The Myth of the Machine: I. Techniques and Human Development,"* in *Lewis Mumford: Public Intellectual*, ed. Thomas P. and Agatha C. Hughes (New York: Oxford University Press, 1990), 152–63.

3. On Mumford and Odum, see Allen Tullos, "The Politics of Regional Development," in Hughes and Hughes, *Lewis Mumford*, 110–20.

4. The full title was *La Technique ou l'Enjeu du Siècle* (Paris: Libraire Armand Colin, 1954); translated literally, it means *Technique: The Stake of This Century*. The reason for the new English title is unclear, but commercial considerations may have been the cause.

5. Mumford to Melvin Kranzberg, April 20, 1968, Mumford Correspondence, Lewis Mumford Papers, Special Collections, Van Pelt Library, University of Pennsylvania. The review appeared in the *Virginia Quarterly Review* 43 (Autumn 1967): 686–93.

6. Mumford to Eric Larrabee, September 15, 1957, Mumford Papers. Larrabee was then editor of *Harper's Magazine*.

7. Mumford, *The Culture of Cities* (1938; reprint ed., New York: Harcourt Brace Jovanovich, 1970), 492. Meanwhile, in cases where he analyzes the potentially positive aspects of technology—as in *Technics and Civilization*—only to have been overly optimistic in retrospect, he nonetheless congratulates himself in his 1963 new introduction to that work for somehow having anticipated three decades earlier technology's potentially negative aspects. Conversely, however, in his 1959 reappraisal of that same book he laments his retrospectively naive hopes for transcending technology and, as a partial cause

of that regret, his earlier failure to treat atomic power more seriously. See Mumford, "An Appraisal of Lewis Mumford's *Technics and Civilization* (1934)," *Daedalus* 88 (Summer 1959): 532–34.

8. See Mumford, "Fashions Change in Utopia," *New Republic* 47 (June 16, 1926): 114–15.

9. Ironically, the model garden city shown in the 1939 film *The City*, for which Mumford wrote the narrative, has since been criticized for its sterile, stagnant qualities and for its resemblance to too many modern suburban communities.

10. Mumford, *Findings and Keepings*, 373.

11. Mumford, *The Story of Utopias* (1922; reprinted New York: Viking Compass Books, 1962), new Preface, 7. A good example of Bloch's writing on utopianism is *A Philosophy of the Future*, tr. John Cumming (New York: Herder and Herder, 1970), esp. 84–144.

12. Mumford to Catherine Kraus Bauer, July 1930, reprinted in *Findings and Keepings*, 353. See also his note there regarding his use of this phrase elsewhere.

13. Mumford, *The Story of Utopias*, 6, 7.

14. To repeat political theorist George Kateb's apt lines, "There is not, for the most part, skepticism about the capacity of modern technology and natural science to execute the most vaulting ambitions of utopianism; on the contrary, there is a dread it will" (*Utopia and Its Enemies* [New York: Free Press, 1963], 14–15).

15. Mumford, "Bellamy's Accurate Utopia," *New Republic* 68 (August 26, 1931): 51. This is a retrospective review of the book, an updating of his treatment of it from *The Story of Utopias*.

16. Mumford, *The Story of Utopias*, 169; the quotation is from the book's original edition.

17. Mumford, *The Pentagon of Power: The Myth of the Machine: II* (New York: Harcourt Brace Jovanovich, 1970), 229.

18. See Howard P. Segal, *Technological Utopianism in American Culture* (Chicago: University of Chicago Press, 1985), 2–7.

19. Mumford, *Pentagon of Power*, 212.

20. Ibid., 223.

21. Marcuse's position is summarized in an essay interestingly entitled "The End of Utopia," in his *Five Lectures: Psychoanalysis, Politics, and Utopia*, tr. Jeremy J. Shapiro and Shierry M. Weber (Boston: Beacon, 1970), 62–82.

22. Mumford, *Findings and Keepings*, 373. As Mumford sarcastically adds, "Did not the president of a great university the other day publicly salute . . . Fuller . . . as another Leonardo da Vinci, another Freud, another Einstein?" (ibid.)

23. Mumford to Arthur C. Clarke, May 24, 1975, Mumford Papers. See Clarke's criticism of Mumford in his *Profiles of the Future: An Inquiry into the Limits of the Possible*, 2d ed. (New York: Harper and Row, 1972), 94–97.

Mumford does praise Fuller's "aerodynamic motor car" or dymaxion car in *Technics and Civilization* (1934; reprinted New York: Harcourt, Brace and World, 1963), 446 and illustration #2 between 276 and 277. But he criticizes Fuller's "completely self-sufficient" dymaxion house as leading to excessive social isolation in his unpublished manuscript, "Form and Personality," Mumford Papers, Box 8, Folder 6, IJb. Ironically, Fuller's own mixed review of *Technics and Civilization* in *The Nation* 138 (June 6, 1934): 652, criticizes Mumford for not understanding inventors' "inspiration." For an interesting comparison of the two men, see Allan Temko, "Which Guide to the Promised Land: Fuller or Mumford," *Horizon* 10 (Summer 1968): 25–30.

24. Mumford to Edward Cornish, April 19 and July 12, 1976, Mumford Papers. On how most contemporary futurists see themselves and their enterprise, see Cornish, Foreword, W. Warren Wagar, *The Next Three Futures: Paradigms of Things to Come* (New York: Praeger, 1991), ix–xi.

25. Mumford, *The Story of Utopias*, 306.

26. See John L. Thomas's illumination of this dimension of Mumford's first book in his "Lewis Mumford, Benton MacKaye, and the Regional Vision," in Hughes and Hughes, *Lewis Mumford*, 79–80.

27. Mumford, *The Story of Utopias*, 281.

28. Mumford, *The Culture of Cities*, 346.

29. See, for example, the reviews by F. Taylor Ostrander in *The Journal of Political Economy* 43 (June 1935): 419–21, and by David Ramsey in *Partisan Review* 1 (June–July 1934): 56–59.

30. Mumford, *The Culture of Cities*, 303. As he claims in *Technics and Civilization*, "the organic has become visible again even within the mechanical complex" (6).

31. For elaboration on Mumford's use and misuse of organicism, see Leo Marx, "Lewis Mumford: Prophet of Organicism," in Hughes and Hughes, *Lewis Mumford*, 164–80. See Werner Stark, *The Fundamental Forms of Social Thought* (London: Routledge and Kegan Paul, 1962), for a comprehensive study of the organic and mechanical conceptions of the social order and of the changing relationship over time between them. On the nostalgia of Mumford and other "urbanologists" of the 1920s and 1930s for smaller American cities prior to the closing of the rural frontier, see Zane L. Miller and Patricia M. Melvin, *The Urbanization of Modern America: A Brief History*, 2d ed. (New York: Harcourt Brace Jovanovich, 1987), 169–70.

32. Mumford to George Weller, 1939 (no specific date), Mumford Papers.

33. On these experiments, see Segal, "'Little Plants in the Country': Henry Ford's Village Industries and the Beginning of Decentralized Technology in Modern America," in *Prospects: The Annual of American Culture Studies*, ed. Jack Salzman, 13 (New York: Cambridge University Press, 1988), 181–223.

34. Mumford, *Technics and Civilization*, 226.

35. Waldemar Kaempffert, review of *Technics and Civilization*, *New York Times Book Review* (April 29, 1934): 17. In this regard see Mumford's later

hopes for successful industrial, educational, and demographic decentralization in North Carolina in his "A Thought for a Growing South," *The Southern Packet: A Monthly Review of Southern Books and Ideas* 5 (April 1949): 1–5. I am indebted to Allen Tullos for bringing this article to my attention.

36. Mumford, "Thirty Years Before McLuhan," in *Findings and Keepings*, 328–30; these are excerpts from *Technics and Civilization*. See also his criticisms of McLuhan in *The Pentagon of Power*, 295–97.

37. Mumford, *The Pentagon of Power*, illustration #5 between 180 and 181.

38. Mumford, "If I Were Dictator," *The Nation* 83 (December 9, 1933): 631, 632, 632. The essay was one of a series that publication ran with the same title.

39. Mumford, Foreword, *Planned Society: Yesterday, Today, Tomorrow*, ed. Findlay MacKenzie (New York: Prentice-Hall, 1937), x.

40. See the modest Lilienthal correspondence—from Lilienthal only—in the Mumford Papers. It reflects Lilienthal's characteristic praise of someone who might be of service to him later and his simultaneous boasting/defensiveness regarding the degree of grass-roots democracy in TVA.

41. On decentralization's varied meanings and applications today, see Langdon Winner, "Decentralization Clarified," in his *The Whale and the Reactor: A Search for Limits in an Age of High Technology* (Chicago: University of Chicago Press, 1986), 85–97. Winner is also properly skeptical of decentralization as a panacea.

42. Mumford, *Findings and Keepings*, 381.

43. Mumford, as quoted, uses the term "human scale" at least as early as his 1933 *Nation* essay. See also Kirkpatrick Sale's *Human Scale* (New York: Coward, McCann, and Geoghegan, 1980), which praises Mumford, among others, for advocating and practicing that philosophy. In this context see also Casey Blake's overview of Mumford's work, "Lewis Mumford: Values over Technique," *democracy* 3 (Spring 1983): 125–37.

12. HIGH TECH AND THE BURDEN OF HISTORY

1. On the questionable performance of high-tech weapons systems during the 1991 Persian Gulf War, see [no author] *Eye of the Storm: The Technology of the Gulf War* (Lexington, Mass.: Raytheon, 1991); Bob Kuttner, "The High Cost of High-Tech Weapons," *Boston Globe*, January 25, 1991, 19; Andrew Pollack, "In U.S. Technology, a Gap Between Arms and VCR's," *New York Times*, March 4, 1991, A1, D8; Fred Kaplan, "The War's Lessons: Triumph? Overkill?" *Boston Globe*, March 27, 1991, 22; Paul F. Walker and Eric Stambler, "The Surgical Myth of the Gulf War," *Boston Globe*, April 16, 1991, 15; Alan Radding, "Raytheon Ads Get Patriotic," *Advertising Age* 61 (April 22, 1991): 41; Kaplan, "Patriot: Was It A Hit Or A Miss?" *Boston Globe*, April 16, 1991, 25, 33; Kaplan, "Did Arms Work? Amid Questions, Little U.S. Data," *Boston Globe*, April 23, 1991, 20; Kaplan, "Patriot: For All Involved, A War Hero," *Boston Globe*, ibid.; Kaplan, "Patriot's Failure to Stop Scud Attack Blamed On Computer Glitch," *Boston Globe*, May 21, 1991, 11; Paul Hemp,

"For Now, Patriot Missile Will Remain On The Line," *Boston Globe*, June 1, 1991, 15–16; Kaplan, "Defense Study Cites Flaws in Gulf War Effort," *Boston Globe*, July 17, 1991, 3; [no author] Associated Press, "U.S. Caused Needless Deaths in Iraq, Rights Group Says," *Boston Sunday Globe*, November 17, 1991, 23; Jonathan Yenkin, Associated Press, "Critics Question Effectiveness of Patriot Missiles," *University of Maine Campus*, January 20, 1992, 16; Hemp, "Data Could Have Thwarted Scud Hit in Gulf, GAO Finds," *Boston Globe*, February 27, 1992, 3; Randolph Ryan, "Patriot Propaganda," *Boston Globe*, March 21, 1992, 9; John Aloysius Farrell, "U.S. Downgrades Patriot Success: Army Team Cites Firm Evidence For Fewer Scud Kills," *Boston Globe*, April 8, 1992, 1, 7; Farrell, "Pentagon Pats Itself On Back In War Report," *Boston Globe*, April 11, 1992, 1, 6; Farrell "House Report: U.S. Erred On Iraqi Troops: Field Estimates Called Too High," *Boston Globe*, April 24, 1992, 1, 26; [no author] "A \$124.3 Million Contract for 180 Patriot Missiles," *New York Times*, May 21, 1992, D5; Jim Drinkard, Associated Press, "Patriot Successes Found Overstated," *Boston Globe*, September 30, 1992, 3; and [no author] "Report Critical Of Patriot Fails To Get Vote," *Boston Globe*, October 2, 1992, 67. See also Harry G. Summers, "Is Our High-Tech Military A Mirage?" *New York Times* Op Ed Page, October 19, 1990, A17.

2. See David Cushman Coyle, "Decentralize Industry," *Virginia Quarterly Review* 11 (July 1935): 321–38. Coyle uses the terms "high-technology country" and "high-technology system" (338).

3. See W. Warren Wagar, *The Next Three Futures: Paradigms of Things to Come* (Westport, Conn.: Greenwood, 1991), 26.

4. Alvin Toffler, *Future Shock* (1970; reprinted New York: Bantam Books, 1971), 9, 11.

5. Ibid., 2.

6. Ibid., 25, 266, 124, 125.

7. Ibid., 7, 1.

8. Ibid., 5.

9. Ibid., 478, 470.

10. Ibid., 391.

11. Toffler, *The Third Wave* (1980; reprinted New York: Bantam Books, 1981), 349. In 1975 Toffler published *The Eco-Spasm Report* (New York: Bantam Books), a short book that succinctly provided the same basic thesis as *The Third Wave* but called the phenomenon "Super-industrialism."

12. Toffler, *The Third Wave*, 10, 182, 11.

13. Ibid., 424, 442.

14. Ibid., 391, 357.

15. Edward Cornish, quoted in review of *The Third Wave* by Jerry Adler, *Newsweek* 95 (March 31, 1980): 86.

16. Toffler, *The Third Wave*, 1.

17. Toffler, *Previews and Premises: An Interview with the Author of "Future Shock" and "The Third Wave"* (New York: William Morrow, 1983), 89.

18. Ibid., 208, 213, 214, 215.

19. Toffler, *Powershift: Knowledge, Wealth, and Violence at the Edge of the 21st Century* (New York: Bantam, 1990), 3, 11, 75.

20. Ibid., 18, 19.

21. Ibid., xix.

22. John Naisbitt, *Megatrends: Ten New Directions Transforming Our Lives* (New York: Warner Books, 1982), 8.

23. Naisbitt disagrees with Toffler regarding the appeal of "electronic cottages," claiming, with some justification, that most people want to go to offices and other workplaces and to associate with one another, not work at home. See Naisbitt, 35–36.

24. Ben Bova, review of *Megatrends*, *Washington Post Book World* 12 (October 17, 1982): 1.

25. Naisbitt, *Megatrends*, 1.

26. Bova, *Post* review, 1.

27. Naisbitt, *Megatrends*, 252.

28. Naisbitt and Patricia Aburdene, *Megatrends 2000: Ten New Directions for the 1990's* (New York: William Morrow, 1990), 11. In 1985 Naisbitt and Aburdene published *Re-inventing the Corporation: Transforming Your Job and Your Company for the New Information Society* (New York: Warner Books). Where *Megatrends'* purpose was to describe the "new world" outlined above, this book's mission was to tell corporate executives and others "what to *do* about those and other new changes which compel us to rethink every aspect of corporate life" (4). Perhaps *Megatrends 2000* will soon be followed by a similar corporate operations manual.

29. Naisbitt and Aburdene, *Megatrends 2000*, 311.

30. Ibid., 309.

31. On Infomart, see Toni Mack, "Crow's Feat," *Forbes* 134 (December 17, 1984): 216, 220; Peter Petre, "Selling: Computer Marts: A New Way to Hawk High Tech," *Fortune* 111 (February 4, 1985): 64; Jim Hurlock, "Information Processing: Slow Starters—Or White Elephants? High-Tech Trade Marts Haven't Drawn Many Crowds—Or Exhibitors—But Backers Remain Optimistic," *Business Week* 2933 (February 17, 1986): 78; Lisa M. Keefe, "The Soft Sell and the Crystal Palace," *Forbes* 139 (June 15, 1987): 130–31; Dennis Eskow, "Infomart: A Boon for Busy IS Managers," *PC Week* 6 (September 25, 1989): 81, 85; and Peter H. Lewis, "The Executive Computer: Connectivity Comes to Life in a Technology Supermarket," *Sunday New York Times*, September 29, 1991, Business, 11.

32. Quoted in 1985 or 1986 untitled Infomart brochure.

33. [No author] "The Crystal Palace Story," *Infomart Directory First Quarter 1992*, 2.

34. See Paul Goldberger, "Javits Center: Noble Ambition Largely Realized," *New York Times*, March 31, 1986, B1, B2. On the Crystal Palace itself, see Folke T. Kihlstedt, "The Crystal Palace," *Scientific American* 251 (October 1984): 132–43.

35. Letter to me from Janice Collins, account executive, Tracy-Locke/ BBDO Public Relations, September 17, 1986.

36. See [no author] "Videoconferencing: A New Mindset in Corporate Communications," *Infomart Magazine* (First Quarter 1992): 14–15.

37. On Leonardo da Vinci and advertising for Xerox and other high-tech companies, see Brian Moran, "Leonardo Sighs: High-Tech Companies Adopt Artist's Image," *Advertising Age* 57 (October 6, 1986): 118, and [no author] "What's New Portfolio," *Adweek* 26 (January 16, 1989): 34. Moran's article discusses the competition among Xerox and two other high-tech companies using Leonardo in their ad campaigns to claim originality in their historical appropriations, with the two others also claiming greater historical sensitivity than Xerox.

38. On the models of inventions from this traveling exhibit and their use in later museum exhibits, see [no author] "Exhibit Showcases da Vinci's Inventions," Associated Press article in *Bangor Daily News*, June 27–28, 1987, 12. On the builder of these models, Roberto Guatelli, see John Culhane and T. H. Culhane, "The Master Modeler: Leonardo as a Lifelong Inspiration," *Science Digest* 93 (December 1985): 66–71, 86–87. On a different, less ideological exhibition of Leonardo's art and inventions, see Ros Herman, "Leonardo's Bequest: Leonardo da Vinci Museum of Science and Technology, Milan," *New Scientist* 130 (June 8, 1991): 50.

39. Richard Terrell, quoted in Eskow, "Boon for Busy IS Managers."

40. A computer virus is a program planted secretly by one or more malicious programmers. Hidden on infected floppy computer disks, the virus spreads to (in this case IBM-compatible) computers when the infected disks are used to start (or boot) them up. Once this happens, the virus program writes itself into the computers' memories, and, if the computers have internal hard drives, or memory devices, infects them too. And if the infected floppy disks are used in other computers, the virus will spread to them as well. The result is the loss of invaluable data often not backed up on either additional disks or hard copies. On the Michelangelo computer virus, see Josh Hyatt, "Leading Edge Attacked By Rogue Virus," *Boston Globe*, January 29, 1992, 65–66; Hyatt, "Computer Killers," *Boston Globe*, March 3, 1992, 35, 45–56; and Hyatt, "Happy Birthday, Michelangelo," *Boston Globe*, March 7, 1992, 25. But see also John Markoff, "Virus Threat Is Overstated, An I.B.M. Study Concludes," *New York Times*, September 9, 1992, D4, questioning current theories about the actual prospects for the kind of widespread computer virus described above.

41. See Lawrence M. Fisher, "Apple to Give the Public Its First Look at Newton," *New York Times*, May 29, 1992, D3. On Isaac Newton, apples, and gravity, see I. Bernard Cohen, *The Birth of a New Physics*, 2d ed. (New York: Norton, 1985), Supplement 14.

42. These ads appeared in, among other places, several issues of *Newsweek* in 1990 and 1991. Michael Schrage, "Like All Art, Telecommunications Movement Needs A Great Patron," *Boston Sunday Globe*, November 15, 1992,

Business, A2, ironically calls upon the "Baby Bells" to sponsor art that would look to the future rather than the past. "Don't just commission works of art," he suggests, "commission networks of art" using high-tech media.

43. On Charlie Chaplin's Little Tramp and advertising, see [No author], "Critic's Corner: A Rose for IBM," *Advertising Age* 53 (August 30, 1982): M-29; Daniel Burstein, "Using Yesterday to Sell Tomorrow: How the Unlikely IBM–Charlie Chaplin Marriage Came to Be," *Advertising Age* 54 (April 11, 1983): M-4, M-5, M-48; Bob Marich, "Fortune Jabs Little Tramp," *Advertising Age* 55 (May 21, 1984): 1, 96; Patricia Winters, "Little Tramp Ends Stint as IBM Front Man," *Advertising Age* 58 (April 6, 1987): 80; and Jon Lafayette, "IBM's Little Tramp Returns to Ads," *Advertising Age* 62 (September 2, 1991): 5. Marich's article discusses the attempts by two small computer companies to use the Little Tramp in ad campaigns that followed IBM's. See also Charles J. Maland, *Chaplin and American Culture: The Evolution of a Star Image* (Princeton, N.J.: Princeton University Press, 1989), 362–70.

44. Coincidentally, the Computer Museum's new "People and Computers" exhibition has both a video and a photo of but, alas, no comment on the television version of the IBM Little Tramp advertisement. On the Computer Museum overall, see chapter 7 above.

45. Among other places, the Sun Microsystem advertisement appeared in the *Boston Globe*, February 24, 1992, 9; the Storer Communications telegraph operator advertisement in *Advertising Age* 54 (May 9, 1983): 30–31; the Storer Pony Express rider advertisement in *Advertising Age* 54 (July 18, 1983): 54–55; and the Lockheed advertisement in a 1988 issue of *Newsweek*.

46. *ElAl* 41 (January–February 1992): 2.

47. On Jacob Bigelow's *Elements of Technology*, see Segal, *Technological Utopianism in American Culture* (Chicago: University of Chicago Press, 1985), 78–81, 180 n. 7, 208 n. 15, 208 n. 16, 209 nn. 19, 20, 21, 210 n. 28.

48. Interestingly, R. L. Polk, a high-tech company, had an advertisement using Leonardo and his proposed inventions with the caption "State of the Art Technology" in *Advertising Age* 58 (May 18, 1987): 8.

49. See Jeffrey L. Meikle, *Twentieth-Century Limited: Industrial Design in America, 1925–1939* (Philadelphia: Temple University Press, 1979), chap. 9. On the history of world's fairs, see the very useful *Historical Dictionary of World's Fairs and Expositions, 1851–1988*, ed. John E. Findling (Westport, Conn.: Greenwood Press, 1990). Not surprisingly, perhaps, Findling's Preface, xiii, implies a belief that world's fairs not only will persist into the twenty-first century but also that they should.

50. See Frank Vizard, "Electronics: The Flavor of CES," *Popular Mechanics* 167 (April 1990): 42, 44, and Jerry O'Neill, "Show Reports: Photokina," *Lighting Dimensions* 13 (January 1, 1989): 80, 86–87.

51. See Steven Greenhouse, "Playing Disney in the Parisian Fields," *Sunday New York Times*, February 17, 1991, Business, 1, 6; Sarah Catchpole, "Foreign Journal: Paris Chic Hits Mickey Mouse Code," *Boston Globe*, Febru-

ary 3, 1992, 2; and Ronald Koven, "French Debate 'Better Mousetraps,'" *Boston Globe*, April 13, 1992, 5. The French intellectual credited with the Chernobyl reference varies with each story.

52. Michael L. Smith observes a similarity in both layout and purpose between EPCOT and the 1939–40 New York World's Fair. See his "Back to the Future: EPCOT, Camelot, and the History of Technology," in *New Perspectives on Technology and American Culture*, ed. Bruce Sinclair (Philadelphia: American Philosophical Society, 1986), 70.

53. See Priscilla Painton, "Fantasy's Reality," *Time* 137 (May 27, 1991): 52–59.

54. Mike Wallace, "Mickey Mouse History: Portraying the Past at Disney World," *Radical History Review* 32 (March 1985): 49.

55. Marty Sklar, quoted in Jennifer Allen, "Brave New EPCOT," *New York* 15 (December 20, 1982): 41, 43. Mickey Mouse, Donald Duck, and other Disney cartoon characters *are* banned from EPCOT in the name of seriousness. On the genuinely serious crop research at EPCOT in the Kraft-sponsored Land pavilion, see John Rothchild, "EPCOT: It's a Stale World After All," *Rolling Stone* 403 (September 1, 1983): 38; David Hall, "The Green Earth—Care of Disney," *New Scientist* 103 (July 26, 1984): 41; and Judie D. Dziezak, "EPCOT Center Adds New Exhibit: A Plant Biotechnology Laboratory," *Food Technology* 42 (December 1988): 110, 114–15, 117. On EPCOT's semieducational exhibits and computer terminals, see Elting E. Morison, "What Went Wrong with Disney's World's Fair," *American Heritage* 35 (December 1983): 77.

56. Craig Hodgetts, quoted in Jeff Kramer, "Recreating Make-Believe," *Boston Globe*, June 14, 1992, 2.

57. On these professional theme park and world's fair organizers, see Mark Zieman, "Jinxed Effort: New Orleans Prepares For Its World's Fair And Plenty of Criticism," *Wall Street Journal*, March 26, 1984, 1, 12, and Louise Zepp, "IAFE Sets Goal At 500 In Membership Drive," *Amusement Business: The International Newsweekly for Sports and Mass Entertainment* 102 (May 7, 1990), 1, 52. IAFE refers to the International Association of Fairs and Expositions.

58. Ray Dykes, "How PR Packed 'Em In at Expo '86: Interview with George Madden," *IABC Communication World* 4 (February 1987): 13.

59. Findling's Introduction to *Historical Dictionary of World's Fairs and Exhibitions* does note that in the earliest world's fairs held in the United States, American participation, unlike that of European countries, "was undertaken by private means; there was much resistance to government support among Americans used to a sense of isolation and nonentanglement with the Old World" (xviii).

60. See [no author] "Debate Flares on U.S. Role at a World's Fair," *New York Times*, February 12, 1990, B12; Michael K. Frisby, "Budget Woes Imperil U.S. Pavilion for '92 Fair," *Boston Globe*, November 14, 1991, 22; Jonathan Kaufman, "Money Constraints Leave U.S. With Modest Showing at Expo '92," *Boston Globe*, April 20, 1992, 1, 9; and Alan Riding, "Seville Journal: The

World's Fair Opens, but Where's Columbus?" *New York Times,* April 21, 1992, A4.

61. Quoted in 1986 *Infomart Fact Sheet,* no page number, prepared by Tracy-Locke/BBDO Public Relations.

62. See William E. Schmidt, "The Desolate Legacy of Knoxville's World's Fair," *New York Times,* May 18, 1984, A10; Dale Russakoff, "'82 World's Fair Pavilion: From Dazzler to Disaster," *Washington Post,* June 9, 1987, A3; Zieman, "Jinxed Effort"; and Wayne King, "Failed Fair Gives New Orleans a Painful Hangover," *New York Times,* November 12, 1984, A16.

63. See, as an example of this, [no author] *Selling the World of Tomorrow,* catalog for 1989–90 exhibit of same name on the 1939–40 New York's World Fair (New York: Museum of the City of New York, 1989).

64. David L. Groves, "Comparison of the 1982 and 1984 World's Fairs from the Participant Outcome Perspective," *World Leisure and Recreation* 31 (Summer 1989): 37.

65. Henry Raymont, "A $6-million Shortfall for Columbus," *Boston Globe,* November 25, 1991, 11. On the Seville World's Fair, see also the articles cited in n. 60 above.

66. See John Barber, "Pavilions of Promise: The Best of Expo '86," *Maclean's* 99 (March 17, 1986): 24–26; Christopher S. Wren, "Vancouver Unwraps Its World's Fair," *Sunday New York Times,* April 20, 1986, Travel, 15; and Eleanor Wachtel, "Expo '86 and the World's Fairs," in *The Expo Story,* ed. Robert Anderson and Wachtel (Madeira Park, B.C.: Harbour, 1986), 29.

67. See Clyde Haberman, "Japanese See a 'Made in Japan' Future And Feel Reassured by That Vision," *Sunday New York Times,* May 5, 1985, A12.

68. Henry Adams, *The Education of Henry Adams: An Autobiography* (1907; partially reprinted in *Changing Attitudes Toward American Technology,* ed. Thomas Parke Hughes [New York: Harper and Row, 1975], 168, 170–71).

69. A related plea is in Langdon Winner, "A Postmodern World's Fair," *Technology Review* 94 (February/March 1991): 74.

70. See C. P. Snow, *The Two Cultures: And a Second Look* (New York: Cambridge University Press, 1964). The original version of the book, entitled *The Two Cultures and the Scientific Revolution,* appeared in 1960.

71. See, for example, Fred M. Hechinger, "About Education: Foundation Urges Drastic Change," *New York Times,* September 29, 1981, C4; *The New Liberal Arts: An Exchange of Views,* ed. James D. Koerner (New York: Alfred P. Sloan Foundation, 1981); Edward B. Fiske, "Technology Gaining a Place in Liberal Arts Curriculums," *Sunday New York Times,* April 29, 1984, 1, 20; John G. Truxal et al., "Liberal Learning and Technology: Building Bridges," *Change: The Magazine of Higher Learning* 18 (March/April 1986): 4–41; J. Ronald Spencer, *The NLA: Retrospect and Prospect* (New York: Alfred P. Sloan Foundation, 1988); John P. Brockway, *Technology and the Liberal Arts: Mixing Differing Thought Patterns* (New York: Alfred P. Sloan Foundation, 1989); and Samuel Goldberg, "On Behalf of the Foundation," *NLA News* 8 (May 1992): 4–5.

72. Lee Smalley and Steve Brady, *Technology Literacy Test: A Report* (Menomonie: University of Wisconsin–Stout, 1984), 1.

73. On "doing" technology rather than merely talking about it in the context of the New Liberal Arts, see Morton Travel, "The Evolution of Vassar College's STS Program and Its Interaction with the 'New Liberal Arts,'" *Science, Technology, and Society: Curriculum Newsletter of the Lehigh University STS Program* 56 (November 1986): 4.

74. See Snow, *Two Cultures*, 29–33.

75. David P. Billington, "In Defense of Engineers," *The Wilson Quarterly* 10 (New Year's 1986): 89, 87. See also the comments in Fiske, "Technology Gaining a Place," of engineering professor Truxal of the State University of New York at Stony Brook regarding the differences between science and engineering; *Technology and Science: Important Distinctions for Liberal Arts Colleges,* ed. John Nicholas Burnett (Davidson, N.C.: Davidson College and Alfred P. Sloan Foundation, 1984); and Henry H. Bauer, *Scientific Literacy and the Myth of the Scientific Method* (Urbana: University of Illinois Press, 1992), 13–14, 124–28.

76. See, for example, Samuel Florman, "Technology and the Tragic View," in his *Blaming Technology: The Irrational Search for Scapegoats* (New York: St. Martin's, 1981), 181–93, and Florman, "The Education of an Engineer," *American Scholar* 55 (Winter 1985–86): 97–106.

77. See Judith Axler Turner, "Project to Include Technology in Liberal-Arts Curriculum Deemed Successful So Far, But Goal Remains Elusive," *The Chronicle of Higher Education* 31 (November 27, 1985): 20. The phrase "technological modes of thought" comes from Goldberg, "The Sloan Foundation's New Liberal Arts Program," *Change* 18 (March/April 1986): 14. See Goldberg, 14–15, and Nannerl O. Keohane, "Business as Usual or Brave New World? A College President's Perspective," ibid., 28–29, for differing perspectives on the need to transform the entire undergraduate curriculum in order to accommodate Sloan's vision of appropriate technological literacy. Keohane's reference to Huxley's classic dystopia reveals a healthy skepticism of the New Liberal Arts missing in most other writings of administrators and faculty involved in the enterprise.

78. Dennis W. Cheek, *Thinking Constructively About Science, Technology, and Society Education* (Albany: State University of New York Press, 1992), 9. See also Hechinger, "About Education," *New York Times*, August 3, 1988, B7, regarding the limits of scientific and, by extension, technological literacy.

79. Truxal, quoted in Fiske, "Technology Gaining a Place," 1.

80. See, for example, the 1990 commencement address of University of Michigan President James J. Duderstadt, a fervent advocate of uncritical ahistorical technological literacy, before his institution's College of Engineering, abridged in *Michigan Today* 22 (June 1990): 14. See also the similarly uncritical, ahistorical approach to contemporary math and science education detailed in *Research News: University of Michigan Division of Research Development and*

Administration 43 (Spring 1992). Ironically, as historian Bruce E. Seely has shown, the history of technology has for generations been deemed important within undergraduate engineering education at several progressive engineering schools and organizations. See his "The History of Technology and Engineering Education in Historical Perspective" (paper delivered at annual meeting, American Society for Engineering Education, Toledo, June 24, 1992).

81. The National Association for Science, Technology, and Society, which has held annual technological literacy conferences since the mid-1980s, and the now-defunct Council for the Understanding of Technology in Human Affairs, which published nine volumes of *The Weaver: Information and Perspectives on Technological Literacy*, have been much more sensitive to these nonquantitative concerns than the Sloan-funded programs and publications.

82. Truxal, director of this program, recognizes this dilemma. The teaching of technology, he says, "should not be restricted to students who will be future leaders; most of our students do not fall into this category" (Truxal, "Learning to Think Like an Engineer: Why, What, and How?" *Change* 18 [March/April 1986]: 12).

83. See Langdon Winner, "On the Foundations of Science and Technology Studies," *Science, Technology, and Society: Curriculum Newsletter of the Lehigh University STS Program* 53 (April 1986): 6. See also Winner, "Conflicting Interests in Science and Technology Studies: Some Personal Reflections," *Technology in Society* 11 (Fall 1989): 433–38, and Stephen H. Cutcliffe, "Science, Technology, and Society Studies as an Interdisciplinary Academic Field," ibid., 419–25.

84. On the need for such a broader, critical approach to literacy in general, see Myron C. Tuman, *A Preface to Literacy: An Inquiry into Pedagogy, Practice, and Progress* (Tuscaloosa: University of Alabama Press, 1987).

85. Nicholas Rescher, "Technological Progress and Human Happiness," in his *Unpopular Essays on Technological Progress* (Pittsburgh: University of Pittsburgh Press, 1980), 3–22.

86. Ibid., 19.

INDEX

. . . . •